C000241782

NEVER SAY NO

By the Same Author

Peter Fleming
Monarchs of the Glen
Armada
Wildings – the Secret Garden of Eileen
Fighter Pilot
Hitler's Games
The House the Berrys Built
When the Country Went to Town
Fauna Britannica
Raoul Millais
Among the Deer
Philip de Laszlo
The War that Never Was
Man of War
Our Land at War

Novels

The Megacull
Spider in the Morning
The Gold of St Matthew
The Heights of Rimring
Level Five
Fire Falcon
Horses of War
The Man-Eater of Jassapur

As Editor

The Letters and Journals of Sir Alan Lascelles
End of an Era
In Royal Service
King's Counsellor

NEVER SAY NO

A memoir by Duff Hart-Davis

Left Field
Editions
2018

First published in 2018 by Left Field Editions

British Library in Cataloguing Publishing Data:
A catalogue entry for this publication is available
from the British Library

ISBN 978 1 5272 1842 0

Printed in Great Britain by
TJ International

CONTENTS

For
My Family

INTRODUCTION

Early in the Second World War my sister Bridget and I were evacuated to America, but we returned home in 1943, when she was eight and I seven, to find that we had a new brother, Adam, born in July. We lived in Bromsden Farm, an isolated Chiltern farmhouse tucked away in a corner of the Nettlebed estate, which belonged to the writer and traveller Peter Fleming. For a boy endowed with the hunting instinct, that was an idyllic base: in the school holidays I helped on the farm, and clung like a limpet to Harry Brown, the gamekeeper, on his rounds of the woods and fields.

For the rest of the war my father Rupert was away in the army, coming home whenever he got leave; and when peace returned he resumed his former occupation as a publisher. This meant that he spent the week in London, coming down at weekends, and it was my mother, Comfort, who bore the burden of looking after the family. Small, stubborn and immensely energetic, a resourceful cook, a skilled gardener and a gifted French teacher, she managed the family and the primitive house with love, skill and courage.

Innocents that we were, we children did not know that my father had been briefly married before, to the actress Peggy Ashcroft; and we were slow to realise that in 1947 he had fallen in love with Ruth Simon, a highly intelligent and attractive woman in London (whom he later married). He managed the affair as discreetly as he could, but inevitably my mother got to know of it, and suffered cruelly. Thanks to her fortitude and devotion, we continued to live at Bromsden, and went through school with the advantage of having a solid home base. I loved my father, but found it hard to forgive him for switching allegiance as he did.

Our family was alive with writers. In the 1920s and 1930s my maternal grandmother, the American author Mary Borden, had produced a stream of popular novels, and later she wrote vivid accounts of the private hospitals which she took to France and the Middle East to nurse the wounded in two World Wars. My godfather and great uncle Duff Cooper wrote distinguished biographies, among them *Haig* and *Talleyrand,* and his own memoir, *Old Men Forget.* My other godfather, Peter Fleming, was celebrated for his iconoclastic travel books *Brazilian Adventure* and *News from Tartary,* both best-sellers in the 1930s, and for his despatches as an idiosyncratic and far-ranging correspondent for *The Times.* My father was widely known as publisher, author and editor in the book world of the 1940s, 1950s and 1960s. He had a huge range of literary friends, and in 1967 was knighted for Services to Literature, in particular for his leadership of the fund-raising campaign to save the London Library from the clutches of the Westminster County Council.

With all this in my background, it was perhaps not surprising that I, too, should want to be an author. When I was still at school, and well-meaning grown-ups asked what I proposed to do for a living, I usually said I wanted to write – whereupon most of them replied, 'Forget it. Find a proper job.' In spite of their discouragement, I persisted, and after university I secured a humble place in journalism as a graduate trainee on the *Western Mail* in Cardiff, where I enjoyed reporting on every kind of event, from Mozart concerts to wrestling matches, sometimes both in the same evening.

I should have done at least two years in Cardiff, but after only a few months, by a sudden stroke of luck, an unexpected vacancy opened up in London on the new *Sunday Telegraph,* whose first issue was due to appear in February 1961, and in January I joined the newspaper as No 3 on the books page, working under the Literary Editor, Tony Curtis, and his deputy, Rivers Scott, at the princely salary of £900 a year.

So I gained a toe-hold in Fleet Street. I could scarcely have found a more congenial slot, for Tony and Rivers were both erudite, experienced book men, and as friendly as could be. Between them they recruited numerous heavyweight reviewers, notably the playwright Nigel Dennis, the poet John Lehmann, the philosopher Antony Quinton (later President of Trinity College, Oxford) and the *grand dame* of 1960s Eng. Lit., Dame Rebecca West.

We had an early flurry of excitement when our secretary, who was engaged to an Italian policeman, eloped to Paris with a married London taxi-driver; but the curse of our existence was lack of space on the books page. In its first incarnation the *Sunday Telegraph* based its appeal to readers on the fact that it was a *compact* newspaper, of only twenty-eight pages, unlike its main competitor *The Sunday Times,* which was already starting to bloat with supplements. The restriction may have been a useful advertising gimmick, but it made life difficult for all departments.

Tony and Rivers agreed that, whatever the pressures, each week's lead reviewer must have a decent amount of space, and generally set a limit of 1,000 words. Most of our stars were fairly professional about keeping to length, but Dame Rebecca – still firing on all intellectual cylinders in her late seventies – usually passed the 1,000-word mark like a racehorse at full gallop, and pulled up, snorting with indignation, at 1,500 words or worse. Cutting her reviews to size was a fearful problem, for she hated losing a single word, and often somebody had to hasten in person to her flat in Princes' Gate, bearing a proof, to negotiate a partial surrender by both sides.

Other reviewers took cutting more lightly. One week Tony Quinton over-ran disastrously; but we decided that the first eight column-inches of his review were waffle, and deleted them. When he announced that he was coming in to correct his proof, we awaited his arrival with trepidation. In he sauntered, big and boisterous as usual, well oiled after lunch, and we held our breath while he read. His only reaction was: 'Since the room is full of pedants, I propose, at this point, to introduce a comma' – and, having done so, he departed in high good humour, not noticing that his first 400 words had gone.

Life on the book page was agreeable enough – and nothing was more enjoyable than the weekly floggery, in which we carted off surplus review copies to Gaston, the second-hand book dealer who lurked in an alley near St Bride's, and returned with handfuls of £20 notes. More important, I learnt a good deal from my colleagues about how to handle difficult authors. But I also began to look for chances to write myself, either for other sections of the paper, or outside.

My first major opportunity came in 1967, when NASA, the American National Aeronautics and Space Agency, commissioned an earth station on Ascension Island, in mid-Atlantic, in support of the Apollo moon-shot programme. Somehow I got myself detailed to cover the official opening, and flew down with a party of journalists. The aircraft in which we travelled was a turbo-prop Britannia designed for long range, but even that had to make a refuelling stop at Dakar in the middle of the night. Then we took off again, and at dawn, fifteen hours out of Heathrow, we at last sighted our target – a speck of land in a boundless expanse of ocean. From the moment we glided smoothly in to touch down between rust-red volcanic cones rising from beds of tumbled black lava, I was so fascinated by the place that I wrote not only a full-page report for the *Sunday Telegraph*, but, in due course, a history of the island.

So a pattern was set. The first chapters in this book take in National Service, and two journeys made before I had a job; but once I was employed by a newspaper, again and again an assignment gave me an idea for some larger enterprise – either for a factual book, or for a novel – and for the rest of my career I have combined journalism with more solid literary projects. I tended to follow up any lead that caught my interest, with the result that I took on a wide variety of unrelated subjects – as it were, scattering my shot. I see now that I might have made a greater impact if I had specialised in one area – say military or natural history – but I might also have become a thundering bore.

CHAPTER ONE

Soldier
1956–57

In the mid-1950s no fit young man could escape National Service – which meant two years in the Army, Navy or Air Force. Looking back, I wish I had tried for the RAF and learned to fly, or opted to learn Russian; but, being naturally conformist, I followed tradition and enlisted in the Coldstream Guards, which had been my father's regiment during the Second World War.

Our eight weeks of basic training at the Guards' Depot, Caterham, were hellish. In bitter winter weather our Brigade Squad, of twenty-eight potential officers, was housed in an ancient wooden hut, heated by a single coke stove, which burnt out overnight, so that when a bugle sounded Reveille at 06.30 in the dark of a February morning, it took a fierce mental effort to roll out of bed and make a dash for the ablution block 200 yards away.

Our hut was supervised by Trained Soldier Banks – a huge Liverpool Irishman of such limited intellect that he had not even become a lance-corporal. The only redeeming feature of getting-up was the pantomime which developed between him and a seriously laid-back recruit called Christopher Brett. Every morning, with the rest of the hut on their feet and dressing, Brett would remain horizontal for as long as he dared. From the end of the hut the Trained Soldier, also still in bed but up on one elbow, would yell, 'If you don't get out of that bed in one second flat, Brett, I shall come and bloody *kill* yer!' With that he would take a sudden rush down the centre of the hut, still in his pyjamas, and turn Brett's bed upside-down – but by then the occupant had shot to his feet and was hastily pulling on clothes. Part of the entertainment was the fact that Banks felt obliged to invent a new threat every morning: 'I shall come and bloody *drown* yer ! ... I shall come and bloody *skin* yer! . . I shall come and bloody *kick yer to death!*'

Outside, the aim of the non-commissioned officers was to knock the shit out of us public-school boys – and in this they quickly succeeded, yelling at us on the drill square, chasing us on cross-country runs and marches, hustling us over the assault course, threatening us with close arrest, bullying and denigrating us into submission. We soon realised that the only hope of surviving, then or in battle, was to obey orders without question – exactly what our tormentors wanted. We also learnt never to volunteer for anything, however innocent a question might sound. 'Anyone here play the piano?' asked the weapons instructor at the entrance to the firing range – and when someone foolishly put up a hand, it was 'Right – you carry the ammunition to the 100-yard firing point' – an absolutely crippling task.

What rendered life just about tolerable was the incredible profanity of the instructors' language: it made our day to have a sergeant scream into someone's ear, from a couple of inches' range, 'You syphilitic heap of cat's piss!' or to hear a corporal roar up at a 6′ 7″ recruit, 'If I ever see shit piled any higher, I'll send you a fucking *telegram*!' Memorably revolting new expressions were coined every day, and outbursts of (possibly simulated) rage were so extreme that several of the sergeants, we felt certain, would finish their careers in the mental hospital hard by the depot. Like the language, the food was disgusting, but we were always so ravenous that we ate anything we could get hold of. One indelible memory is of an ape-like cook suddenly shouting 'Buckshee buns!' and hurling bullet-hard rock-cakes into our tables with all the force he could muster. If one of the missiles had hit someone in the eye, a serious injury would have resulted.

The man we hated most was our platoon sergeant, a Coldstreamer, always immaculately smart, ferociously critical of any small lapse in turnout or drill, and apparently lacking any vestige of humour. Not for six weeks did we realise how skilfully he had been handling us. Then at last his demeanour softened: he began to make jokes and for the first time treated us as human beings. He could afford to, for that first, brutal demeanour had earned our allegiance. Now we saw what an excellent man-manager he was. One particular exchange created a bond between us, when he translated the Scots Guards' regimental motto *Nemo me impune lacessit* as 'Touch me not with impurity.' 'No, no, Sergeant,' several of us chorused. 'It means "Nobody fucks me up and gets away with it.' After a moment his face broke into a grin and he conceded victory. From then on life became less frantic.

When the course ended, after a few days' leave the survivors moved on to the Officer Cadet Training Unit at Eaton Hall, a monstrous Gothic house near Chester belonging to the Duke of Westminster, now demolished. So enormous was the building that an elephant's head, mounted with trunk outstretched on a turn of the main staircase, in no way hampered progress up or down. Once in an outburst of exuberance we carried an Austin 7 aloft and drove it back and forth along the first-floor landing; another time we did the same with a flock of sheep.

For anyone who had endured the rigours of Caterham, Eaton Hall was a picnic: the regime was far more relaxed, and the surroundings – soft Cheshire farm land – far more attractive, especially as spring turned to summer. All the same, the pressure was too great for some cadets, a few of whom ended their misery by jumping off the roof of the house.

Again we lived in wooden huts, and – extraordinary as it now seems – we were allowed not only to import sporting guns, but also to keep them in the lockers beside our beds. One night this led to an incident that came within seconds of finishing my attempt to gain a commission. Another course had just passed out, and, as usual, its members ran riot in the camp after dinner. I had gone to bed and was fast asleep when I suddenly awoke to find the hut under attack. Intruders had burst in and were turning beds over, throwing things about and yelling like madmen, obviously drunk as lords. Without thinking I grabbed my beloved Atkin 12 bore, loaded both barrels, stuck them out of the window and fired two shots upwards into the trees.

The immediate result was most gratifying. Our assailants took fright and vanished into the night. But, a few seconds later, disaster threatened. In rushed a Military Policeman in a state of high excitement, shouting 'Who fired those shots?' As I was standing with a gun in my hands, and smoke was still curling from the ends of the barrels, I seemed to be in deep trouble. Yet in that crisis inspiration struck. 'I don't know,' I said. 'While I was asleep one of those bastards grabbed my gun out of the locker and fired off through the window. I had to drag it back off him.' Why the M.P. believed me, I shall never know – but he went off cursing in pursuit of the revellers, and I collapsed into bed shaking with relief.

Another incident stands out from that time. One of our intake, Benjy Mackworth-Praed, had a dark-green 1930s Bentley coupé, and one afternoon he loaded up the whole of the cricket team – eleven players, plus umpire and scorer – to drive out to the playing field. With thirteen people on board, the car made slow progress, for the rear mudguards were forced down onto the tyres by the sheer weight of passengers, and we were crawling past the magnificent wrought-iron gates in front of the house when out charged the terrifying figure of Regimental Sergeant-Major Lynch, all 6′ 4″ of him, in a towering rage. Puce in the face and roaring like a bull, he hit the gates with a terrific clang and hung on to them, an enraged beast loosing off volley after volley of invective in his Irish twang. The immediate result was that the entire team was placed in close arrest, for 'wilfully riding in a vehicle they knew to be over-loaded.' Our cricketing opponents were left with no-one to play, and we lost all privileges for the next fortnight.

In spite of this and other misdemeanours, I passed out successfully, and so became a second-lieutenant in the Coldstream Guards. Posted to the First Battalion, I found myself in London, quartered in Chelsea Barracks. As it turned out, my stay in the capital was fairly short, its most stressful point being the day we lined the Mall, in full uniform of scarlet tunics and bearskins, for a state visit by the President of Portugal. For those stationed at the east end of the Mall, as my platoon was, this proved a nerve-racking occasion. Once we had taken up position, facing the road, with our backs to St James's Park, neither I nor any of my men was allowed to move. I was supposed not even to look left, towards

Buckingham Palace, to gain an idea of what was happening. The same applied to all the platoon commanders down the line.

Our task sounded simple enough: to present arms when the presidential cavalcade came past. But this was not as easy as it sounded. If a vehicle started up the Mall from in front of the Palace, and the platoons on our left began to present arms, one after another, the only sensible thing to do was to follow suit– and the result was a series of false alarms. Again and again, from our left, came the crash of boots on tarmac and rifles coming to the slope, growing louder as the noise rippled towards us. Again and again I brought my platoon to attention and shouted the command, 'Pre – sent ARMS!' – only to see a single Volkswagen Beetle or taxi potter past.

When this had happened several times, the Sergeant-Major lurking behind us became restive. 'There's something horrible happening at the far end of your platoon,' he hissed, in a menacing stage whisper easily audible to the crowd on the pavement. 'Get a move on your men, Mr Hart-Davis. Get a move on your men!' I knew nothing was happening, and in any case I could do nothing to get a move on anyone. My only course was to ignore the barracking, which naturally had the desired effect of making me even more nervous. In the end, when the presidential procession did come past, we presented arms adequately, and soon were marching back to barracks.

That was the autumn of the Suez Crisis, when British and French troops joined the Israeli army in an attempt to seize control of the Canal from President Nasser. Rumour had it that our battalion was next-in-line to be deployed to Egypt; but the war ended so suddenly, when Britain succumbed to diplomatic pressure from the United States and the Soviet Union, that we were not needed, and we went instead to join the British Army of the Rhine.

Our battalion landed in a former German army barracks at Krefeld, on the western edge of the Ruhr, not far from the Dutch border – a depressing place surrounded by dead-flat farm land. Ten years after the end of the world war, relations with the Germans were still uneasy. Clearly, the British could not behave with the aggression they had shown earlier, when they crashed about the defeated country doing as they liked: we had to fraternise with the local population as best we could, and they, in turned, maintained a cool but polite front.

Late in 1955 tension between East and West was high. In the depths of the Cold War the whole of Eastern Europe was sealed off by the inter-zonal border and occupied by Soviet forces. It seemed perfectly possible that the Soviet army might launch an invasion across the frontier – and members of British Special Forces were preparing to carry out a potentially suicidal mission in that very event: behind any Soviet advance, they would go to ground and live troglodytically for as long as possible, so that they could report troop movements back to Allied headquarters.

Tension eased a little in February 1956, when the Soviet President Nikita Khruschev made his astonishing speech in the Kremlin, suddenly denouncing his predecessor Stalin as a mass-murderer, and condemning the regime of 'suspicion, fear and terror' over which the dictator had presided. Khruschev, it seemed, wanted better relations with the West. Even so, the task of the British Army of the Rhine remained to slow down, to the best of our ability, any invasion that the Soviet Union might launch. How effective we might have been, it is impossible to say; but my impression was that we would have been quickly overcome by sheer weight of numbers. Nevertheless, we trained as best we could.

There was nothing like a trip down the border between West and East Germany to bring home the repulsive nature of Soviet Communism. Soviet and East German propaganda claimed that the watch-towers, high metal fences, barbed wire entanglements, anti-vehicle ditches, minefields and dog-runs were designed to prevent Fascist infiltrators penetrating the peace-loving Deutsche Democratische Republik. In fact the purpose of the 850-mile-long barrier was to prevent citizens escaping – and very effective it was.

To look at the frontier, we could get occasional trips with Brixmis, the military mission which patrolled the border. Its members were based in the DDR, but they also had vehicles in the West, and were glad to show visitors sections of the barrier. I particularly remember one view-point –

a large wooden platform built expressly to give a close-up view into the Socialist paradise. Through the wire one could see straight into the houses of a small town or village, only a few yards away. It was extraordinary, and shocking, to think of people living there like animals in a cage – but not all the inmates were subdued. As soon as a sizeable crowd of voyeurs had assembled, a girl in the window of one of the houses launched into a striptease act, which she finished by presenting her naked backside and letting down a large white sheet on which was written: PLEASE SEND NYLONS TO HARDENBERGSTRASSE 47.

One activity in which it was easy to fraternise with the Germans was shooting. Officers were invited to join the great hare drives in which farmers specialised, and other-ranks were welcomed as beaters. Operations were conducted on a large scale. Fifty or more guns and maybe fifty beaters would assemble at the rendezvous, and after a satisfactory amount of horn-blowing everyone would walk out – gun, beater, gun, beater – to form an immense *Kesseltreibe,* or encirclement. At another horn signal everyone would start walking inwards, the guns firing at anything that moved. Every hare that got up was greeted with shouts of *'Hase! Hase!'* but as the Germans, like rural people everywhere, tended to truncate the word, it emerged as one syllable instead of two. Instead of *'Ha-se!'* it came out phonetically as 'Arse! Arse!' – a cry which the guardsmen eagerly took up. When the circle became dangerously tight, new horn calls rang out to signify 'No more shooting inwards' – but there always seemed to be one or two guns who ignored it and continued to blaze away, thereby incurring fines, which were exacted during the closing ceremony.

I think we conducted ourselves with reasonable decorum in public. Of course there were exceptions – as when a young Grenadier officer, emerging from a night club in the small hours, was displeased to find a Volkswagen Beetle parked in front of him, and walked straight over it, fore to aft. The owner, who was sitting at the wheel, about to drive off, was not amused, and leapt out to remonstrate.

In barracks our behaviour sometimes became positively frenetic, fuelled by ridiculously cheap alcohol – witness a letter which I wrote to my parents after Christmas 1955. Festivities in the officers' mess began with a cocktail party given for all the families stationed in and around Krefeld. 'Everyone got pretty drunk,' I reported, and the guests didn't stagger away until about 10 pm.'

> Just after they'd gone an officer called Anthony Bedford-Russell suddenly poured a whole fire-bucket of water down my front. He was pretty tight, and so I was I, but less so. I retaliated, and soused him from head to foot with another bucket. Later he came after me with another pail of filthy brown water.
>
> Not wanting that lot over me, I ran off down a passage, chucking yet another bucket into the air, to ward him off. He thundered after me, failed to see the one I'd thrown, and ran slap into it. It hit him between the eyes and cut him quite deeply at the top of his nose, so that he poured with blood. We took him off to the M.O., and he lay on the operating table, calling for a whisky-and-soda, which we gave him. As the doctor deftly sewed him up he kept shouting 'One thing I'm not having is any bloody stitches!'

Throughout the holiday one crazed ritual followed another – none more ridiculous than the Officers v. Sergeants football match, for which the players wore fancy dress. The first half, lasting only ten minutes, was fairly normal, and the officers scored one goal; but, as I reported, things warmed up after half time.

> I was a reserve, and we brought out a sackful of thunderflashes, which we let off by the dozen. We also set off four smoke canisters, which were so efficient that the whole field was blotted out. We then ran a coil of barbed wire across the pitch, dropping coloured smoke grenades as we went.
>
> Meanwhile the sergeants had manned a fire hose, with which they soused everyone in the officers' goal-mouth. They succeeded in putting out a couple of the canisters, and when the smoke cleared, the sergeants were seen to be scoring a goal. It was then noticed that

> there were three balls on the field, so the goal was not given, and the officers won 1- 0. Afterwards an officer called Jeremy Whitaker was thrown into the swimming bath by the sergeants, but we managed to get seven of them in as well – so we came out of that one best. After that we formed a sort of procession, and marched round the barracks with the band ... As you can imagine, by Boxing Day everyone was feeling considerably the worse for wear.

Early in the New Year I got a surprise when I learnt that I had been appointed Brigade Transport Officer at the headquarters of 4th Guards' Brigade. This was promotion of a kind, for the post was normally held by a captain. Being a mere second-lieutenant, I hoped for a pay-rise. In spite of persistent haggling by my supporters, none came; but the change meant leaving my friends in the 1st Battalion and moving about twenty miles east, to the headquarters at Hubbelrath, a village on hills above the outskirts of Düsseldorf.

Naturally I was apprehensive, for although I had a reasonably mechanical turn of mind, I knew nothing about organising transport, or about how a brigade headquarters worked. Luckily I found an ace awaiting me in the form of Jim Dargie, a Scots Guards sergeant who had been at Hubbelrath for months and had a firm grip of the transport section. An exceedingly helpful fellow, he taught me what I needed to know and covered-up my mistakes. Another bonus was that the officers' mess was in a substantial country house – once the home of a well-to-do German – down a lane about quarter of a mile from the barracks. There we had comfortable rooms, and were waited-on by a tubby and rubicund old German butler, Frederik, whose inevitable greeting in the evenings was 'Whisky, Sah?' We were never sure whether he was saying 'Whisky, Sir?' or 'Whisky sour?' – but the answer was always, '*Ja, bitte.*'

Having survived a week-long course learning to drive ten-ton lorries on ice, I concentrated on training. Throughout spring, summer and autumn our main activity was going on exercises, leaving barracks and dispersing for a few days into the countryside further east, towards the Iron Curtain – as we would if or when hostilities broke out. My main tasks were to make sure that the headquarters lorries and jeeps were properly maintained, and to deploy them into woods, farm buildings or other hiding places for the duration of the imagined emergencies. There were no restrictions on where we could go. We did our best not to damage crops by driving heavy vehicles over them, and most farmers tolerated our presence with good humour, but of course there were occasional flare-ups. Having taken a few quick German lessons in England before we left, I was gaining confidence with the language, and could usually de-fuse confrontations.

Small incidents stand out sharply. One night our radio network was all to blazes: we could not contact any of our own units, and only one alien operator kept coming through loud and clear, endlessly repeating his call-sign: 'BOWstring,' in a faintly ridiculous northern accent, with heavy emphasis on the first syllable. 'BOWstring ... BOWstring.' Answer came there none. Where he was or who he was, we could not tell, but he sounded very close, even though he evidently could not hear us repeatedly telling him to switch frequencies.

Hostilities culminated with the arrival in our headquarter van of the formidable Brigade Major, Major the Earl Cathcart, DSO, MC, who, having endured a few minutes of the sing-song intonation, seized the microphone, pressed the SEND switch and roared, 'Bowstring! If you don't get off the bloody air AT ONCE, I shall have you put in close arrest!' To which blast there came the inevitable riposte: 'BOWstring.' The Brigade Major departed in a rage, exasperated by the fact that he had no means of carrying out his threat.

One evening on another exercise I had a struggle to get all my vehicles and people settled in a wood, and so was late for supper at a pub which colleagues had pin-pointed as the rendezvous for an evening meal. Arriving half-starved (having had no lunch), I spotted a vacant place at the table and sat down between two friends. Hardly had my backside touched the chair when a waitress placed in front of me the most magnificent tournedos I had ever set eyes on – a great, circular chunk of meat, thick, steaming, glistening and slightly charred on top, with fried potatoes alongside. 'My God!' I exclaimed. 'Whose is that?' Nobody claimed it. Nobody, apparently, had ordered it. So without ado I ate it, thinking of the Austrian drinking song favoured by Clarissa, sister of my friend and fellow Coldstreamer David Caccia:

Wer kann das bezahlen?	(Who can pay for that?)
Wer hat das bestellt?	(Who ordered it?)
Wer hat so viel Stinky-Binky?	(Who has that much Stinky-Binky?)
Wer hat so viel Gelt?	(Who has that much cash?)

The questions were never answered. The kitchen had apparently made a mistake, and I got a miraculous free supper.

Another night proved far less amusing. I was asleep in the hay-loft of a farm when someone ran into the stable below yelling that there had been an accident. I shone a torch on my watch: 3 am. Already dressed, I scrambled down a ladder, out into a cool, clear, summer night and into a waiting jeep. The accident had happened only a mile or two down the road, so we were quickly on the scene.

On a sharp bend one of our open jeeps had rolled over, ending on its side and pinning the driver by the midriff between the metal bar along the top of the windscreen and the trunk of a wayside tree. The man was conscious, but he was hanging in mid-air and obviously in great pain. The only way to get him down was to hitch a steel cable from the side of the jeep to the front of a three-tonner and ease the lorry backwards while two men stood by to catch the casualty gently as he was released.

With the nightmarish scene illuminated by the headlights of other vehicles, a three-tonner was soon in position to give a pull, but I felt impelled to order the driver to get out of the cab and let me take over. Although he was an excellent man, with a good record, I thought that if there was a disaster and we managed to kill the injured man, the responsibility must be mine. I tried to explain this in a few words, but I could feel the guardsman's resentment as I climbed up into the driving seat.

Keeping the three-tonner's engine at high revs, I eased the clutch out millimetre by millimetre, until my left leg began to shake, partly with effort, partly with nerves. As the heavy vehicle crept backwards, the linking cable went taut. After few more seconds the windscreen of the jeep began to release its grip, and two men were able to lower the casualty on to a stretcher.

I cannot now remember why our own medical facilities were not available. Somewhere, there must have been a military ambulance and crew, standing by for emergencies; but – possibly because of a communications black-out – we could not reach them, and we had to get our man to hospital as quickly as possible. We were in thickly-forested country, with confusing minor roads snaking between the hills; but somebody remembered seeing a red-and-white sign saying '*Krankenhaus*' not far back along our previous day's route, so we headed in that direction.

By the time we reached the sign, dawn was breaking. In the half light a large, white building, buried among trees, looked more like a country house than a hospital. I ran to the entrance and pressed a bell. No response. I tried again. Still no answering sound. 'Keep ringing,' I told the corporal with me. 'I'll try at the back.'

Round the corner, through one of the tall ground-floor windows loomed the figure of a weird-looking woman – old, white-haired, white-faced, wearing a white night-dress, and barely visible in the grey dawn light, she was swaying from side to side and making vague, airy sweeps with her hands. '*Unfall!*' (accident) I shouted, and clapped one fist into the other hand to indicate a collision, but my gestures made no impression. 'Mad,' I thought. 'This is a loony bin.'

But no – as I hurried back to the front, the door opened and the place sprang to life. Nurses took the casualty in, and – as we heard afterwards – gave him skilful preliminary treatment before moving him on to a more highly-equipped hospital. When I visited him there a few days later, I found him horizontal, with one leg in traction, but in high good humour and on the road to full recovery. Fifty years on, other details of that night have faded; yet the images of a limp body hanging in mid-air, and the ghost of Miss Havisham floating around inside her window, remain pin-sharp to this day.

For recreation, we were well off, at any rate in winter. There was a squash court in the barracks. In cold weather we could skate, and those with cars could go off skiing at weekends. I played rugger as a second-row forward for the Battalion and the Headquarters, and had some enjoyable matches – but we were not very successful, for most of the guardsmen had no firm grip of the rules, and in moments of excitement tended to pass forward, which of course brought many a promising movement to a halt.

Riding was also possible, for several of the officers had horses, and the country behind the barracks was open farmland, entirely without fences, and with dirt tracks running through it. My first outing ended in disaster. I rode out with two friends, and at first all went well; but when the others broke into a canter, my horse – a 16-hands gelding called Harry – suddenly took off at full gallop. Nothing would stop him. I could not even slow him down; it was all I could do to stay on board, and I was carried away across country until I was out of sight of my companions.

Eventually I managed to turn my beast round and start back; but what nobody had told me was that he had been trained for dressage, and when I inadvertently gave him some aid that he remembered, he abruptly went into a prancing, high-stepping gait which carried both of us sideways at an angle into a field of beautifully-ordered cabbages. *'RAUS!'* came an angry yell – and there was the farmer, gesticulating furiously from the edge of the crop. I waved back, shouting apologies; but the more I kicked and the harder I pulled, the higher Harry stepped, mincing one row of cabbages after another. *'RAUS !'* roared the farmer, *'SOFORT! WEG DA!'* – but I think he could see that I was out of control, and as soon as we began to move straight forward again, his objurgations faded. Yet that was not the end of my problems. When Harry decided to canter straight under a tree, I was swept off into the branches, Absalom style, and the horse galloped back into barracks riderless, to the great delight of my men.

Goaded by an urge to write, and being short of money, I spent every minute of my spare time composing short stories aimed at women's magazines. Few were even acknowledged, and none (perhaps mercifully) was accepted. A more ambitious project was to write a play, and when

I had sketched out a few scenes I persuaded an English girl working in the Consulate to type out my draft. As a reward, I suggested I should take her to the opera in Düsseldorf, where the newly-built (and startling pink) *Deutsche Oper am Rhein* had just been hailed as an outstanding achievement in the reconstruction of the shattered city.

Anna was new to opera, so to give her an easy start I bought (or thought I had bought) tickets for *Die Fledermaus,* which was playing in repertory along with other works. During the twenty-minute drive into town I tried to outline the plot – a great party given by a Russian prince (probably sung by a woman), everyone in masks, and so on. By the time we reached the opera house, I'm sure Anna was thoroughly confused.

We arrived late, at the last possible moment. As we shuffled to our seats in the front row of the stalls, the conductor was already on the podium, and he swung round to glare at us, irritably tapping his baton on the bare wooden rim of the orchestra pit. Then he turned and raised his right hand. At his signal the bass drum gave out three menacing rolls – brrrrrrmBOM, brrrrrrmBOM, brrrrrrmBOM – and I knew straight away that this was not *Die Fledermaus,* but *Il trovatore.* To my intense embarrassment, I had got the wrong night. In the crescendos of the overture I tried to explain that this was not about a fancy-dress ball, but about medieval witchcraft – and it was hardly surprising that I never saw Anna again.

CHAPTER TWO

Flash and Dash
1957

In January 1957, at the end of my National Service, I had eight months clear before going to university, and I managed to fit two long journeys into the break. Both were engineered by my godfather, Peter Fleming; but it was Tony (later Sir William) Keswick who launched me on the first.

One of the Tai-pans, the family who ran the great, far-Eastern trading firm Jardine Matheson, Tony was a large and jovial fellow, and a close friend of Peter, who, though addressing him as 'Pompous', greatly enjoyed his company. He returned the compliment by calling Peter 'Flamingo'. When Peter somehow persuaded him that I might be a useful recruit to his business, Tony arranged for me to get a taste of foreign trade by sending me as a supernumerary on a merchant ship sailing to the coast of West Africa and up the rivers into Nigeria. His second barrel (as he called it) was a plan to post me to Canada, where I would see something of the Hudson's Bay Company, of which he was a Governor.

On 20 March 1957 I travelled to Liverpool to join the S.S. *Exedene,* a long, low cargo vessel, painted black along the sides, with white upperworks and a single derrick fore and aft. To my landlubber's eye she seemed pretty large: she was 430 feet long, with a beam of 56 feet, and was rated at 4,908 gross tonnage. I went aboard in a roaring gale, nervous of the whole enterprise, for in this strange environment I had no idea what my status or duties might be.

I need not have worried. From the start I was treated with kid gloves: I was allotted a comfortable cabin of my own beside the bridge, amidships, and told I would mess with the officers. The captain, a taciturn Scot, had such a broad accent that at first I had trouble understanding him; but he was very affable, and he impressed on me that I was to take things easy. 'Dinna bust yersel,' he said. 'Do just as much work as ye like' – and that was more or less his only instruction. At breakfast next morning I was fascinated by his habit of chomping eggs and bacon, toast and marmalade, all in the same mouthful. After twenty-four hours on board I reported in a letter home: 'The officers hardly speak at all, and eat incredibly slowly, but they are very well meaning.'

Our first port of call was Swansea, where we picked up 1,500 tons of steel tubes. While loading was in progress I had nothing to do, so I walked up the steep hill behind the town, in drenching rain, and took refuge in an abandoned stable, looking down over all the glistening slate roofs, stricken by misery at thought of being separated from my girlfriend, Phyllida Barstow, for the next two months, with huge distances between us (I am glad to say that, more than fifty years later, she and I are still happily married).

As soon as we put to sea, homesickness vanished. After a couple of days of rough weather, beset by rain and fog, we emerged into brilliant sunshine, which lasted unbroken all the way down past the bulge of Africa. The heat steadily increased, and soon, working on deck all day, I wore nothing but a pair of shorts. There was plenty to do, chipping away rust and re-painting bare patches, but life was very relaxed: there was never any hurry. I was pleased to find the captain reading *One of Our Submarines,* a best-selling account of wartime service by Edward Young, and when I told him the book had been published by my father, he seemed tremendously impressed, and set me to do his typing, which I enjoyed. Although amiable for most of the time, he occasionally exploded in a fit of exasperation over some idiocy committed by one of his crew, but it never lasted more than a minute or two.

The crew-member with whom I had most in common was the Second Mate, the friendliest and most intelligent of the officers, who shared my interest in books and music. Coarser by far was the purser, a diminutive Portuguese who introduced himself by announcing, 'I'm the little man with the big dick,' and boasting about the number of women he had laid in ports all round the world. Nearest to me in age were two apprentices, Mark and Dan, seventeen or eighteen – who were friendly enough, but wary of me, sensing that I came from another world, and not sure how to treat me. I, a typically buttoned-up ex-public-schoolboy, made deplorably little effort to get to know them or explore their backgrounds.

I had plenty of time for reading, but I was also trying to write, and I drafted several short stories – none of which saw the light of day. When the *Exedene* put in to Dakar, in Senegal, to re-fuel, I got my first, unforgettable smell of West Africa – an acrid stink of malfunctioning drains, of rotting vegetation, of heat, of darkness. Quickly away again, the ship headed south and then east. As we passed Sierra Leone, Liberia and the Ivory Coast, the sea turned from deep blue to green. Whales surfaced on all sides, flying fish skimmed beside us, and porpoises gambled alongside our bows. Our next port of call, at the beginning of the Gold Coast, was Takoradi, where we unloaded our steel and other cargo. In the evenings we had wonderful swimming at the European club in a pool scooped out of rocks on the edge of the sea, with the temperature of the water in the high eighties, surf exploding over the rocks, and brilliant moonlight glittering off the spray.

I knew that at Obuasi, a short distance inland to the north, my step-grandfather, Major-General Sir Edward Spears, would just be finishing his annual visit to the Ashanti Goldfields Corporation, of which he was Chairman. For two months every spring he and my grandmother went out and lived in state in a spacious bungalow which he himself had had built; they were driven about in an Armstrong-Siddeley limousine, and were worshipped by the workers in the mine, who regarded them almost as deities. Spears fancied his role as a big bwana, and loved the Ghanaians' simplicity, often telling the story of a man who, for a fee of sixpence, had himself made invisible by a spell from some local juju. After a shift in the mine, confident that no one could see him, he swaggered out through the gate with a gold bar wrapped in a towel tucked under his arm. At first all went well. The sentry on the gate did not challenge him, and for a moment he thought he was clear. But then, to his dismay, he suddenly realised that although *he* was invisible, the gold was not: the sentry must see it, moving through the air. So he panicked, ran, and was apprehended.

I did not mention Spears to my ship-board colleagues, for fear that I might seem to be boasting about family connections. But I thought of him often as we forged on along the Gold Coast, across the Bight of Benin and into the Benin River.

The ship had a small library, and among its few books was a copy of Conrad's novella *Heart of Darkness,* in which the narrator, Marlow, tells the story of his journey up an African river 'on an old tin-pot of a steamboat' to rescue the mysterious Mr Kurtz, chief agent of a company trading in ivory at the 'Inner Station'. By the time we reached the coast I was gripped by the author's descriptions of the river and the menace of the primeval forest through which it ran. 'Going up that river,' he wrote, 'was like travelling back to the earliest beginnings of the world, when vegetation rioted on the earth and the big trees were kings.'

Conrad, I knew, had worked as captain of a steamer on the Congo – a river far bigger than the Benin; but the environment we were poised to enter was surely much the same. At the mouth of the river we stopped in mid-stream to take on our pilot, Black Komi. Black as night he was, gaunt-cheeked and bald, save for a little silver fuzz. Out he came in his speeding dugout canoe, propelled by two henchmen paddling like fury to keep ahead of a flotilla bearing other, spurious pilots trying to thrust their services upon us. He beat them by a few yards, and we hoisted him aboard, canoe and all, leaving the others yelling and chattering with disappointment. Then we steamed slowly up-river for an hour before anchoring in mid-stream for the night.

On both banks the jungle was so dense that for most of the way all we could see was a solid wall of foliage. Now and then, at points where the trees were lower, endless vistas of mangrove swamps stretched away to infinity beyond them. Every few miles a tiny native settlement huddled into a niche in the bank; the huts, made of leaves and wattle, were half in the water, and it looked as though the inhabitants practically lived in their dugouts.

The moment we hove-to for the night, the clanking rattle of our anchor chain fetched out a swarm of canoes, which shot away from the nearest village loaded with men, women, boys and girls, clad, if at all, in a few rags. Within a minute or two they were alongside, and up came a shrill chorus of 'Dash me, Johnny! Dash me, Johnny!' Any dash (present), like a cardboard box or a tin can brandished over the side, provoked screams of anticipation, and the sight of an empty bottle raised excitement to fever pitch. The boys were incredibly quick at diving; they swam like fish, and if there was the least chance of securing some prize, a whole boat-load would plummet into the water simultaneously.

As night came down, the scene grew more and more bizarre. When we switched on the floodlights, huge insects fizzed into the beams and whirled round our heads as we crowded along the rail. Down below, eighteen canoes jostled together beside the ship, with a mass of black faces glinting up at us. We would wait till a dozen or so of the boats were nicely lined up, then throw a bottle as far as possible ahead of them. Every splash-down sent off a frantic race. Each canoe had a boy poised on the bow, ready to jump or dive, and anything up to twenty bodies would hit the surface simultaneously. There would then be a furious *melée* in the water, as the combatants screeched, jabbered and beat each other over the head with paddles, until one managed to get the bottle into his own canoe.

For the ship's crew, well used to the game, there was a single objective: in return for a dash, to obtain a flash. The answer to 'Dash me, Johnny' was 'Flash me, Bonny', and to provoke the launch of a missile over the water a girl in one of the canoes would turn a somersault or do a handstand, shamelessly revealing her all and provoking raucous applause from the spectators above. Audience and players alike displayed phenomenal stamina and kept the game going for hours: it was ten o'clock before the supply of dashes ran out. Then the last of the canoes floated away into the darkness, and farewell shouts came ringing back over the stream.

Next morning we advanced up-river. Hoping to learn some secrets of navigation, I went on to the bridge to talk to Black Komi, only to find him immersed in a battered copy of Kennedy's Latin Primer. What he thought the book was about, I never discovered, for his English was fragmentary, and no matter what question I put to him, he answered by merely rolling his bloodshot eyes. I don't think it made any difference to him that some schoolboy had carried out the traditional emendation of the cover, so that the title read *Kennedy's Eating Primer*.

But if Komi's Latin was sketchy, his knowledge of the river was superb. The stream wound back and forth between the mangroves, and many of the bends were so tight that on the outside of turns ships failing to come round hard enough had punched huge, v-shaped dents into the banks, forcing trees and their writhing roots apart. Komi negotiated the channels so skilfully that although we several times came within feet of an impact, we never touched.

Our next port of call was Sapele, a wood-working town a hundred miles from the sea. There we moored alongside the jungle, and soon the outer flank of the ship was crowded with huge rafts of hardwood logs – light-coloured obeche, mahogany and sapele, a dark wood like mahogany which had given its name to the town. On shore all kinds of sawn timber were being produced, but we were after the big stuff: whole trunks weighing several tons apiece which had been floated downstream. Loading them was a skilled operation, as lumberjacks, standing on the slippery round boles, had to lasso each one by separating it from its neighbours and passing a canvas band underneath at either end so that it could be hoisted by one of the derricks.

Life on board was rendered far less comfortable by the arrival of a swarm of Kroo boys – extra labourers, from a tribe who traditionally furnished visiting ships with a temporary extra work-force. They lived on deck for the duration, cooking and sleeping in the open, and created a hideous mess, as well as a noisome, animal smell. In the suffocating heat our chipping and painting slowed to a minimum. The midday temperature was 95 F in the shade and 135 F in the sun, the humidity terrific. Mornings and evenings were the most pleasant times of day. As dawn broke, the jungle was always steaming slightly, and the river lay still as a vast silver mirror, on which pencil-thin silhouettes of dugouts hung motionless. Evenings brought glorious sunsets, as the sky caught a reflection of the jungle and turned a delicate shade of green.

My bartering ability increased rapidly. Africans were constantly coming alongside in canoes laden with fruit, for which they demanded outrageous sums. At first I was timid about beating them down, but I soon hardened and realised that they were happy if they got quarter of their starting prices. One day I bought a stalk of about 90 bananas for 2s 6d – and immense pineapples, eighteen inches high, could be got for a shilling. Paw-paws and mangoes cost almost nothing.

On several evenings we hired dugouts, only to find that they were wildly unstable, and much harder to manoeuvre than we had expected. On our first outing, with two of us aboard one canoe, it took us half an hour to reach the middle of the river, where we spun round three times and toppled overboard. Luckily the dugout didn't go down, and we swam to the shore and righted it. Later, gaining some mastery of the craft, we explored creeks going up into impenetrable jungle. We must have been lucky not to pick up any infection from the river, for the water was anything but salubrious. Dead bodies came floating downstream in various stages of decomposition – and if a duty policeman saw one, he did nothing except cheer it on its way.

After five days in Sapele we penetrated still further north into the interior, creeping up channels that seemed barely wide enough for the ship to pass through. Now we really were in Conrad's heart of darkness. The natives, living in ramshackle mud huts along the banks, looked wilder and more primitive than the people down-river. They wore no clothes; their voices were harsh and animal-like, and at night the sound of their drums rolled out across the water.

I had just come to the end of the novel, with its feverish climax, in which the old steamer is assailed by volleys of arrows, and the helmsman is killed by a spear. Marlow, reaching his goal at last, finds Kurtz's bungalow surrounded by tall stakes, each surmounted by a decomposing human head. The old man, at the point of death, is carried aboard, and expires as he is borne down river.

I had found the final pages of the book so vivid that I kept scanning the dense vegetation on the banks, in case hostile savages were flitting through the trees beside us, bent on launching an attack. I had to remind myself that it was more than fifty years since Conrad had written his story, and that he had no doubt amplified the evil power of the environment, which made Kurtz croak out, as he died, 'The horror! The horror!'

Abonema, our most northerly port, proved to be a substantial town, with one or two concrete buildings rising above a mass of huts, the whole dominated by the grey stone shell of an enormous church. Evidently some zealous missionary had begun building it, and, when he went elsewhere, left funds for it to be completed. But the money disappeared and the interior was never finished – so the building was used to house animals and became known as the Church of the Holy Goats.

This time we anchored in mid-river, surrounded on both sides by great rafts of logs. We heard that the town's white inhabitants – all six of them – lived a separate existence on the bank opposite the main settlement; but one night the apprentices and I decided to go into town for a drink. As we were leaving, the purser armed us with a vicious-looking knife, telling us not to hesitate, but to use it if we hit trouble. 'Leave most of your money behind,' he said, 'and watch out for yourselves. If the cops find a body in a ditch tomorrow morning, they won't give a damn, whatever colour it is.'

Quickly we realised that going ashore had been unwise. The town was pitch dark. The stinking streets were unlit, and the only illumination came from a few candles flickering in the windows of huts. Word of our presence soon spread, and gangs of youths began to follow and jostle us, eager to start a fight; but we took things easily, and after a couple of beers in filthy bars we withdrew to the safety of the ship. It was a relief to be afloat again.

With a full load of logs, and several tons of rubber, we slipped back downstream to the coast and eastward to the Bonny River. Once more, our passage through a chain of creeks demanded expert navigation. Several times we had to go astern and forward again, manoeuvring to negotiate the bends. Our destination, Port Harcourt, was much the largest jungle town we visited, and our main task there was to pick up 800 tons of peanuts and peanut oil, for which the *Exedene* had one deep tank amidships; but I am ashamed to say that I remember practically nothing about the place.

Somehow I fell in with two young British expatriates living in the town. Who they were, and what business they had there, I do not know. All I can recall is that they were friendly and civilised: they had records of classical music – Mozart sonatas particularly – and they were powerful imbibers. Invited for a drink, and then for supper, I became totally plastered – the drunkest I have ever been. I vaguely recall one of my new friends taking me back to the ship in the small hours, and thinking, as I saw dimly-lit trees flash past the windows of the car, 'Thank God someone here knows how to drive, because I couldn't, to save my life.'

The next thing I knew, I came round groggily as someone poured a bucket of river water over my head. Daylight! I found I was lying up the steeply-sloping gangplank, with one leg stuck in a gap between steps, from which I extricated myself with difficulty. Later someone told me I had tried to attack the native watchman at the bottom of the steps, but he, recognising me, had sensibly kept his distance until I had lost interest and lurched upwards.

At sea once more, we put in again at Takoradi to take on one last batch of cargo. Then, with everything loaded, we decanted the Kroo boys – and glad we were to be rid of them, for they had created filth wherever they had settled and made the whole ship noisome. As we sailed out of the harbour we threw tons of their rubbish overboard and washed the decks down from stem to stern. It was as if the *Exedene* had sloughed off an old skin: she came up different, and shining, and we went at her furiously with our paint pots, keen that she should look her best when we reached home.

I came back eager to write about the trip; but other things intervened. I never went to Hudson's Bay, or joined Jardine Matheson; and it was not until the next summer, when I had a holiday job on the *Bolton Evening News,* that I at last got down to the task of composition. High on the edge of the moor above the town I found a wooden hut, with a bench outside, poised above an inspiring view. Whose the building was, I never knew, but it seemed to be open to all comers. Climbing up to it after work on long, light evenings, I scratched away at an article with pencil and paper, draft after draft, until I felt satisfied. I wanted to call the article 'Hot for Certainties', after George Meredith's

Ah what a dusty answer gets the soul
When hot for certainties in this our life!

But several people persuaded me that this would be pretentious. 'Rubbish!' said my father crisply. 'You've had an adventure, not a dusty answer. Go for something simpler.' So I changed the title to 'Flash and Dash', and sent the piece to *Blackwood's Magazine,* who, to my delight, accepted it, published it, and paid fifteen guineas – a modest success, but my first break-through into print.

CHAPTER THREE

Go to Moscow and Turn Right
1957

'Come to Russia,' said my godfather Peter Fleming by way of greeting. I was flattered by the invitation, but, knowing that he had made similar, sudden approaches to other people, inciting them to join him on outlandish expeditions (for instance to the Mato Grosso), I was also cautious. That very day I had landed back from West Africa, and I had only just regained my land-legs. Yet within twenty-four hours the idea of a foray inside the Iron Curtain seemed so exciting that I agreed to go.

I was just 21, and politically naïve, having never paid much attention to international affairs; but the summer of 1957 was a stirring time, for in May the Soviet Union suddenly announced that it was about to open its western frontier to tourist cars – a startling development, considering the state of East-West relations at the time.

In the depths of the Cold War, the whole of Eastern Europe was frozen under Soviet rule. East Germany - the *Deutsche Democratische Republik* - was a closed Communist state, cut off from the West by border defences armed with mines and electrified wire, allegedly to keep foreigners out, but in fact to prevent citizens escaping. Czechoslovakia was dominated by its Soviet-backed Government. The People's Republic of Poland was another Soviet satellite. In November 1956 the Soviet Army had invaded Hungary and crushed the people's revolution with tanks.

The idea of driving through parts of the Soviet empire and into Russia was novel and slightly alarming. The decision to admit Western motorists seemed to herald a slight thaw in east-west relations. Some commentators saw it as a follow-up of Khruschev's speech denouncing Stalin.

Peter, then 50, was still well-known from his best-selling pre-war travel books *Brazilian Adventure* and *News from Tartary*. His many outlandish journeys included visits to North and South America, to Japan and to China, where he had managed, against great odds, to interview the Communist leader Mao Tse-Tung. His younger brother Ian was also gaining recognition with novels about his secret-service agent James Bond, the first of which, *Casino Royale,* had appeared in1953; but so far no one had made a Bond film, and the books did not as yet command any following in Russia.

Now, in 1957, Peter had hit the headlines again with the publication of *Invasion 1940,* his historical study of Operation Sealion, Hitler's plan to invade England. The book, which came out in May, attracted enormous coverage, not least in America, where the *Chicago Herald Tribune* called it 'an incredible, fascinating story.'

Many people, disconcerted by Peter's taciturnity, found him a difficult character; but he and I had spent so much time in each other's company that we understood each other very well, and had no need for constant chatter. Nor did I resent his habit of addressing me as 'You great oaf,' because I knew it denoted affection. Casual acquaintances did not realise how funny he was. In fact he loved jokes and was constantly making them, most effectively in his books and articles. In a typical throwaway line about the start of one of his own journeys he wrote, 'With the possible exception of the equator, everything begins somewhere'; and when somebody was described as being driven by worry to his wits' end, he remarked, 'No very great distance, I imagine'.

It was twenty years since he had last been in Russia, but during the 1930s he had travelled widely in the Soviet Union, and he retained what he called 'a perhaps rather masochistic affection' for its people and atmosphere. He also had what he called 'an execrable but resolute' grasp of Russian; and, as a connoisseur of the barely-credible inefficiency of the Communist system, he was keen to make another visit, to see how things had changed. He therefore suggested to *The Times* that he should pioneer the motor route to Moscow and on to Yalta in the Crimea. The Editor, Sir William Haley, agreed that the newspaper would pay the expenses of the journey, and fees for an unspecified number of articles. Early in June Haley mentioned the project to the Soviet Ambassador to London, Ivan Malik, who was enthusiastic, and said that the more people who took the road to Moscow, the better.

The distances involved looked formidable. We worked out that Yalta was at least 3,000 miles from base in Oxfordshire – so we would cover more than 6,000 miles in all. There was only one way of arranging a trip, and that was through the Automobile Association, which in turn dealt with Intourist, the official Soviet tourist organisation. The cost, payable in advance, was £156 a head for twenty-seven days' first class board and lodging (the equivalent of £3,270 today). This, in theory, included four meals a day, a hotel room, a private bathroom, and the services of an interpreter/guide. In return for payment, we were given one small coupon – the only proof of our entire arrangement; but we were assured that we would be accompanied by our interpreter 'at all times' throughout the tour. Petrol, oil and repairs would have to be paid for in roubles exchanged at the rate of twenty-seven to £1 – but as a gallon of petrol cost only six roubles, the cost did not seem daunting.

Our hotel rooms were booked in advance, and only one route was permitted. From the frontier at Brest-Litovsk we would drive through Minsk and Smolensk to Moscow, then south through the Ukraine to the Crimea. We would not be allowed to deviate from the prescribed road; the restriction sounded tiresome, but in practice it presented no problem, for, as Peter remarked later, 'It's easy enough to get to Yalta. All you have to do is go to Moscow and turn right.'

That was true enough. But as he was totally un-mechanical, and could hardly tell a gearbox from a gasket, he needed not only a co-driver for the journey, but also someone to look after his car. One of the reasons why he chose me was that (as I have recounted) during National Service, I had acted as Transport Officer of 4th Guards Brigade, and had learnt a little about engines. Even so, my knowledge was sketchy; and, assuming there would be no efficient garages in Russia, and certainly none with any knowledge of western vehicles, I went on a crash maintenance course with Gowrings, the firm in Reading who had supplied Peter's dark-blue, convertible Mark II Ford Zephyr, the big Ford of the day. Meanwhile our passports disappeared for weeks into the impenetrable bowels of the Soviet Embassy in London.

Peter, who had a penchant for teasing Communist officials, nearly grounded our enterprise before take-off by suggesting to Intourist that we should travel outwards first class and return second class. His aim was to find out, and report on, how hotels and other facilities differed from one class to the other; but the request cast the bureaucrats into a morass of suspicion and confusion, and caused such a delay that our tickets and visas arrived only just in time.

A week or so before we left for Russia, we had a briefing from a man in a pinstripe suit who came down to Oxfordshire from London and, with the utmost urbanity, made various suggestions, asking if we could do him a favour by keeping an eye open for military facilities along our route. 'Just after you've cleared Dnepropetrovsk,' he murmured, 'if you wouldn't mind looking to your right to see if you can spot any aircraft on the ground ...'

We left England on 27 June, flying with the car by Silver City Airways from Lydd to Le Touquet, armed with a copy of Baedeker's *Russia* (1914) and a supply of whisky. It might have been comforting to have a pistol in the dashboard pocket, but we decided that the presence of a weapon would be sure to cause trouble sooner or later.

The first night found us at Hubbelrath, where we lodged comfortably with friends in 4th Guards Brigade. I stayed with Henry and Janet Gibbs, and Peter was most hospitably put up by David Toler, the Brigade Major, and his wife Judy. Then it was into the unknown: a long, scorching-hot day slanting south-east through Germany brought us to Frankfurt and Nuremberg, and thence through a lovely, soft evening, alive with the smell of pines and warm hay, to the Czech frontier. There, under the gaze of guards perched in wooden watch towers, slovenly officials took an hour to peruse our documents before posting us through three separate barriers, the middle one made of barbed wire and guarded by machine-gun posts.

By the time we reached Plzen, late at night, no doubt we were tired and unappreciative, but the dining room of the Continental Hotel struck us as ineffably dreary, its sub-fusc décor made even more depressing by the band, which played tunes like 'Roll out the Barrel' again and again. As we ordered more vodka and waited for our Schnitzels, Peter kept urging me to go across and accost a raven-haired, ferociously made-up harpy who sat alone at a distant table; but I could not face trying to start up a conversation in German, let alone in Czech, at that stage of the evening. In the morning a visit to the grandiose State Bank was no more inspiring. For Peter the place evoked memories of his earlier Soviet travels, as he once again sensed 'the feeling of a bureaucracy without purpose or hope, and with very little to do'.

Later in the morning we reached Prague. I longed to stop and explore the streets of handsome buildings which had escaped destruction in the war, many still looking much as Mozart must have known them; but Peter (as usual) was determined to press on, and we drove straight through the city with positively philistine disregard of its attractions, to reach the Polish frontier at tea-time.

At the barrier a prim little girl searched every cubic inch of our luggage. She was stumped by my Loeb edition of Herodotus in ancient Greek and English, suspecting (I thought) that the peculiar script embodied some sort of code; but she passed our crate of NAAFI alcohol without a word, and in no time we were on our way towards Breslau. In one three-hour stretch we saw six other cars, and in Breslau itself I was shocked by the devastation: heaps of rubble – the remains of buildings shattered in the war – still lay everywhere. Improbably enough, we spent a luxurious night in the bridal suite of the Hotel Metropole.

The next day was June 30. Our visas authorised us to enter the Soviet Union on 1 July, but because we suspected we were competing with other journalists to be first into Russia, we decided to press on and see if we could jump the gun by a few hours. I fear we paid as little homage to Warsaw as we had to Prague. We did have a quick look at the Old Town, which had been smashed to rubble during the war but had already been miraculously restored, with its tall houses painted in soft pastel colours. That was a pleasant surprise. Not so the dreadful Palace of Culture and Science, a 'gift from the Soviet Union to the people of Poland,' completed two years earlier. A colossal skyscraper nearly 800 feet tall, reminiscent of the Empire State Building in New York, but clearly a product of brutalist Soviet design, and (as we soon saw) a blood brother of the tower in the Moscow State University, this monster towered over the city, utterly out of proportion with the rest of the buildings

Chilled by the sight of it, we headed for the Russian frontier, which we reached at 7.30 on a lovely evening. The Polish barrier, on the bank of the River Bug, was manned by a charming officer, who rang up his opposite number across the water. Half an hour later a small car came speeding out onto the bridge, stopped and turned round in the middle. Our genial Pole walked out with our passports, handed them over, and came back. The Russian waved to us to join him; as we drove forward, the Polish barrier dropped behind us with a clang, and we were in.

At Brest-Litovsk, four kilometres away, through woods alive with soldiers, we were surprised to find the customs checks perfunctory. Our luggage was not searched: we simply filled in forms declaring how many firearms we had (nil), and how much gold (nil), opium and hashish (nil) we were carrying. But we found that our premature arrival had flummoxed the Intourist officials, and that no accommodation had been booked for us. Our only option was to stay in the palatial station building, all pink and white marble inside, where we got a room containing three upright, chrome-plated iron-beds, an electrically-operated samovar and an oppressively large tree. Over an excellent meal in the station restaurant I gave an impromptu English lesson to four large and jolly waitresses, detailed to learn the language for the benefit of the tourists who (they were confident) would soon be flocking through. Peter, meanwhile, managed to file a brief report for *The Times*.

To our chagrin we found we had been beaten to the post by Pat Smiley, an intrepid girl from the *Daily Express,* who had arrived two hours ahead of us, travelling on her own. In the morning we picked up our interpreter, Valentine, a small fellow in his thirties with adequate English but zero curiosity about us or our journey. As we set off for Moscow, the sun blazed down, and it was a joy for us, in the front seats, to have the roof down. Less so for Valentine, pinned in the back by the slipstream and deafened by the roar of the wind. Expecting that he would try to plant a microphone somewhere in the car, we had decided not to discuss any sensitive matter while we were driving, and we had devised a simple code for alerting each other if we saw anything unusual. Any mention of fruit would mean we were being followed, any name of a tree (beech, oak, maple) that we had spotted something of interest.

Only the one broad highway lanced through the immense, flat landscape, whose sheer size I found exciting. The scale of the country was huge, the road hypnotically straight. We covered twenty-four miles before we came to the first gentle curve, in a village. After that, there was no other bend for seventy-four more miles. The surface of the road was tarmacked, but undermined by subsidence and vilely graded into humps and hollows which limited our speed to 50 or 60 mph. A few side-roads meandered off into the hinterland, but they were mere dirt tracks, and there were no sign-posts to show where they led. Now and then we met a convoy of grey military trucks, but the only civilian vehicle we saw all day, apart from horse-drawn carts, was one ancient tractor. With no fences between the fields, the country looked depressingly bare and empty – except for a few black storks, which paced about in the fields. Occasionally a clumsily-executed hoarding saluted some achievement by workers who had heroically exceeded their norm, but of commercial advertising there was not a sign.

As we drove, history was all around us. We talked of Napoleon, marching his immense forces, 600,000 strong, towards Moscow in the summer of 1812, heading deeper and deeper into trouble as he made to attack the capital. For his troops in their heavy uniforms, the heat must have been crippling. Part of the Emperor's undoing was that, as usual, he relied largely on local crops for feeding his horses; and he was dismayed when the Russians, retreating ahead of him, set fire to their fields of hay and corn as they went. From the dry, brittle look of the wheat and barley we saw, we reckoned that fire-raising would have been easy enough. And it was down the very road on which we were driving that the shattered French army straggled in retreat when winter set in.

Our first day brought us to Minsk, a large city almost completely rebuilt since the war. An enormous youth festival was in progress, with singers and dancers in traditional costume performing rather like Morris men in the street right under the windows of our hotel. Yet the appearance of a western car proved a powerful counter-attraction.

Word of our arrival spread at amazing speed: within minutes a crowd began to cluster round the Zephyr, prodding its flanks and stippling its paintwork with fingerprints. By the time we reappeared after signing-in, about 300 people were scrutinising the car with the kind of wonder they might have accorded a space-ship. They were intensely curious about us, too, and stared at us as if we were freaks. Being fair-haired and blue-eyed, I was several times mistaken for a Dane, a Dutchman or a German – an impression reinforced by the fact that the only language in which I could communicate *was* German. Quite a few of the men could speak it, and they seemed happy to use it, even though memories of the war were still raw.

Presently one small, serious-looking fellow, maybe in his forties, looking thin and under-nourished, emerged from the crowd and introduced himself in reasonable English. 'I am schoolmaster here,' he said. 'Welcome to city of Minsk. But please tell me, why are you here?'

'We're tourists,' I said. 'Your Government has opened the road. We're on our way to Yalta.'

'Yalta! That is very far. You are a student?'

'That's right.'

'And this gentleman is your father?'

'No – my godfather.'

'*Krestnyy otets! Horosho!*' There was a pause while he passed the information on to the crowd. Then I said, 'My godfather has travelled many times in your country.'

Turning to Peter, he asked, 'Where have you been?'

Launching into his monosyllabic Russian, Peter mentioned his passage to China on the Trans-Siberian Railway in 1933, but kept his account of the journey so short that the little teacher seemed disappointed.

'I think you are not allowed to talk to me.'

'What d'you mean?'

'Your government forbids it.'

'Nonsense!' I said. 'Maybe *your* government forbids it. But we can talk to anyone we like.'

He looked at me for a few seconds, then said, 'In that case, tell me, please. There is one thing I would like to know. How did you get this car?'

'It belongs to my godfather.'

'*Nyet, pozhaluysta.* I realise you have to say that, for reasons of propaganda. But I would like to know the truth. Clearly, it is not possible for a private citizen to own such a vehicle.'

Useless to tell him that in the West thousands of people had cars of this kind – so much so that traffic jams were a nightmare. The man was so saturated by Soviet disinformation, so cut off from Western news or events, that he could not believe us when we persisted with our story, and in the end he concluded that we were lying. His manner, which had been friendly, cooled rapidly. 'I am sorry you cannot speak freely,' he repeated, and drifted away.

Next day, trouble. We had just set out for Smolensk, 220 miles away, when Peter began to feel ill, with agonising stomach cramps. Soon he was in such pain that he curled up, sheet-white, in the passenger seat, and I drove as fast as the undulating road would allow, stopping frequently for him to stagger out on to the side of the road and be sick. The moment we reached our hotel, he went straight to bed.

Medical personnel, summoned by Valentine, came in waves to examine him. First a very large woman, clad in white, gripped him ferociously round the midriff, making him groan with pain; then a single male specialist appeared, then two more women. 'It is *appenditzit,*' the specialist announced. 'Appendicitis. An immediate operation is necessary.' '*Nyet!*' Peter croaked. 'My appendix was taken out when I was a boy.' This news caused a protracted discussion, during which the patient gasped out a short despatch for transmission to *The Times,* dictating it to me. Naturally our booked call came through just at the medical exchanges were reaching their climax. I sat in one corner of the room, shouting down the telephone to London, while the Russians jabbered away round Peter's bed – and somehow the man in Printing House Square managed to take down what I was saying. A chaotic evening eventually calmed down when Peter, having refused to go to hospital, consented to some pain-killing injections, first in his back, then in his arm.

In the morning he was more comfortable, but comatose from sedatives, so I bundled him into the car and drove all-out for Moscow, 250 miles away. About 80 miles short of the capital a huge black limousine came speeding towards us, screeched to a halt and disgorged a squad of news agency photographers, who shot reels of film. When we started again, an athletic black-haired man with an extraordinarily long neck dangled from the rear window of the car with a movie camera to capture the Zephyr in motion.

On the outskirts of the city we were met by a car containing a delegation from the British Embassy, who led us in. Luckily there was very little traffic apart from trams and buses, but without Valentine to explain the rules, I would soon have been in difficulties. The main streets were far wider than any in England, with two lanes separated by a kind of no-man's-land, marked off by thick white lines on either side. Between these were stationed blue-uniformed policemen, sending out ambiguous instructions with their white truncheons and letting off occasional blasts on their whistles. The overhead signs at junctions were very small, and to a newcomer, driving on the right of the road, it was by no means clear where or when one was allowed to turn left.

Our destination, the Savoy Hotel, had been the last word in luxury at its inception in 1913. Now the five-storey building was showing its age, but it retained an aura of imperial days, partly manifest in the *babushki,* the substantial ladies, dressed in black, who sat at desks outside the lifts and monitored the comings and goings on every floor, doubtless reporting anything suspicious to the KGB.

By the time we arrived, Peter had developed a high fever and again retired to bed. The doctor from the British Embassy swiftly came round, only to be baffled by his symptoms; but his temperature gradually subsided, and he was delighted when a reporter from Moscow Radio, after recording a brief interview, signed off by saying, 'Pardon me for interrupting your disease.'

Our status as official tourists secured us tickets to the Bolshoi Theatre. Peter, still not feeling well (and in any case being notably un-musical) passed up the opportunities; but I went eagerly to performances of *La Bohème* and *Prince Igor.* I remember little about the production of *Bohème,* except that I was disconcerted by the crudity of the singers' make-up: Rodolfo's lipstick and rouged cheeks were as bright-red as those of the women. Someone told me it was part of the Bolshoi's tradition – but I found it uncomfortable. *Prince Igor,* in contrast, made a tremendous impression: a huge cast (including real horses), all-out singing and dancing, and stunning stage effects. In one glorious scene the sun gradually set, growing larger and redder as it sank down the back-cloth towards the horizon, and in another, when the citadel was sacked, live flames licked high up the walls.

Many of the audience, I suspected, had been awarded tickets and transported to the capital in return for heroic efforts in exceeding their work norms. With their drab clothes and air of slight bewilderment, they looked uncomfortably out of place, wondering how they had landed in those gilt-laden surroundings. On my left sat a tiny woman who perhaps came from some Arctic Siberian province: very dark of skin and desiccated-looking, she was dressed in black and gave off a powerful smell of kippered fish, as if she herself had been well smoked. Throughout three acts of the opera and two intervals she never stirred – and what she thought was happening on stage, it was impossible to imagine. My right-hand neighbour was utterly different: a large and restless French lady who heaved about in her seat, palpably bored. At the end of the tumultuous and thrilling Polovtsian dances she gave a loud *whoosh* of relief, exclaimed, '*Enfin – c'est fini!*' and departed, not waiting for anything worse.

Another privilege for tourists was that of going to the head of the queue which snaked away across Red Square from the squat granite pyramid of the Mausoleum. Part reddish pink, part black, the hideous building, rising in ledges from a plinth, then housed the corpses of Lenin and Stalin, with their names displayed in big capital letters above the entrance.

Giving way only to a delegation of blue-shirted East Germans, our guide led us down steps into a dimly-lit cavern, where we joined the line of worshippers gazing at the two monsters who had sent millions of Soviet citizens to their deaths. Down in the vault the air was cold and carried a faintly sweet smell, not unpleasant, but sinister. Both bodies were brilliantly illuminated in coffins with steeply-raked glass sides. Lenin – if indeed it still was he – lay on his back, eyes closed, wearing a white shirt with collar and tie, his head propped up at an angle, little sandy beard jutting, hands resting on his stomach. Thirty-three years after his death, the skin of the face was shiny – and I wondered whether I was looking at a body or a wax replica. Whatever the truth, the object was too close to be comfortable – only a few feet away. The same was true of Stalin, especially as he seemed unnervingly real. He too lay on his back, his arms in the same posture, clad in a military uniform jacket, with a row of medals on his chest. Only three years since he had died, he looked all-too lifelike: coarse black bristles, sprouting from his chin, showed that his beard had continued to grow after death. [1]

What were the good Soviet citizens thinking as they filed silently past? They stared for as long as they could, but the steady movement of the queue kept pushing them forward, and their faces remained expressionless. The only sound was the shuffle of feet on the floor.

It was a relief to emerge into the fresh air, and see more of the city's sights. We had acquired a different interpreter – Vladimir, who spoke good American and knew Moscow well. He gave us the inescapable tour of Gum, the immensely-long state department store, with its ornate, colonnaded façade, which runs down one side of Red Square; and although it was obviously not his fault that the goods on show were so few and so shoddy, somehow his sub-fusc personality matched the surroundings and made them even more depressing.

Outside, we found the ubiquitous Soviet propaganda oppressive, and I was constantly pestered by young men asking if I had any spare clothes

1 In October 1961 Stalin's body was removed from the mausoleum and buried.

or shoes to sell – or indeed if I would part with the check shirt and denim trousers I was wearing. Rather than linger in the city, we soon set off for the first of what Intourist called our 'cultural objectives,' Yasnaya Polyana, the home of Leo Tolstoy, near Tula, about 80 miles south of the capital.

The great writer spent almost all his life on the 4,000-acre family estate, working with his peasants on the harvest, swimming in the lakes in summer, skating on them in winter. Nearly 50 years after his death, his presence was everywhere about the elegant, two-storey house, long and low, with white walls and green roof, set on a slope among enfolding woods. Here were his library of 20,000 books, his simple bedroom, his study, and the leather couch on which not only he but all his thirteen children had been born. It was fascinating to think that the characters of Anna Karenina, Alexei Vronsky, Stiva Oblonsky, the Bezhukovs, the Bolkonskys, the Kutuzovs and countless others all gradually took shape here on the author's desk as he scrawled out draft after draft of his novels in his tiny hand-writing. Peter – another literary squire – felt Tolstoy's presence also in the surrounding woods, where he lies buried in a glade beneath an oblong grassy mound. The rusticity and isolation of Yasnaya Polyana appealed to both of us, and seemed a million versts from the deadening futility of Soviet Communism that prevailed outside the bounds of the estate.

The intellectual level fell sharply at our next stops – the regional headquarters of two of the local *Sovnarhoz,* the new regional economic councils recently created by Khruschev in an attempt to de-centralise control from Moscow. One of these offices was in chaos, with furniture being unloaded in what Peter called 'an atmosphere of genial despair.' In the other, the staff at least had desks on which to put their feet up until something started to happen.

In sharp contrast, Spasskoye Litvinovo, home of the 19th-century writer Ivan Turgenev, near the town of Orel, proved a delight: another white house, smaller than Yasnaya Polyana, with wooden balustrades, set in the heart of another well-wooded estate. Here Turgenev – a tall, broad-shouldered, solitary youth – grew up in the early 1800s, and here, after his father had died when he was only sixteen, he constantly prowled about the countryside on solo shooting expeditions, not least to escape from the harangues of his tyrannical mother. His forays after game led to the book which first made his name – the collection of essays entitled *A Sportsman's Sketches.*

Spasskoye was sadly run-down: the paint on the house was peeling, the paths overgrown with weeds. But the spirit of Turgenev was strongly in occupation, and a charming guide – a little old woman with a few words of English – explained that all the pictures and furniture had belonged to the author himself. Every exhibit elicited the same carefully-pronounced explanation. As we came to a desk, 'Here is Turgenev ... writing.' As we passed a picture, 'Here is Turgenev ... shooting.' 'Here is Turgenev ... walking', and in a bedroom, 'Here is Turgenev ... sleeping.' Lying on a table was an English translation of *A Sportsman's Sketches,* no doubt put there for our benefit, and by chance it was open at the first page of the story called *Bezhin Meadow,* which I had read and loved.

Starting with a pin-sharp description of a summer evening, the piece describes how the author gets lost after a day shooting blackcock, and as dark falls stumbles into an encampment of peasant boys minding horses turned out to graze. Every sight, sound and scent is recorded with wonderful clarity: the red glow of the boys' fire, the coolness of the night air, the munching of unseen horses, the splash of fish in the river. Reading a couple of pages took me back into another age. It was magical to be in Turgenev's own environment, at the time of year he described: another country, another world.

We did our best to re-visit earlier times, walking out through the park after supper. In the warm dusk we met a party of lively lads from the Orel technical institute, who, taking us for Germans, plied us eagerly with questions about the West. They thirsted for western music – Louis Armstrong and Bunk Johnson were their heroes – but since no British or American records were available in the Soviet Union, the only way they could hear real jazz was on the radio.

Next morning we were on the road again, heading south through the *Chernozem* or Black Earth Belt, the most fertile part of the Ukraine.

The sun grew hotter by the hour, and the harvest was coming in from huge, gently-rolling wheatlands. Memorial pillars and tanks on pedestals alongside the road reminded us that during the Second World War savage battles had been fought across this open landscape. In urban parks all the trees were still small: their predecessors had been blitzed into oblivion, and the new generation had had barely a dozen years in which to grow. Statues – some still of Stalin – were invariably painted silver.

During one of his earlier journeys Peter had visited the anti-God museum in Moscow. That ludicrous institution had long since gone, but we found an echo of it in a poor little de-consecrated church. The onion dome had been taken off and lay on the ground beside the building, and the chancel had been converted into a bowling alley, with a huge poster-photograph of Lenin glaring down from where the altar had been.

Being in charge of refuelling, I had to keep my wits about me, for filling stations were often more than 100 miles apart. Only two grades of petrol were available. The standard variety – which was not at all to the Zephyr's taste, and made the engine pink – came from hand-operated pumps, most of which were out of order. When we were reduced to using it, I had to clean sludge out of the filter bowl at the bottom of the carburettor every morning. The car went better on the vintage variety, which our Intourist coupons entitled us to buy; but this higher-octane stuff was kept in tins, under lock and key, and could be got only through the good offices of the man in charge of the station, who often had disappeared for lunch when we drew up. Even if he was present, the odds were that he had no funnel – so that filling-up was a messy and time-consuming business. Sometimes it took an hour and a half to refuel. We carried one spare can, refilled it at every opportunity, and frequently had recourse to it.

Once, as an experiment, we turned off the highway down a fork that led away to the right. Before we had gone quarter of a mile, and before Vladimir had begun to remonstrate, a man in military uniform rose up out of a ditch beside the road and waved us down. '*Zhal!*' he said. 'Sorry. The road is closed.' His manner was genial enough – but the speed with which we had been intercepted gave us the unpleasant feeling that our progress was being monitored every mile of the way.

Ordinary Soviet citizens, on the other hand, were as friendly as could be, and we never felt the slightest hostility. On the contrary, people longed to communicate, sparked up by their first-ever contact with foreigners. In Kursk, when we came out of a restaurant after lunch, we found five policemen holding back a crowd of several hundred and blowing their whistles furiously to maintain order. As we got into the car, women hoisted their children to have a look at us, as if we were Martians. There, as everywhere, people were casually dressed, the men in open-necked shirts, the women in faded cotton frocks that had been through the wash many times. Almost all the men wore caps, and most of the women head-scarves.

It was the same at every stop. In any town or village people surrounded us, like cattle converging on a picnic party in a field, and although amusing at first, this soon became tiresome. The first questions were always about the car: '*Amerikanskiy? Angliyskiy*?' How much does it cost? How many cylinders in the engine? How fast will it go? How far to a litre? Would I please lift the bonnet so that the engine could be inspected?' Sometimes, after an agreeable but taxing session of question and answer in two or three languages, I felt we were doing a microscopic bit to improve east-west relations. We deliberately avoided asking political questions, for fear that they would arouse suspicion and lead to our being arrested for attempted subversion. Perhaps we were excessively cautious, but in that oppressive atmosphere restraint seemed the safest option.

On we went, through Kharkov, Dnepropetrovsk and Zaparozhe, between vast fields of wheat, sunflowers and maize, with hoopoes flying beside us and flamingos standing round ponds. The heat increased steadily until the daytime temperature was well into the eighties. Being troubled by lack of exercise, I sometimes took to jogging for a mile or so in the cool of the morning, while Peter kept the car crawling behind.

The hotels varied from moderate to awful. In all of them the bathrooms were primitive, and in one there was no running water. We soon gave up the hope that any of them would have a swimming pool, and I incurred the wrath of one manager by forcing open the French windows in our bedroom. I do not think those windows had ever been opened before:

they were sealed shut and painted over, so that the temperature in the south-facing room was insufferable. Brute force was the answer: when I exerted all my strength, they gave way with a loud crack. The glass did not break, but old paint, putty and bits of wood exploded all over the floor, and in came blessed air.

The food, on the other hand, was better than we had expected: borsch and chicken Kiev were always reliable, and I developed a passion for *varenyky* (known elsewhere in Russia as *pelmeni),* little dumplings stuffed with minced meat or spiced vegetables and usually served with sour cream. We asked in vain for caviar, but there was never any shortage of vodka, which we had to order by weight – so many grams, measured out into a small decanter.

Leaving the black earth behind, for one whole day we drove through the Nogaisk steppe – a grey, barren stretch of undulating, parched grassland and minimal cultivation. Then at last we came to a tongue of land – a causeway, flanked by the sea on both sides – which brought us onto the Crimean peninsula, and across a dead-flat plain to the town of Simferopol. Thence we climbed steeply over wild, rocky, wooded mountains, before descending through coils of hairpin bends to Yalta, on the coast of the Black Sea.

Of all the towns we had seen, Yalta was much the most attractive: its streets were lined with cypresses and poplars, and it had a holiday air. Once the resort of royalty and the aristocracy, it had become a favourite summer destination for Soviet citizens, hardly any of whom were then allowed to travel abroad. We found the place full of holiday-makers, many lobster-coloured from rash exposure to the sun; but, outside the sanatoria in which they were staying, facilities were limited. There were, for instance, no public lavatories on the beaches, with the result that on the shore people were shamelessly defecating in full view of everyone else. At Gurzuf, a smaller resort to the east, the beach was so filthy that we scrambled out onto some rocks and swam from there. The water, once one got into it, was gloriously warm and clear.

Our comfortable hotel, only a couple of hundred yards from the front, was run by a solicitous, French-speaking woman, whom I described in a letter home as 'by a long way the most civilised person we've met so far.' From her office Peter telephoned a report to *The Times,* claiming a modest scoop – ours being the first British vehicle ever to reach the Crimea.

Naturally we wanted to visit the Livadia Palace, in which Stalin had outmanoeuvred Churchill and Roosevelt in February 1945 at the conference about the future division of Europe. A useless local guide took us to the elaborate, white palace, only to find that it had been turned into a sanatorium and was closed to visitors. Years later I learnt that Churchill had made a wonderful remark there. One evening after dinner, as he gazed out over the sea, he said to his daughter Sarah, 'This is the Riviera of Hades.'

Our real interest lay in the battlefields of the Crimean War, a tantalisingly short distance along the coast to the west. We did not expect to be granted access to Sevastopol, home of the Soviet Black Sea Fleet, on which security was obviously tight; but we hoped that we might sneak a look at Balaclava and the Valley of Death, up which the Light Brigade charged in 1854. Alas for our plan. The coast road, we learnt, had unfortunately been closed by an avalanche – so we switched to a second line of attack.

Another legitimate tourist destination was the16th-century palace of the Tartar Khans at Bakhchisarai, a few miles inland. From there a secondary road led to Sevastopol – and so, hoping that an oblique approach to our target might circumvent the alleged landslips, we left Yalta and headed for Bakhchisarai.

When we reached Simferopol, I happened to be driving, and as we cleared the town I glanced at the rear mirror and noticed a man on a motorbike pull out behind us. 'Apple at six-o'clock,' I muttered.

'Put your foot down, then,' Peter replied.

In no time we were rocketing along an uneven gravel road at 70 mph, trailing an immense cloud of dust. Bakhchisarai turned out to be no more than a village, and we were through its main street in a flash. For a few moments we thought we were clear – but then with a howl of his high-powered engine our escort shot past, and a couple of miles further on we found him with his bike parked across the road, flagging us down. He was coated in white dust from helmet to boots, but when Peter greeted him with '*Dobriye den*', he gave us a broad grin. Much as he regretted it, he said, the road ahead was closed.

'*Lavina?*' we asked anxiously. 'Avalanche?'

'*Da, da – lavina.*'

Back, then, to the Tartar palace, a wonder of its kind, with much woodwork garishly painted in red and gold. Around the walls of its celebrated harem exotically-dressed mannequins lounged on banquettes, in supposedly suggestive attitudes. More fascinating was the marble fountain, set in a wall, with tears of water welling out into seven cups, eternally commemorating the grief of Giray, the Khan whose favourite courtesan pined away and died. Aleksander Pushkin, having visited the palace in 1824, was so moved by the pathos of the story that he composed an epic poem, *The Fountain of Bakhchisarai.*

Turning our backs on the Crimea, we headed for home as fast as the surface would permit – a marathon slog along the road whose idiosyncrasies we now knew only too well. In one long day, ending at a horrible, waterless hotel outside Mtsensk, we covered 480 miles. In Moscow we paused for a couple of days, on one of which we were invited to lunch at the Embassy by the Military Attaché.

After the meal, as we sat outside in a courtyard, a leisurely political discussion set in. Soon I began to find this tedious, but then I noticed, across the yard, a stand-pipe with a hose attached. We knew that drivers of dirty cars could be fined by the police – and here was an ideal opportunity of getting rid of the dust and dried mud that coated the sides of the Zephyr. Choosing my moment, I politely asked if I might make use of the hose. Peter found this a rather boorish intervention, and apologised, saying 'Duff is a great opportunist.' Luckily our host was amused, and said, 'By all means – go ahead.' So the car was restored to its pristine glossiness, and I took a photograph of it parked on the Kamenny bridge over the Moscow river, with no other vehicle in sight, and the golden domes of the Kremlin glittering in the background.

Heading for home, we passed through Smolensk without stopping, sped on our way down the great road by a performance of Tchaikovsky's 1812 Overture on the radio. At Brest-Litovsk we said goodbye to Vladimir, and after we had cleared the frontier we pulled up on a grassy verge. Out came a bottle of Soviet champagne which we had been saving for this moment; but scarcely had I touched the little wire cage on the top when, with an explosion like the despatch of a two-inch mortar bomb, the cork flew out with such force that it cleared the telephone wires beside the road, and the contents of the bottle foamed out over my hands. We were left with an egg-cup full of warm, fizzy liquid tasting faintly of paraffin, and with that we celebrated our escape from the workers' paradise.

CHAPTER FOUR

Supersonic
1966

I often wish I had learned to fly. Whether my eyesight or my maths would have been good enough for me to quality as a front-line pilot, I doubt; but I have always found combat aircraft exciting, and I was lucky enough to hitch several rides in fast jets, besides flights in less dangerous conveyances. In my dealings with the RAF I was always struck not only by my hosts' high level of skill, but also by their friendliness, and their readiness to answer questions put by an enthusiastic but ignorant inquirer wished on them by public-relations officers in the Ministry of Defence.

My first trip was one of the least glamorous, but strange and memorable. Long before dawn one winter morning in 1966 I found myself at RAF Kinloss, on the shore of the Moray Firth, boarding a Mark III, Phase 3 Shackleton bomber for a long-range reconnaissance patrol in the Arctic. At 5.35 am the captain, thirty-one-year-old Squadron Leader Derek Hann, announced take-off with a cryptic message: 'We're eleven souls on board, and here we go.' What did that mean? That not all eleven might get back? There was plenty of time to worry as the old aircraft clawed its way up into the black northern sky.

As one element of the early-warning system maintained to keep a check on Communist shipping coming down from the north, our brief was to patrol a 30,000-square-mile block of ocean off the Lofoten Islands, and to photograph any vessel we found. For the first two hours we flew in darkness, with nothing visible outside the aircraft except the wing-tip lights and the four exhaust manifolds glowing red-hot in the blackness.

Then, almost imperceptibly, the sky began to lighten, and we could just discern white horses plunging wildly 1,500 feet below.

At 8.22 we crossed the Arctic Circle and came on task. Day-break seemed to have been arrested, and even at mid-morning leaden twilight still lowered above the pewter sea. The wind rose to 75 mph – force eleven – and the captain reported a thirty-foot swell, with occasional waves reaching sixty feet. Inside, the Shackleton was noisy but warm and surprisingly comfortable, modified from its original specification as a bomber to form a surveillance and communications centre, crammed with electronic equipment. Its wings, flexing visibly, absorbed much of the turbulence, and cheerful messages emanated from the galley, where one of the crew, who took it in turns to be off-duty, brewed up hot drinks and substantial meals. 'Galley to crew,' came a call on the intercom. 'Anybody not want coffee?' 'Tea for Radar,' was the answer, and 'Orange for Second Nav.'

For hour after hour we saw nothing except water – but that wasn't surprising. Who would be out in such horrible weather? At least the absence of traffic gave the crew the chance to make practice bomb attacks on flares dropped to imitate targets – until at last the man on radar duty came up with, 'I've got a contact. Forty-six miles ahead.'

This turned out to be the weather-ship Mike; but visibility was so bad that we could not see it until we were little over a mile away. Then began the long run home, enlivened by the discovery of two Russian trawlers. A quick inspection satisfied the captain that they were genuine fishing vessels, and not the kind of intelligence-gatherers that in those days haunted NATO exercises, betrayed by their array of aerials and radar scanners. And so we headed for home.

Back in Scotland, we landed in a whirling snow-storm at 4 pm, and found that another aircraft had just gone out on a search-and-rescue mission, so that ours was next-in-line. Having just flown for ten and a half hours, the crew was immediately on two-hour stand-by to fly again. I didn't envy them – and ever since I have remained haunted by the desolate nature of that northern ocean, on which the sun would not rise again until the spring.

Lightning Encounter
1966

The Shackleton was a plodder. A supersonic Lightning was altogether a different beast, the fastest British fighter of the day. 'If you hear the pilot calling "Eject! Eject! Go!",' said the instructor, 'sit well back in the seat and yank the black-and-yellow zebra loop between your legs. You'll probably lose your knee-caps on the under-edge of the instrument panel as you go out – but that'll be the least of your worries.'

I was already clad in a G-suit, which would inflate whenever we went into a hard turn, to stop blood draining down into my legs. On top of that was a heavy immersion suit (in case we came down in the sea). I and all my kit had been weighed, suspended in mid-air from a sling, in order to determine the exact pressure at which to set my ejector seat.

When I asked for something on which to make notes during the sortie – a pad or a notebook – the instructor replied, 'Don't worry, mate. You won't be doing any writing. We had an Italian journalist here last week. He made one a hell of a fuss – he had to record all his thoughts, his sensations, his experiences. When he got down, he'd only scribbled four words: *'Aeroplano no. Projettile si'* – 'This not an aircraft. It's a missile.'

I stopped calling for writing materials, and we were ready to go.

Out on the tarmac at RAF Coltishall, on the Norfolk coast, stood a pair of 18-ton, blunt-nosed silver bullets – each little more than two huge engines, one on top of the other, with small, swept-back fins for wings. One, designated Lima Five for our sortie, was a single-seat operational Lightning, the RAF's swiftest interceptor; the other, Lima Two, was a T-2 trainer, with two seats jammed side-by-side in the cockpit. My pilot was Flight-Lieutenant Brian Cluer, a genial South African in his early thirties who had flown with the South African Air Force and the Royal Canadian Air Force before joining the RAF – a man of wide experience, known to his mates as 'B.C.', with a deep, comforting voice and a relaxed air that quickly inspired confidence.

On a heavy, dark afternoon in late February, snow was lying around the airfield, but the runway and pan were black and shiny. With nerves on edge, I scrambled up a twelve-foot ladder to the cockpit and eased myself down into the right-hand seat, faced by a bewildering array of dials and switches. A helper who had come up behind me sorted my straps – leg-restrainers round calves, lap-straps round waist, negative-G straps between legs, shoulder straps down from above, until I was trussed into the seat.

On with the white bone-dome helmet. On with the black rubber oxygen mask, clamped over nose and mouth. Now I could hear the hiss and rasp of my own breathing. I could see the rate in the doll's eye blinking on the instrument panel: white – in, black – out. Slow it down, I told myself. Suppress the claustrophobia. My helper pulled out the safety pins to prime my ejector seat – one, two, three, four red tags. The canopy snapped shut.

Brian had already briefed me on our sortie. 'We'll take off as a pair, then separate. Lima Five will head out to sea and come back at flight-level four-zero-zero – that's 40,000 feet – acting as a target for us to intercept.'

Now he was finishing his pre-flight checks, his voice clear in my helmet. A rumble and slight shudder went through the aircraft. 'Number One engine turning and burning,' he told the tower, 'and we have no fire ... JPT gauge coming up. Looks OK. Brake pressure coming up. OK ... Number Two engine turning and burning – and again, we have no fire.' He sounded slightly surprised at the lack of any conflagration, but as I could not see his face, I couldn't tell what he was thinking.

We taxied out and lined up on the end of the runway, with Lima Five on our left, wing-tip to wing-tip, almost in touching distance. A brief wait. Then up came a white-gloved thumb in the other cockpit, and over the radio, 'Rolling ... rolling ... GO!'

A terrific thump in the back. Amazing acceleration. Lima Five was still beside us, but beginning to draw ahead. 'Watch his nose-wheel lifting,' said Brian calmly – and up it went.

Seconds later we too were airborne at 200 mph. Again Lima Five had the advantage. He was still only a few feet away, but pulling ahead. 'Bastard!' cried Brian merrily, 'I can't catch him. It's you – your extra weight.' Our partner vanished into lowering snow clouds. Then our own world was blotted out. Our climb was so violent that g-forces piled on. Lead weights seemed to have clamped themselves on my legs and arms. My feet were fastened to the floor, my arms to my thighs. Lead had filled my stomach, forcing it down into the seat. Lead in the eyeballs made it almost impossible to see. Fighting the pressure, I started to sweat.

Out of the cloud we burst into brilliant sunlight and a wonderfully blue sky. As we levelled off, the g-forces vanished. I assumed that we're pausing in our climb. Wrong. 'We're up,' said Brian. 'There.' He pointed at the altimeter, which was reading 36,000 feet. The air-speed indicator showed Mach 0.9 – 650 mph.

I was surprised that he didn't seem to be *doing* anything. I had thought that, like the pilot of an airliner, he would be constantly reaching up to flick switches or twiddle dials. Instead, he was sitting perfectly still. The reason, I learned later, was that most of the controls were on his stick, so that he could manage them without apparently moving.

After a minute or so flying level he said, 'Have a go. Try a roll. Bring the nose up a bit and put the stick on your knee. No sudden movements – just keep it gentle.'

Me? I'd never flown anything. Nevertheless, I tried – and the result was astonishing. Sky and clouds went into a whirling spin – blue, white, blue, white – and before I could correct we had performed two complete rolls.

'This is fantastic!' I shouted. Then for a minute or two I managed to fly level, revelling in the Lightning's response to the slightest touch. I was just thinking, 'This is best thing I've ever done,' when Brian punctured my euphoria by saying, 'OK, we'd better get back on course.' I thought I'd been flying straight, but in fact I'd veered off by sixty degrees.

Again and again an immense cloud came hurtling towards us – and in an instant we had burst through it, back into the blue. The sheer speed of the changes left me gasping. Up came a message from G.C.I. – ground-controlled intercept, who had taken us over from the Coltishall tower: 'Zero Two, stranger in your area.' In a moment we had him on the radar – a blip coming from the right. Then we saw him for real – a white paper dart of a Phantom, slicing across the sky 5,000 feet below us. Nothing to do with us. But only seconds after he had vanished, G.C.I. called again: 'Zero Two, we have a target for you. Range one hundred miles, heading two-one-five on four-zero-zero.'

'Zero Two, roger, roger,' Brian answered. Then to me, 'That's Dave. He'll be turning to come back at us. He's above us, but even so I'm going to dive first, to pick up speed. OK – here comes the power.'

The boost of the after-burners was like a tremendous punch in the kidneys. Our speed built rapidly. No sensation as we went through the sound barrier: Mach 1.1, 1.2, 1.3. Ground Control kept calling the position of the intruder. 'Target three-zero right and fifty miles ... Target three-five right and forty miles.'

Suddenly we wheeled right and dived onto the attack vector in a numbing turn. I saw our speed rocketing – Mach 1.5 ... Mach 1.7 – 1,250 mph. The horizon whirled crazily until the cloud layer was vertical, on its side. A huge, suffocating pressure gripped me from all sides. Again my eyeballs turned to lead. My arms were too heavy to move. My stomach was threatening to erupt. 'You can*not* be sick into your oxygen mask!' I told myself as I swallowed desperately and gasped for breath.

How could Brian fly, navigate, work the radar and keep up such a calm conversation with base?' Then dimly I realised he was talking to me: 'Look at the radar. We'll get him in a second. There!'

'Judy!' he called, telling G.C.I. that he had taken over the intercept. An orange blip was moving in from the right of the radar display. Seconds later a little ring of light came hunting it, twitching and jerking across the screen until it closed over the blip. 'Got him!' Brian cried. 'We're locked on.' Red lights came up on the instrument panel saying 'Missiles armed.'

The enemy was still invisible, but we were climbing at him from underneath, snapping at him from below and behind. Only in the final seconds of the attack did we see him – a tiny black arrow trailing an immense plume of vapour. 'Splash!' Brian called. The intercept was perfect, and in theory our missiles had achieved a kill.

Immediately Brian cut the re-heats. Three or four more minutes at that speed, and our fuel would have run out. Plummeting earthwards almost vertically – 20,000 feet in a minute – we plunged back into the clouds and through them. I found it an immense relief to see the earth again – the grey sea, the snow-laden coast, the lights on the airfield – for although I had never been frightened, I had felt horribly uncomfortable. As we came in at 200 mph I just had time to register the fire-engines and rescue vehicles lined up on the access tracks alongside the runway. Then we were down – *bang* – and juddering to a halt. As we came to a standstill Brian let out a *whoosh* of relief. 'In this aircraft,' he said, 'every landing is a kind of controlled crash.'

Back in the changing room, I had dozens of questions that I wanted to ask; but I was feeling so sick and disorientated that I couldn't summon them up, or even remember my own telephone number. Brian was extremely solicitous, frequently asking if I was all right; but I sensed that he was in a hurry to depart, and I braced myself to ask what his problem was.

'It's my car,' he said, glancing at his watch. 'It's being serviced, and I have to recover it before the garage closes for the weekend.'

'In that case,' I said, 'can I give you a lift to fetch it?'

So I took him to the garage, and he invited me back to his quarter, where I met his smashing wife Gay and gradually settled down over a cup of tea until I could think straight.

Had I not made that mundane offer in the changing room, I should never have gained a lifelong friend. While still in England Brian gave me the most generous help in furnishing information for the opening sequence of my thriller *Spider in the Morning,* in which my fictional reporter Sam Sholto narrowly survives an emergency during a Lightning sortie very like the one I had flown. I remain indebted to him for that – and for giving me what I could call, without exaggeration, the fastest half-hour of my life.

Brian built his whole career round aircraft. He went on to train Saudi Arabian cadets to fly supersonic jets, and after leaving the RAF he became General Operations Manager for Cathay Pacific Airlines in the Far East. His final (and, as he said, most amusing) job was Controller of the Government Air Service in Hong Kong, where he learnt to fly helicopters and much enjoyed chasing sea-borne smugglers who were trying to sneak expensive items like Ferraris into mainland China. Eventually he and Gay retired to live in Canada and settled at Whistler, in British Columbia, which he describes as possibly the most beautiful place in the world.

His tour as an instructor on Lightnings in the Middle East was made all the more hazardous by the fact that his pupils tended to be both cowardly and boastful – a dangerous combination. These proclivities were graphically illustrated – not in his presence – by an incident at the Basic Flying Training School at Linton-on-Ouse, where students learnt to go solo in the Jet Provost. One morning a Middle-Eastern student took off successfully but almost at once crashed into the middle of a wood. By extraordinary good luck, the aircraft did not catch fire, and he was able to extricate himself from the cockpit and walk away unharmed.

When the Jet Provost went down, an emergency was proclaimed, and fire-crews rushed out to the wreck, only to find no sign of the pilot. He was next seen in the officers' mess cradling a gin-and-tonic, and when questioned about the crash, denied all knowledge of it. Confronted by his signature on the Form 700 which he had filled in for the sortie, he said, 'It's a forgery.' There was no way of penetrating his mendacity; but part of his aircraft, inscribed with a description of the incident, was mounted on the wall of the crew room, where it remained for all to see.

CHAPTER FIVE

Mid-Ocean 1967

'This is one of the strangest places on the face of the earth,' wrote a Victorian naval officer of Ascension Island, and when I first arrived there, I saw what he meant. As I stumbled out of the long-range Britannia at 7 am after an all-night flight from England, I was hit by a blast of baking hot wind, and blinked in disbelief as the sun, newly risen out of the sea, raked low across rust-red, conical hills and fields of broken black lava.

Volcanic remains are Ascension's most striking feature; but another is its isolation. Nearly a thousand miles from the closest point of Africa, and eight hundred from its nearest neighbour, the island of St Helena, it is a mere triangle of rock with sides about seven miles long, poking up out of an infinity of ocean. Until 1815 it was uninhabited by humans, except for the odd castaway; then it was manned by a garrison of the Royal Marines, to prevent any French attempt to rescue Napoleon from his incarceration on St Helena, and it has remained British ever since. At the start it was called H.M.S. *Ascension,* the Navy's only stone frigate.

A hundred and fifty years after its first occupation, space-age technology arrived on the island. In May 1967, as one of a posse of journalists, I went out to inspect the Earth Station built by the British firm Cable & Wireless in conjunction with Marconi to support the Apollo space programme, the American attempt to land a man on the moon.

For the Apollo controllers it was essential to have accurate information about the trajectory of rockets going into earth orbit, and Ascension is the first bit of land over which they pass after launch from the east coast of America. Thus, on our first morning, we visitors were taken to inspect the gleaming, white dish aerial of the Earth Station, rising from a wilderness of lava known as Donkey Plain. Its role would be to relay signals from missiles and spacecraft and pass them up to the Atlantic Intel satellite poised 23,300 miles above the earth in synchronous orbit, for immediate transmission back to America.

It was disappointing to find that, because of delays in other phases of the programme – principally the disaster when the Apollo 1 capsule caught fire on the launch pad at Cape Canaveral, killing all three astronauts, in January that year – the station was not yet in action; but there were any amount of strange discoveries to be made elsewhere. Our hosts – members of Cable & Wireless resident on the island – kindly drove us about the few rough roads, showed us the sights and told us a bit about the island's past. On that initial visit I stayed for three days, and although I was impressed by the space technology, I became even more fascinated by Ascension's history and texture, and in particular by its wildlife.

In 1815 the members of the naval garrison found themselves in charge of an astonishing landscape. Towards the south-east side of the island one high hill had shrubs and trees growing round its summit, and it had already been called Green Mountain; but the rest of the terrain was starkly barren, consisting almost entirely of volcanic debris, with cones of red cinders sprouting from fields of jumbled black and grey lava, much of it piled high into petrified jungles.

The shores of the island dropped so steeply into the sea that it was impossible to form an enclosed harbour, and the best the sailors could achieve was to build a pier about thirty yards long running out from a sheltered landing-place on the west coast. Even with this completed, getting ashore was a hazardous business, for enormous waves known as 'rollers', up to forty feet high, were liable to come in suddenly, so that anyone wanting to land by small boat had to be prepared to make a last-minute jump.

On shore the sailors lived in tents at first, but in due course they built a barracks, storehouses, two forts, a church, and a house for the

Commandant on a ledge above the landing, all of cut stone, and called the settlement Georgetown. In the early days almost all their food had to be imported, but over the years they made heroic efforts to initiate production on the island. The only area on which rain fell in useful quantities was around the summit of Green Mountain, and there, more than 2,000 feet above the baking lava plains, they struggled to establish a small farm.

Merely to render the high ground accessible demanded an immense physical effort. Working by hand, helped by a few detonations, members of the garrison carved a zig-zag track out of the face of the mountain: a sequence of short, steep straights, many with a gradient of one-in-three, linked by more than twenty cripplingly tight hairpin bends, which they called 'the Ramps'. Up on the heights they built a cottage, a mountain barracks and (later) a hospital.

Even in a Land-Rover, 150 years on, an ascent of Green Mountain was electrifying: one could scarcely imagine what it must have been like for the driver of a cart with a recalcitrant mule. The higher we went, the cooler the air became, and until the road ended on a level terrace festooned with greenery, and with a cottage in a garden full of vegetables. There we met Peter Critchley, a farmer from the West Country, and his wife Grace, who had already spent ten years on the island, long outstaying the rest of the transitory inhabitants, and had achieved miracles of production on the twenty acres flat enough for cultivation. The friendly welcome they gave us was enhanced by the exhilaration of being 2,000 feet up in mid-Atlantic, looking down over extinct craters and lava flows, and out over 6,000 miles of ocean.

From the Critchleys I gained a useful outline of the island's recent history. In 1899, the installation of the first transatlantic cables had put Ascension in touch with the outside world, and when the Marines finally departed in 1922, the Eastern Telegraph Company (which later became Cable & Wireless) took over as almost the sole occupants. Then, in March 1942, an American task-force 1,500 strong suddenly swept in to build an airfield, giving planes on their way to Africa an essential touch-down point in mid-Atlantic ('*If we miss Ascension, Our wives get a pension,'* went the pilots' song.). The energy of the engineers and the power of their machines were phenomenal. In ninety days they blasted and bull-dozed a 1,000-yard runway through the valley between two hills on South West Plain, and so established Wideawake Airfield.

The Critchleys also explained about the Saints – the St Helenians who had been coming up from their own island to work for the past forty years. Courteous, easy-going people of every colour from black to *café au lait* – a mixture of African, Indian, Chinese, Portuguese and British – they were, and are, an essential part of Ascension's life, working at first as labourers and servants, but later filling many high offices. From the Saints' point of view, the northern island has been a life-saver, for it is the only place in which most of them can find employment.

Short as it was, that first visit fired my curiosity, and I longed to know more about the island's past. In London again, I began to research Ascension's history, only to find that no book about it existed. Cable & Wireless had little information about earlier years, and I soon realised that the most substantial source would be the Victorian naval reports in the Public Record Office.

I was still working on the *Sunday Telegraph* in Fleet Street, but luckily for me the public records were then housed in Chancery Lane, only a few hundred yards away, so that at lunch time and in other spare moments I could nip up and put in an hour or two studying ships' logs and reports from the garrison. The material was riveting, made all the more enjoyable by the formality of the Victorian prose in which officers of the garrison and ships' captains couched their messages. (John Bell, one of the mountain gardeners, wrote to the Commandant: 'I now beg to draw your serious consideration to the question of Manure.')

When the death of Napoleon in 1821 removed the need to keep an eye on St Helena, the main role of the Ascension garrison became to support the ships waging the Royal Navy's campaign against slavery on the humid, fever-ridden coast of West Africa. Again and again a man-of-war would appear off the island, desperate to rid herself of hands stricken with disease, and ships' logs were punctuated by the lugubrious phrase, 'Departed this life ... Departed this life ...'

In 1823, when the twenty-gun sloop HMS *Bann* anchored close inshore, the plague spread to the garrison and killed more than fifty men. After that disaster no contaminated vessel was allowed near the settlement; invalids were put ashore in a bay a couple of miles to the north – a small, sandy beach hemmed in by slabs of lava, called at first Comfort Cove, and then, more aptly, Comfortless Cove. Food and water were brought out and deposited at a safe distance; a shot was fired to signify the arrival of supplies, and the sufferers were left to their fate. Many were buried behind the bay in any little declivity that could be enlarged from the ash beds between heaps of black basalt slabs, and to this day pathetic crosses stand guard over their graves.

Because of its isolation, the island was a wildlife vacuum. When the Marines arrived, the only large animals were a few wild goats, probably put there by some ship's captain as a potential source of food for stranded mariners. There were also black rats which had got ashore from wrecked ships, and land-crabs, which lived high on the mountain but came down to breed along the edge of the sea. At certain times of year huge green turtles came up the beaches to lay their eggs in the sand. In contrast with the lack of terrestrial life, sea-birds thronged the coast in thousands: sooty terns (soon known from their shrill, incessant calls as 'wideawakes'), fairy terns, red-footed, masked and brown boobies (a form of gannet), red-billed and white-tailed tropic or boatswain birds and, most spectacularly, huge, cannibalistic frigate birds, the males sporting scarlet gular pouches.

When the Marines began to introduce new species, in the absence of natural controls their efforts frequently proved disastrous. The obvious answer to rats was cats; so cats were imported, but soon they made off into the lava, preyed for preference on the sea-birds, multiplied fast and grew extra-long hind legs to cope with the difficult terrain. The answer to cats was dogs, and cat-hunting became a favourite sport. Donkeys, brought in for pulling carts, also went wild and established themselves so securely in the lava fields that their smooth-coated descendants flourish to this day. Goats escaped and survived for many years. Pigs were less fortunate: many got away, but all were eventually rounded up and eaten..

Insects inadvertently brought in on plants were another menace. They devoured crop after crop, and in efforts to suppress them the Admiralty sent out partridges, pheasants and guinea fowl, all of which survived for a while. Mynahs brought from Mauritius also proved effective. On the other hand rooks – obtained with great difficulty from rapacious dealers in London – all died, as did owls recruited to stiffen the campaign against rats. Land-crabs, which were at least native to the island, ate their way through one crop after another.

The constant heat was too much for many of the imported species. 'I am sorry to inform you.' wrote the Commandant to the Admiralty in 1827, ' that only one Hare (a male) has reached us alive, four of the Partridges died, and one of the Pheasants ... A great mortality has occurred among the Bees.' In fact most of the bees were blown out to sea by the ceaseless trade wind, but the insects which remained on land were so destructive that even Joseph Spearing, the most persevering of the mountain gardeners, in the end had to be taken away 'in a condition of quiet dementia.' As the garrison surgeon reported, 'At 3 a.m. the symptom of Formication came on, this led him to believe that not only his bed but his whole house was swarming with ants ... He became very violent, but then calmer.'

Enormous amounts of time and effort were given to 'the destruction of vermin', and victims were paid for in money or rum:

> It is the Commandant's direction that Sergeant Constant will from this date forward to Headquarters every Monday morning the tails of all the cats and rats for which he may have to issue spirits ... The tails, heads and claws of the vermin killed are to be sent to the Garrison every Saturday morning for the Sergeant Major to count, and report the number to the Marine Office. He is then to cause them to be thrown into the sea.

All work on the island had, in theory, to be sanctioned by the Lords of the Admiralty, from their comfortable perch 4,000 miles away in

London, but as it took at least three weeks for a message to travel in either direction, the Commandant often felt able to ignore orders. Not so the surgeon, Dr. Cronin, who, when he asked for regular blue-jacket nurses to be sent out, was rebuffed by an Olympian rebuke:

> The Lords direct that Dr Cronin shall be informed that he takes a very erroneous view of the position. It is no part of his duty to select the Marines for nurses.

This was all entertaining stuff; but I soon realised that, to make best sense of it, I would have to visit the island again and spend some time there. In those days there was no scheduled air service to Ascension, and the only ship that called there was the monthly mail steamer which put in on its way to St Helena. Since it then went on to Cape Town before starting its return voyage, a round trip took many weeks. In any case, nobody was allowed to visit Ascension without permission from one of the organisations working on the island. I therefore approached the only one I knew – Cable & Wireless – and explained what I wanted to do. The response was generous: the company agreed to put me on one of their charter flights, and also to arrange accommodation at the far end. Further, they undertook to buy 2,000 copies of my book for world-wide distribution to their staff, and this enabled me to obtain a contract from the publishing firm Constable.

Thus armed, in March 1969 I again boarded a long-range Britannia and endured the 15-hour journey. This time, however, I had the thrill of being on the flight deck as we approached our destination, and spotted the minute dot of land when it eventually appeared ahead of us in the light of dawn – truly a precious jewel set in a silver sea.

It took a while to acclimatise. Day in, day out, the temperature remained in the eighties, and the hot, south-east trade wind never ceased to bluster at 15 or 20 mph, bringing with it brick-red dust which, to the chagrin of housewives, coated every surface. Billeted with a hospitable family, given free access to local historical society's records, and furnished with an ancient car which made appalling noises but nevertheless kept going, I settled down to collect information.

One of my main aims was to explore the surface of island, and in this I was greatly assisted (a) by having the car and (b) by the friendly help of John Packer, one of the Cable & Wireless staff, who had already amassed extensive knowledge about the island – the geology, flora, birds, animals and the marine life around the coast. Not only was he a storehouse of information, and extremely helpful with it: he was also an indefatigable pedestrian, with very long legs, and had walked over more of Ascension's daunting terrain than anyone else in living memory.

It was my great good fortune that he was glad to share his knowledge, and also that he enjoyed leading two-man expeditions over the clinker to the extremities of the island. The going was hard and extremely hot, but the views were awe-inspiring, and the texture of the island's surface endlessly fascinating. Curled sticks of lava rang with the hollow chime of porcelain when struck against other rock, and volcanic bombs lay everywhere, some weighing several hundred pounds, some the size of peas, but all bearing marks of their violent passage through the air after they had been spewed from the throat of the mountain.

During my stay there was a startling incident which had nothing to do with my research. One day we heard from a friendly U.S. Air Force officer that a ballistic missile test – the launch from Cape Kennedy Air Force Station in Florida of a rocket with multiple warheads – was due to take place in the evening, and at sunset a small crowd of spectators gathered on the shore of Mars Bay, looking out to the west. Our American hosts were in radio communication with the launch-pad, and when lift-off was confirmed, they could predict within seconds the time of impact on the target, which lay forty miles off Ascension's west coast.

For twenty minutes of growing anticipation we waited, gazing into the sky to the west, as the missile headed towards us over 6,000 miles of ocean. Then the U.S. chief said quietly, 'Coming in, coming in,' and suddenly, without a sound, a ball of intense white fire blazed out of the darkness. Then another flared, and another, and another – seven altogether. I had expected the warheads to spread out, as from a rocket in a firework display – but no: they followed each other in a curve, all hurtling down the same beautiful, white-hot arc, right to left. Seconds later an immense, Wagnerian bass roar came thundering over the sea, so powerful that it almost knocked us down. The boom was caused not by any explosion – for the warheads were inert – but by the re-entry of the rocket into the atmosphere.

I think the watchers were slightly shaken, as much by the spectacle as by the blast of noise. 'What sort of accuracy can you get at that range?' I asked the Chief. 'Is it a matter of hundreds of yards?' 'No, no,' he replied. 'Feet. Feet.' Then out of the dark came another American voice: 'Get a load of that, you Russian sons-a-bitches.'

No greater contrast could be imagined than between that ballistic missile, with its fearful precision, and the green turtles blundering in to nest on Ascension's beaches. Prehistoric creatures, up to five feet long, weighing 500 lbs or more, and on land as clumsy as can be, they swim 1,400 miles from the coast of Brazil, guided to their pin-point of a target by some agent not fully understood. One theory is that they follow a chemical trace in the water which emanates from the island and spreads out as it drifts down to the south-west; another, that they are obeying instincts millions of years old, implanted from the time before South America and Africa moved apart. In that incredibly ancient era (the fossil record indicates) the turtles nested around a line of volcanic islands close to Brazil; then (some experts believe) as the tectonic plates shifted and the continents drew apart at the rate of less than an inch a year, the islands gradually moved out to sea, forming the feature now known as the Mid-Atlantic Ridge, causing the turtles to venture further and further in search of their ancestral breeding grounds.

Whatever the explanation, these prehistoric monsters are miraculous survivors, and I found it intensely moving to watch the females come ashore after their marathon swim. They had mated in the sea (the males never land), and some of them flopped down exhausted in the edge of the surf; others at once began to labour up the beach, with starlight glinting off the wet plates of their shells, their flippers churning a double trail out of the sand like that of a caterpillar tractor.

Having chosen an appealing spot, each turtle started to dig. Powerful backward thrusts from her front flippers sent sand flying yards behind her as she excavated a shallow depression, big enough for her to lie in. Then, with amazing delicacy – considering that she could not see what she was doing – she fashioned an egg-pit with her rear flippers, scooping out sand to form a hollow about fifteen inches wide and eighteen deep beneath her tail. Into this, groaning with the effort, she deposited nearly a hundred soft-shelled white eggs, in batches of four or five.

Next, after another short rest, she covered the clutch with sand, and set off back to the sea. During the night she would repeat the operation four or five times. She would never see her offspring, or know that out of every hundred baby turtles hatched, at least ninety per cent would be eaten by predatory birds and sharks as they erupted from the sand and scuttled for the water. And yet, year after year, for perhaps half a century, instinct would bring her across the ocean and propel her through the same laborious routine as had driven her ancestors since the days of the dinosaurs.

After three weeks on the island I felt I had garnered enough material for my book, and ought to head for home. This was easier said than done, as Cable & Wireless had no charter flight in the offing; but luckily the U.S. Military Air Command came to my rescue and offered me free passage to Antigua in a C-141, a huge, four-jet transport aircraft known as a StarLifter, with wings so long that when it was on the ground they drooped towards the tarmac. My clearest memory of the flight is of the loadmaster giving instructions as a few passengers boarded. 'You see that round opening in the roof? You may not think you can get through that. But if we have to ditch, by heck you will.'

In London again, after a while I began to feel exhausted by research: the hand-writing on many of the Admiralty papers was hard to decipher, and the task of ploughing through them seemed unending. Then a new idea dawned on me.

Why not write a novel about an imaginary island, using some of the knowledge gained in recent months? The idea grew quickly. My island would be like Ascension, but I would call it St Matthew, after a place which appeared on maps for centuries, but in fact never existed. In the 18th century that great mariner Captain Cook believed firmly in its existence; thinking it was somewhere in mid-Atlantic, he was eager to find it. 'I had a great desire to visit the island of St Matthew, to settle its situation,' he wrote in his journal. 'But as the winds would not allow me to fetch it, I sailed for the island of Fernando de Noronha on the coast of Brazil.'

Like Ascension, St Matthew is (in my imagination) isolated, volcanic, hot, and inhabited only by the employees of a telegraph company, as well as by a work force of Saints, and an American contingent running the airfield. The narrator, a boisterous young Fleet Street reporter called Sam Sholto, is detailed to cover the opening of a space station on the island. Seeking background information before the trip, he goes to the P.R.O. and among the naval records he discovers a nineteenth-century report from one Captain John Costello, describing how he captured a 'piratical schooner' on the African coast, seized the gold bars it was carrying, and buried them on the island. Further research in family papers reveals to Sam exactly where the gold is hidden – at the bottom of a fumarole, a bell-shaped cavity formed by the escape of gas when lava is cooling after an eruption.

He goes out on a charter flight and soon finds the treasure. But before he can organise any means of removing it, up out of the South Atlantic sails a lone yacht, piloted by a sinister South African called Bok, whose only crew is Catkin, a striking blonde. Bok claims to be an ornithologist, come to study the frigate birds, but Sam soon senses that he has some other agenda.

He is in the pay of the K.G.B., and his mission is to sabotage the space station. In this Sam manages to frustrate him, but he ends up losing on all counts. Catkin, with whom he has had a scorching affair, is killed, and he loses control of the gold. His trip to St Matthew ends in disaster.

The novel came out in 1967, entitled *The Gold of St Matthew.* Reviews were short but friendly – and I naively hoped that no one in Cable & Wireless would notice them. But of course somebody did, and before long

I got a mildly aggrieved letter from one of the senior managers saying that although he had found the story amusing, he was disappointed to see that, after the company had given me so much help and invested money in my transport and lodging, this was all I had managed to produce in the way of a history of Ascension. I at once wrote a grovelling apology, explaining that the novel was just a *jeu d'esprit:* that I had written it as light relief from my historical researches, in which I had got rather bogged down, and that the real, serious book was on the way.

Returning to the PRO, I buried myself in the records once more, and settled down to finishing my account. *Ascension – the Story of a South Atlantic Island* came out in 1972, and was generously welcomed by the company. But in my introduction to the book I made a serious mistake, when I wrote that the island had 'never played any major role in history, and probably never will.' That sentence taught me never again to pass unnecessary remarks. Barely ten years later the outbreak of the Falklands War suddenly invested Ascension with huge strategic importance. Although almost 4,000 miles from the war zone, Wideawake Airfield was the only base from which the R.A.F. could launch bombing raids on the runway and Argentine military installations at Port Stanley.

The Black Buck raids were operations of astonishing complexity. On the first, on 30 April 1972, two veteran Vulcan V-bombers took off from Ascension, supported by no fewer than eleven Victor tankers, to re-fuel them in mid-air. Technical problems forced one of the Vulcans to turn back, but it was replaced by its partner. After repeated in-flight rendezvous with the tankers, this single aircraft reached its objective, and in a diagonal pass straddled the Port Stanley airfield with a stick of twenty-one 1,000-lb bombs, one of which blasted a large crater out of the centre of the runway. Afterwards, there was much debate about the efficacy of the raid. The crater was soon filled-in well enough for Hercules C-130 transport planes to take off and land, but at least Argentinian jet fighters could not use the airfield during the remainder of the conflict.

With peace restored, Ascension had a new role: that of an indispensable air-bridge between Britain and the Falklands. Far from having no strategic value, the island became a vital stepping-stone on the

8,000-mile flight to and from the far south. Without it, we could never have maintained our garrison there at any effective strength. So much for my summary dismissal of the island's usefulness.

In 1992 I made a brief return to Ascension, to gather material for a second edition of my book. This time I went in one of the RAF's big TriStar jets, which cut the journey time from England from fourteen hours to eight. Once again I landed soon after dawn in the first blaze of sunlight, and I fell into such agreeable conversation with a young man in a loud red-and-blue checked shirt that I failed to pay attention to my suitcase. The next thing I knew, it had gone on to the Falklands. As a result, at a cocktail party given in my honour by the island's Administrator, I had nothing more decorous than a T-shirt to wear; but everyone was so welcoming that I soon stopped feeling uncomfortable – and I was delighted to find that the man who had diverted me on the airfield was none other than the Chief Justice of St Helena.

My plan for a second edition of the book fell flat. I collected a good deal more information – about the Falklands support operation, and the changes on the island since then – but no publisher would take the project on – which seemed a pity, as several thousand servicemen and women now pass through Ascension every year, and a paperback would surely have found a market among them. But I remained fascinated by the island, and in 2015 I was delighted when Marc Holland, the Administrator, and his wife Rachel invited me to return yet again on the occasion of the bicentenary celebrations held in October.

Phylla came with me, and we were splendidly looked-after, not only by the Hollands, but by everyone we met. I found great changes, not least in the view looking inland from Georgetown, for Mexican thorn, spread by the wild donkeys, had colonised much of the middle ground, turning large areas from their former grey or rust-red to brilliant green. Another innovation had been the creation of a professional and well-equipped Conservation Department, set up to study the island's natural resources, both on shore and at sea. One of our principal benefactors was Stedson Stroud, the genial Saint who had become Warden of the National Park around the upper slopes of Green Mountain, and had done wonders re-establishing the tiny herb *Anogramma ascensionis,* one of the very few indigenous species. Another was Johnny Hobson, the genial Northern Irishman who combined the role of dentist with managing the Obsidian Hotel.

In spite of many differences, I found that the island had lost nothing of its strange attraction. I came home with enough new material to bring my history up to date, and – thanks to the enterprise of a publishing friend, Merlin Unwin – a handsome new edition of the book came out in the autumn of 2016.

CHAPTER SIX

Long Road Home
1970

In the summer of 1970 some friends in Oxfordshire surprised us with a splendid offer. David and Naida Hildred, who farmed nearby, had bought land in Australia, and planned to go out to inspect it; but because David had a keen interest in the history of India and the North-West frontier, they also planned to drive as far as Delhi, leave their Land-Rover there, and fly the rest of the way. To our great excitement, they asked if we would fly out and bring the vehicle back.

Who could refuse such an offer? We quickly decided to take it up; but various factors limited the length of time that we could afford to be away. One was my job at the *Sunday Telegraph,* where I was working as a feature reporter; another was the fact that our indestructible Nanny Barker (who had brought up me and my sister) would need help looking after our children.

In the office I managed to negotiate a six-week break by arranging to write articles on the drug route from India, which was constantly in the news at the time; and the second problem was solved by Phylla's sister Olivia Stewart-Smith angelically agreeing to take over our house and family for the duration. This was no light undertaking, for the establishment included Nanny, our children (Alice and Guy, aged seven and five), Olivia's husband Christopher, their children (Katy, five, and Christy, three), a retired racehorse, a Thelwell-type pony, sundry chickens and two cats, Fat and Thin.

Dove-tailing our movements with those of the Hildreds was not as easy as it sounded, for the regulations of the day laid down that if a foreign vehicle entered India, only the driver who had brought it in was allowed to take it out again. This meant that either I or Phylla would have to fly to Pakistan, join the Hildreds there, and then drive in through the frontier, while the other flew to Delhi. For both of us preparations were bedevilled by the need to obtain visas and permits for all the countries through which we would pass – India, Pakistan, Afghanistan, Iran, Turkey, Bulgaria, Yugoslavia, Austria, Germany and France. At the *Telegraph,* when I asked 'Tap' Tapsell, the scruffy and amusing Picture Editor, for sixteen passport photographs, he blew up with 'CHRIST! With less trouble than it's taking to get you home from Delhi, I could ship a fucking APE to BOMBAY!'

The vehicle for the journey was a Carawagon, a long-wheelbase Land-Rover specially fitted for expeditions and admirably equipped with double bed, gas cooker, refrigerator, wash-basin and chemical loo, as well as lockable steel cages on the front mudguards which held jerricans for water and petrol. Across the front of the roof, above the windscreen, ran a steel box full of spare equipment – fan belts, water hoses, gaskets and so on. With the release of six catches the main section of the roof rose in a kind of tent, giving six feet of headroom.

When the Hildreds kindly offered to lend the car for a couple of days' experience, we drove it up to Yorkshire, where my father was living, and spent a comfortable night camping on the moor above Swaledale. I also went on a one-day course at the garage which had supplied the vehicle, learning how to take up the brakes and check the various oil levels.

As we were preparing for take-off, my rich and generous great aunt Joyce Balokovic came over from America on one of her periodical visits. She had a strong interest in Eastern mysticism, and when she heard we were going to India, she said, 'Surely you're going to Kashmir as well?'

'No,' I hedged. 'I don't think so.'

'Why ever not?' she exclaimed. 'If you're going to Delhi, you can't *not* go up to Srinagar. What's the problem? Is it lack of time or shortage of money?'

'A bit of both,' I admitted – whereupon she wrote out a cheque for $300.

We left home in the middle of October. I put Phylla on the plane for Karachi, and then, next day, caught a flight to Delhi. Not until we eventually joined forces at the Claridge's Hotel did I learn that the Hildreds had met her, as promised, in Pakistan, but that Pan American had lost one of her suitcases. As this contained dried rations for our overland journey, the loss was potentially tiresome – but luckily the bag came back from Calcutta in time for her to reclaim it.

The delay was irritating – but at least it gave us a chance to explore a bit of Delhi. Also, it made me confident that I would have no difficulty in writing about the drug trail, for, as we wove our way on foot through the never-ending tide of pedestrians, rickshaws and wandering cows, smooth young men kept appearing at my elbow murmuring, 'Sir – you buying hashish? Very good quality. Very cheap'. Passing taxi drivers seemed desperate to do deals. 'You want *charas* ? (the strongest local form of cannabis), they cooed out of their open windows. 'I take you good place now.' Having been warned that the city was alive with informers – almost certainly paid by the police – we refused all offers until we were on our way.

Instead of buying the real stuff, I invented a phantom cargo. In each of the jerricans (I pretended to ourselves) we had secreted ten kilos of *charas* in sealed packets. Even if some officious customs man ordered us to open a can, with water filling the space on top, the drug would be undetectable. In Delhi the top price for ten kilos would have been £200, but I calculated that in England the haul would fetch £7,000 – or over £100,000 at latter-day rates.

Feeling no hurry to be off, we spent two days sight-seeing in Delhi, greatly helped by the *Telegraph's* resident correspondent David Loshak and his wife Molly, both of whom guided us, fed us and generally went out of their way to ease our path. We then drove down to Agra, and were duly astounded by the sight of the Taj Mahal, which we saw both at dusk and at dawn. Scarcely less memorable, we found, was the abandoned, red-sandstone city of Fatepur Sikri, 25 miles out in the desert to the west – an enormous maze of courtyards, colonnades, cloisters, towers and minarets, dating from the reign of Queen Elizabeth I, and scarcely inhabited since.

The Carawagon had withstood the 6,000-mile outward journey pretty well, but it needed servicing, and we left it in the Raj Nath repair station (motto 'Denting and Painting') while we flew for a couple of days and nights to Kashmir. Luckily that volatile region was in a period of relative calm, and although we witnessed one minor riot, we had a magical night in a houseboat on the Dal Lake outside Srinagar, followed by a hideously uncomfortable stay at Gulmarg, nearly 9,000 feet above sea level, which was just beginning to be developed as a ski resort. Our hotel – accurately described as 'picturesque' – was flimsy, made entirely of wood, and, as we watched the sun went down on 28,000-foot Nanga Parbat, turned cold as ice. Nevertheless, we felt grateful to Aunt Joyce for giving us a glimpse of another world.

Back in Delhi, we were anxious to get going – but of course the Land-Rover was not ready for the road. 'Relax yourself, Sir,' said Mr Chaturvedi, the tubby garage proprietor. 'Relax yourself absolutely. Most certainly, you will have it in the morning' – and I was astonished when he lived up to his promise.

Kipling called the Grand Trunk Road 'the river of life'. No doubt in his day traffic flowed at a leisurely pace – but it no longer did in ours. Stately trees set back on either side gave the great highway a certain dignity; flights of green parrots skimmed past above the trees, and fork-tailed kites soared in effortless circles; but the road itself was a miserably narrow strip of pot-holed tarmac, flanked at either side by a six- or eight-inch drop onto broad, dusty earth verges. Down the middle roared gigantic lorries, grossly overloaded, listing to port or starboard and often carrying an extra cargo of humans perched like monkeys on the top. Almost all the trucks were plastered with lurid, highly-coloured paintings or stencils of people, buildings and animals, and all sent out a cacophony of raucous blasts or jaunty, high-pitched trumpetings. Someone told us that, in order to stay awake, the drivers relied mainly on Allah, but also on hashish, which they smoked or ate ground up with nuts – so clearly it was in our interest to steer clear of them.

Whenever two monsters met, one had to give way and lurch down on to earth or sand, sending up a cloud of dust. We had no option but to do the same: the Land-Rover was no match for the oncoming pachyderms, and we kept having to take evasive action, which landed us among the unending stream of bullock carts, cows, pedestrians, bicycles and the occasional camel, all wending their way listlessly beside the highway. Wrecks littered the verges: buses upside down or lying on their sides, trucks of every size and shape. One twelve-wheeler had collapsed right on the tarmac, where it lay with its front axle propped on a pile of old tyres.

Through this chaos we made slow headway. As long as we could keep moving, plenty of air came in through the open windows, but in towns, when were forced down to a crawl by the drifting mass of pedestrians and animals, we and the engine became seriously over-heated.

We soon established a routine, of stopping for a picnic lunch in the most isolated spot we could discover, and then towards evening – not wanting to risk a night unprotected in the open – pitching up in the compound of some friendly-looking hotel or guest house, and sleeping in the Carawagon.

One basic fact of life we soon discovered was that no stretch of the Indian countryside is uninhabited: whenever we pulled off the highway into what looked a deserted space, people rose up out of hollows or ditches, to come and stare silently at point-blank range. Any *al fresco* meal inevitably attracted an audience: a couple of boys, a camel, a pair of oxen, a dog, two or three men and a vulture.

The pervading inertia had the paradoxical effect of increasing our urge to press on. Passing through Amritsar, we steeled ourselves not to stop for a glance at the Golden Temple, and after another twenty miles we came to the frontier between India and Pakistan at Hussainiwala, the village at which an elaborate ceremony of flag-lowering takes place at sunset every evening, with much marching, stamping and goose-stepping by soldiers of either side. There we were maddened by a long, hot wait before a grizzled official, sitting at a table in an old army tent, broke off his argument with a tall, turbaned Afghan and got round to scrutinising our documents.

'You are exporting this vehicle from India? Yes? Where is your permit?'

'No. We're not exporting it. My wife brought it in.'

'Then why you leaving India?'

'We're touring – Afghanistan, Iran.'

'Afghanis very bad people.' He made a throat-cutting gesture.

I said nothing as he riffled through the pages of my passport.

'What is your termination?'

'We're going to England.'

'England? I think you are making joke. England is too far.'

This went on for some time before the bureaucrat, having cranked up his telephone and put through a couple of calls, suddenly lost interest, stamped our passports and papers, and handed them back without another word.

In Lahore we paused to inspect Zam-Zammah, the great cannon on which Kim sits perched at the start of Kipling's novel, and then hurried on to Islamabad, the brand-new capital of Pakistan, founded only four years earlier. In strong contrast with all the other towns we had been through, this one had been laid out on a grid pattern – and we thought it would be easy to find the address to which we were invited. Far from it: in the end we became so confused by the straight lines and absence of street names that we had to hire a taxi to give us a lead. No matter: Geoffrey and Joan Cox gave us the warmest of welcomes, and took us into their diplomatic family for two very comfortable nights.

The Khyber Pass lived up to all expectations. The road twisted upwards through continuous hair-pins between towering walls of grey rock dotted with pill-boxes and look-out points – reminders of all the battles that had taken place here in the past. So that I could take photographs, Phylla drove until she was dizzy with the constant turning. Nine miles on, the Afghan frontier post was already in the shade of a rock face, and the air was agreeably cool. The customs official was sitting at a table in the open on a concrete platform shaded by the cliff, wearing a smart, open-necked olive shirt. Mercifully, he did not start any badinage, but simply whacked down his stamps on our documents, and in answer to a question said that Kabul was six hours ahead. That meant we should reach the Afghan capital soon after dark. Clearly it would be safest not to drive at night, even though the country – still ruled by King Zahir Shah – was then fairly peaceful.

Through the frontier, the road surface suddenly changed. All at once we were on smooth tarmac, and driving on the right, for this super-highway had been built by Americans as a friendly gesture-cum-bribe. In little over an hour we reached Jalalabad, an attractive oasis set in a wide and fertile-looking plain. In that open setting it was hard to imagine Dr William Brydon staggering into the garrison in January 1842, during the first Afghan war, sole survivor of the British army's disastrous retreat from Kabul. But when we climbed through hairpin bends, up into the naked rock gorges of the Kabul river – a truly terrifying landscape – the massacre became all too comprehensible. So narrow were stretches of the gorge that only a sliver of blue sky showed between the crags hundreds of feet overhead, and far below the dark-green river surged between.

Emerging from the gorge at dusk, we found Kabul straight ahead, and gave ourselves the luxury of a night in a hotel. In the morning I called on Abdul Tarsi, Director of the Afghan Tourist Board. When I asked about the official position on hashish, he said, 'Well, it's a matter of degree. In a way it *does* become illegal if it gets too conspicuous.' Encouraged by this ambivalent response, we headed for the bazaar, and quickly did a deal with one of the touts, buying a cake of coffee-coloured hash, with the consistency of putty and about the shape and size of a lady's powder compact. I also bought a long, curved sword – more as a souvenir than as a weapon of defence – and the vendor was so keen to demonstrate its sharpness that he cut himself – whereupon, to his amazement, Phylla patched him up with supplies from our first-aid box. In another part of the bazaar we were fascinated by rows of open sacks containing highly-coloured powder. Red looked like ground peppers, yellow like cumin; but what was the bright green? When Phylla made a gesture of raising some to her mouth, the stall-keeper became seriously alarmed, until a freelance interpreter hove up and explained that the stuff was henna, for dyeing beard or hair.

From Kabul the road climbed steadily onto an immense, stony plain. The city, I knew, was 6,000 feet above sea-level, but soon we were at 9,000 feet, with chains of tawny mountains set back in the distance on either side. The landscape was magnificent, and the air was deliciously cool, but the Land-Rover made heavy weather of the altitude. Its four-cylinder engine was scarcely man enough for all the extra weight we were carrying in the form of special equipment; even on the flat it was labouring, and our top speed was 40 mph. There was practically no other traffic, but occasionally a powerful car – usually American or Russian – overtook us at speed and disappeared into the distance, making me think uneasily what easy meat we would we would be for any unscrupulous predator. We had no means of defence, and, in those pre-cell-phone days, no means of summoning help in the event of an attack.

Now and then we came to a toll-point – a single wooden pole lowered across the road and manned by a lone toll-keeper, who would emerge from his shelter to accept a ten-Afghani note without speaking, and lift the flimsy barrier. There were also little *chaikhanas* selling tea. Here and there groups of nomads' black yurts crouched like small heaps of soot in hollows in the desert, with camels grazing near them; but for most of the way the stony wilderness was empty.

Our original plan had been to go south as far as Kandahar, but when we heard that there was no petrol along that route, we turned right and headed for Herat, through Already we were into November, and in the far north-west winter was setting in. Waking up one morning to find our water-supply frozen, I was reduced to cleaning my teeth with vodka; but later that day in the bazaar we bought two excellent padded cotton quilts for the equivalent of fifteen shillings each, and from then on we were warm at night.

One morning, in the interests of research, I allowed a smooth young man to lure me into the front of his minibus for a discussion. He wanted to sell me some hashish, and he looked like a useful source of information. 'Every month we have sixty men going Iran on horse,' he boasted. 'Three hundred kilos hashish. Always going at night.'

'You carry guns?' I asked.

'BIG guns! Every one, big guns.' Grinning, he held two fingers apart to illustrate some colossal calibre.

'In Iran they shoot people for drug-running,' I told him.

'Bah! They never catch.' He drew the side of one hand theatrically across his throat.

I wished him luck. But rumours picked up elsewhere in Herat undermined our own confidence, and after a couple of days I decided we had better jettison our own small cargo of hash before we reached the Iranian border. This proved easier said than done. Until then, or until recently, the lump had travelled among the junk on the dashboard shelf – but when we tried to evict it, there was no sign of it. We searched in vain, and never found it. The matter remained a mystery - but for days it played on our nerves: what if one of the customs stations had sniffer dogs?

A couple of hours west of Herat we went through the frontier into Iran with no trouble, and breathed again. Our next main target was Teheran, some 150 miles ahead, but we ran into bad weather in the mountains and fell behind schedule. Changing tactics, we decided to aim, first, for a place called Shah Pasand. Since *pasand* means 'pleasant', we thought that one of the Shahs must have liked it, and that therefore it would be attractive.

Dark had fallen; torrential rain was cascading down, and the road was so heavily flooded that duck kept flighting in to land in the pools ahead of us. Suddenly, coming round a corner, we found ourselves in the middle of a gargantuan road-building project: arc lights blazed from gantries, gigantic bulldozers were tearing the guts out of the mountainside, and workmen were creeping about like ants, water glistening on their yellow oilskins. The air was full of steam or fog. As I braked to a halt, the Land-Rover stalled, and would not start again. When I lifted the bonnet to see what was wrong, wild-looking men rushed to our aid, all shouting different instructions. Loudest of all was a fellow with a huge black moustache who kept yelling, 'BENZIN! BENZIN!' When I realised what he was suggesting – that he should soak a rag in petrol, light it and stuff it down into the engine, to dry things out – 'I yelled 'NO! *NON! NEIN! KEIN BENZIN!'* I had a vision of the vehicle going up in flames: end of Land- Rover, end of journey.

Mercifully, the man desisted, and when I tried the starter again, the engine fired. To a chorus of merry shouts – congratulations, I thought – we sloshed forward again, in and out of the bulldozers and dump-trucks, and left the nightmarish scene behind.

As we came down to Shah Pasand, it was nearly midnight. By then we were very tired, but, to our amazement and relief, we found a small hotel, not only lit up, but functioning. Yes – we could have a room. And yes – even better – there was food. Within minutes we were sitting down to some very acceptable pilaf. Since the whole of Iran was officially dry, we could not hope for any reviving alcohol – but then, on a high shelf, I spotted a row of bottles holding what looked like white wine. Alas - it turned out to be cooking oil. Next morning we got another surprise. As we stumbled out of our bedroom in search of breakfast, we found twenty soldiers asleep head-to-tail on the floor of the landing.

Luckily for us, Iran was then in a period of relative political stability. Shah Reza Pahlavi was still in power, and Teheran was pervaded by Western influence. Smart shops and restaurants were flourishing, and elegant women flaunted designer clothes. We were most hospitably entertained by Hushan and Touran Batmanglidj, highly civilised friends of an English friend. Beneath the veneer, however, less attractive behaviour was flourishing. Visiting the Narcotics Bureau in search of information, I found the walls plastered with photographs of convicted drug peddlers. 'What happened to this one?' I asked the young captain who showed me round. 'Shot,' he replied proudly. 'Twenty-eight kilos of heroin.' 'And this one?' 'Shot.' Next day we heard that in the north-western city of Tabriz five more people had been executed – which made me hope fervently that our tiny cake of hashish was not still lurking somewhere in the bowels of the Land-Rover.

Leaning heavily on Mr Tarsi, the Minister of Tourism, and flourishing my *Telegraph* card, I obtained free tickets for flights to the south; and so, leaving the car, we flew down and forgot about drugs for a couple of days as we confronted Persian wonders: the great Mosque of Isfahan, with its astonishing, pale blue dome, and (for me the most splendid and stirring of all) the ruins of Persepolis, the royal palace near Shiraz, standing on a vast terrace cut from the side of a mountain, and built by the Kings

Darius, Xerxes and Artaxerxes, starting in 515 BC. For sheer age and grandeur, I had seen no other site like it.

Back on the road, we headed north-west, wasting no time in Tabriz, but pressing on to the Turkish border at Bazargan. There, for the first time, a customs official did take a cursory look round the Land-Rover, getting me to lift the bonnet and open the spares box; but he waved us through cheerfully, and left us relaxed enough to enjoy the majestic sight of Mount Ararat, a glorious, symmetrical volcanic cone, 17,000 feet high, heavily mantled with snow. How cold it must have been (we thought) for all Noah's tropical animals when the ark landed there.

Our next major target was Ankara, in the centre of Turkey; but first we held to our north-west course, seduced by memories of Rose Macaulay's *The Towers of Trebizond,* that agreeably ridiculous book, half travel, half novel, which opens with the words '"Take my camel, dear", said my Aunt Dot, as she climbed down from this animal on her return from High Mass.' Alas, without Rose riding her white Arabian Dhalur through the streets, and the natives calling 'Goodbye, old trout,' Trabzon, on the shore of the Black Sea, was a disappointment: a drab, undistinguished place, with none of the romance or fun of that eccentric author.

In Ankara we met Mehmet-Ali Kişlali, the *Telegraph's* excellent stringer, and his wife Sevinç, who became a lifelong friend. Mehmet-Ali arranged for me to interview Halit Elver, the Deputy Director of Security, from whom I gained an alarming idea of the scale on which Turkey was trying to combat the drug problem. The Government's principal aim was to reduce the illegal cultivation of opium poppies, but trading was rife. 'Control is the most dangerous job in the police,' said Elver. 'The smugglers shoot on sight.'

By the time we reached Istanbul, we felt that our time was running out; but we gave ourselves one night in the magnificently old-fashioned Pera Palace Hotel (where Ataturk preferred Room 101), before pushing on to the Bulgarian frontier just beyond Edirne. Arriving there at about six in the evening, we were chagrined to see the barrier come down right in front of us, and to be told that it would not open until seven the next morning. 'Why?' we demanded. Because there had been an outbreak of cholera, and transit through Bulgaria was strictly controlled.

There followed the most farcical episode of our journey. At 6.45 am we presented ourselves at the barrier, only to find that we were part of a large and rapidly-assembling queue. A police officer with a megaphone read the riot act. All cars were to proceed in convoy. To avoid contamination of the landscape, there was to be no stopping and no overtaking. Nothing was to be thrown out of vehicles. One police car would lead the column. Another would bring up the rear.

By the time the barrier was raised, at about 7.15, there must have been 200 cars lined up. Many were German – big Mercedes, Opels and BMWs. We were somewhere in the middle. Off we went, and soon reached the dizzy speed of 20 mph. But suddenly everything jolted to a halt. With the leading police car out of sight, nobody could tell what the problem was. We waited. Ten minutes passed. Twenty minutes. Then the inevitable happened. One driver or passenger after another, unable to withstand the urges of nature, slipped out of their vehicle and made a furtive dash for the scrub flanking the road. We, with our on-board loo, were laughing; but for others less well equipped, there was no option. The result was that in the next half hour that stretch of the Bulgarian countryside must have been polluted like no other. So much for the containment of cholera.

Eventually the convoy moved off again – but anyone who has had the misfortune to drive in a column of 200 vehicles will know how peculiarly annoying it is. Some law of dynamics makes it impossible to achieve a steady speed: one moment you are doing 20 mph, then abruptly, for no apparent reason, the cars ahead of you are braking hard. Individual German drivers, unable to control their frustration, kept trying to move up the column by violent overtaking, almost causing a crash as they cut back into the line.

They survived until, all at the same moment, nine or ten of them pulled out on to the left of the road and went roaring ahead in a column of their own. They did not get far. A few seconds later we heard a most satisfactory *screech, crash, thud, bang, thump* – and a few hundred yards further on, there they all were, impacted and crumpled nose-to tail. Delighted to be rid of them, I drove doggedly on, with Phylla cooking and feeding me delicious snacks from behind, until about eight hours later we emerged, exhausted, into Yugoslavia.

Behind schedule now, we hastened back via Zagreb, Vienna and Cologne – where we had the one accident of the entire trip. As we wormed our way through the city traffic, I was squinting up at the majestic twin towers of the Cathedral, which miraculously survived repeated Allied air-raids during the war (and which we later climbed), when I inadvertently nudged the back of a blue Volkswagen Beetle with the sharp corner of one of our jerrican cages. The dent was smaller than my little finger-nail, but the driver, a woman, leapt out in a state of great agitation, making loud lament. Luckily there was a friendly policeman close at hand, who pacified her, tore out the green page of my insurance document and waved us on our way with a cheerful '*Kein Problem!*'

So we came home, to find house, humans and animals all in perfect order. In six weeks we had driven 6,400 miles, stretched our imaginations and given ourselves wide new horizons. What we could not know was that the sights and experiences of the journey would, after a few years' gestation, precipitate a complete change in our lives.

CHAPTER SEVEN

Mercy Mission
1973

My first trip to Nepal, in March 1973, got off to a rather staccato start. My instructions were to present myself at RAF Lyneham, in Wiltshire, by 1.30 am, and Phylla drove me to the airfield in good time. She then returned home, leaving me to await events. My distant objective was Bhairawa, an air-strip just inside the southern border of Nepal, from which emergency food supplies were being flown into the Himalayan valleys, in an attempt to alleviate a famine brought on by two bad harvests. The RAF had promised me free passage in a C-130 Hercules transport, with a warning that the journey would not be comfortable. The first leg of it would be to Akrotiri, in Cyprus.

In the early hours of the morning Lyneham seemed curiously undermanned. Apart from a corporal who checked me in, there was hardly anyone about – until, at around 2.30, a flight crew appeared and walked out to one of the aircraft on the tarmac. Presently the turbo-prop engines fired up, but at least one of the four sounded rough, with terrific backfiring, and soon the crew returned to the terminal. That Herc, they said, was a heap of scrap-metal, and they weren't proposing to fly the effing thing anywhere, least of all to Bhairawa in Nepal.

Someone showed me to a bunk in a wooden hut, and I slept fitfully for a few hours. In the morning I found that take-off had been re-scheduled for midnight – so I had a whole day to kill, and I spent much of it reflecting on how I had managed to land myself in such a tedious delay.

My interest had been sparked by Kedar Man Singh, the *Telegraph*'s excellent stringer in Kathmandu. In the previous November he had reported that an RAF delegation was in town, planning to set up an emergency food-drop in the Himalayas of western Nepal. It sounded as though there might be a great trip in the offing, but when I checked with my contacts in the RAF press office, they denied that anything was afoot. (The reason, I discovered later, was that they did not want a premature announcement in the media.)

Then, early in 1973, our man in Kathmandu again reported the presence of a reconnaissance party – and this time I managed to exact from the Ministry in London not only an outline of Operation Khana Cascade (*Khana* meaning 'food'), but also the promise of a free ride. 'Of course,' said my contact, 'we can't promise you an exclusive. You'll just have to take your chance.'

It sounded as though I would have to share the story with other Fleet Street hacks – so, at Lyneham, it was an agreeable surprise to find no sign of any competitors. When we eventually took off for Cyprus at midnight, there were four other passengers, but they were all RAF personnel, well used to the joys of Hercules travel. 'They've solved this aircraft's noise problem,' some joker said, 'by putting it all inside.' Many a true word ... In the cavernous, forty-foot cargo hold of the plane, the ringing scream of the turbo-prop engines bored into one's brain. Ear-defenders muffled it slightly, but not enough. A few canvas seats were slung along the walls, but the only way to relax properly was to snuggle into one of the hollows in the nets that held down cargo along the centre of the hold.

A seven-hour flight brought us to Cyprus, and to the compensation of a lovely, warm spring morning. Again there was a day-long and featureless wait before another midnight take-off, but at least we passengers could spend much of the day in the sun. After another six-hour flight that night, we staged through Masirah, off the coast of Oman, and by the time we reached Bombay, with a shorter hop across the Arabian sea, it was a wonderful relief to find that we – crew and passengers – were billeted in a cheap but comfortable hotel. After three broken nights and two days sitting around, I found it a huge relief to stretch and wallow in the warm water of a swimming pool.

In the morning we set off early on the last leg of the journey. On the way to the airfield in an RAF truck, our Geordie driver suddenly let out a startled cry of 'Fookin 'ell! Crappers' alley!' – and so it was: in fields on either side of the road Indians were shamelessly squatting at their defecations. 'Dinna fash yerself,' said a Scottish voice. 'It'll grow some cracking melons.'

By now our trusty Herc seemed like home, and when the captain invited me on to the flight deck, it was a joy to be flying in daylight as we headed north-east over the middle of India. The plane had windows wrapped round the sides of the cockpit, so that there was a far-reaching outlook on both sides, as well as forward. Far below, the flat plains of Madhya Pradesh looked scorched and brown in the grip of winter, but the view to the north, towards the Himalayas, was obscured by haze.

Reverting to the belly of the plane, I felt the captain start his descent. Down from the flight deck came a warning, bellowed out by the load-master to those of us not connected to the intercom. Because the runway at Bhairawa was short, the captain was going for a tactical landing. That meant the Herc would bounce up from its first impact, and then come down again. 'Get a bloody good hold of something,' the load-master yelled, 'and don't let go till after the second touch-down.'

I hooked both hands into the mesh of the cargo net and waited tensely as the aircraft wobbled during its final descent. Then came an almighty, crashing jolt, *BANG!,* so violent that I was thrown bodily into the air. Suddenly, with a smaller but still substantial thump, we were down. As the plane shuddered to a halt, a door opened in the side. Outside, a man was pumping his fist furiously up and down, and shouting, 'Fucking RUN!'

We sprinted. By the time I was twenty yards clear, the plane had smoke pouring from the landing gear. The brakes had caught fire – but the excitement was short-lived, as the flames were soon put out. Nevertheless, it was a fairly spectacular arrival.

As I tried to get my bearings, a young RAF officer, very pukka in pressed, short-sleeved shirt and shorts, came up holding a mill-board.

'OK,' he said snootily, 'who are you?'

'Hart-Davis. From the *Sunday Telegraph.*'

'Funny.' He looked down his list. 'I was told you weren't coming.'

'Well – I'm bloody well here.'

'So I see. Where are your colleagues?'

'What colleagues?'

'From the other newspapers.'

'There aren't any.'

The man was temporarily dumbfounded. Clearly, some jerk in the MoD had got things exactly arse-about. It turned out that four other correspondents had been offered the facility, but all had cried off at the last moment. What luck! It meant that, instead of having to take turns at flying, I could join any sortie I chose.

The airfield consisted of little more than a control tower and runway, but rows of tents, designated Kanvas City, had sprung up, efficiently deployed by the Indian Army and a detachment of Gurkhas. Operation Khana Cascade had already been running for a week, and it was going well, ahead of the planned schedule. The whole place was seething with activity. Trucks full of food were arriving. Sacks of maize, wheat and rice, each weighing 87 lbs – the maximum that any Nepalese porter would carry from the drop-zones to the mountain villages – were being strapped onto wooden base-boards by men of 55 Air Despatch Squadron, working stripped to the waist in the fierce midday heat. The air was thick with dust, worst whenever a Herc took off or landed, and the runway was cracking up from the heavyweight pounding of the past few days.

At the start of the operation the laden boards of food had been dropped on parachutes; but so many of them drifted off into inaccessible ravines that the pilots changed their tactics and began flying right down, almost to ground level, above the little air-strips that ran along some of the valleys. The 30-ton aircraft could have landed on some of the grass runways, but, with the ground soft from winter rain, they would probably never have taken off again, and the only alternative method of delivery was for the captain to make a pass at fifty feet and about 120 mph, holding a steady line as the crew in the loading bay pushed loaded pallets out through the tail-gate so that they plummeted straight to the ground. Flying down into the valleys between walls of rock was extremely hazardous, and the air crews exhibited such skill that three of the pilots were later awarded medals.

For me every sortie was an adventure, none more thrilling than the first.

'Ascot Zero Five' called the control tower . 'You're clear for take-off.'

'Roger,' answered the captain, and the Herc trundled forward into a gently-accelerating roll, laden with 280-odd sacks of food. Our destination was Doti, a deep valley 170 miles to the north-west. After a long, lumbering take-off and only a minute climbing, we cleared the ground haze and could see foothills out to our right – crumpled black ridges a mere seven or eight thousand feet high. Another minute, and something else appeared beyond them – a line of white, so high, so remote, that at first I took it for clouds. Then with a lurch in my stomach I realised that it was not clouds at all, but snow peaks – hundreds of them, range after range, piling back to the far horizon.

Out to our right three, four, five, six separate ridges, grey-green, dun-brown or black, marched away towards the beginning of the snow. Beyond them colossal white masses stood out against the sky. 'That's Dhaulagiri,' said the captain casually, indicating a turreted cluster of summits, 'and the one beyond is Annapurna. Twenty-six thousand feet, that fellow.'

I stared speechlessly at the long plume of cloud trailing from its peak. I was brought back to earth by the navigator's voice in my head-set. 'Estimating forty miles. Ten minutes to run. Two more ridges, and the marker should be on the nose.'

The marker, identified by the crew as a good turning-point on earlier sorties, was a conical hill rising out of the junction between two valleys. I kept trying to spot it, but could not take my eyes off the astonishing array of snow and ice.

'Range one-seven miles,' called the navigator. 'Four minutes to the DZ [dropping zone] overhead.'

The pilot began a gentle descent. Then suddenly we slanted right-handed into a twisting, wooded gorge. Below us a small river, bright turquoise, wound between banks of light grey shingle.

Left: Aged two, with father Rupert,1938

Above: Just down from the trees: Takoradi, Nigeria, 1957

Below: Muddied oafs: after the Eton Wall Game, St Andrew's Day 1954, with David Caccia (right)

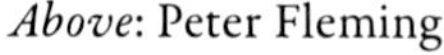

Above: Peter Fleming

Right: Commuting to the *Telegraph* on a Moulton bike, 1966

Below: Return from Yalta: landing back at Lydd with Peter Fleming, 1956 *Photo: The Times*

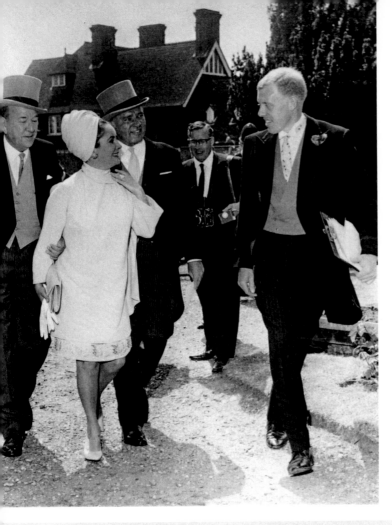

Left: Escorting Elizabeth Taylor, Richard Burton and Noel Coward at the wedding of Simon and Sheran Hornby, 1968

Below: Operation Khana Cascade: A C-130 Hercules twists through the Nepalese Himalayas, 1973

The Chipperfield family circus, 1930s

Gone up in the world. Jimmy with Lord Bath (left) and the Duke of Bedford, 1967

Left: Up the ladder into the cockpit of a supersonic Lightning, 1966

Below: Deer-stalker: with fallow heads in the Chilterns

Our Sherpa team on Annapurna, 1974, with Nima (centre) in white cap

Nettlebed six-a-side cricket team: winners of the tournament at Harpsden, 1976

Above: Rathenny House, Co. Tipperary, 1978

Left: My best horse: on *Dominic* at Rathenny, 1978

DH-D with darted rhino, Chitwan, Nepal,1985 *Photo: Hemanta Mishra*

'Depressurising,' said the Captain. 'Door and ramp clear?'

'Door clear,' came the voice of the load-master, in charge of the cargo bay.

'Gear down,' called the captain – a precaution in case we touched ground during the dropping run.

As the wheels thudded into position, for a few moments our target air-strip was visible, deep in a valley to our right, but we swung left, round the marker pimple, before wheeling into a right-hand turn and heading straight for a precipitous, scrub-covered face. Head-on impact seemed inevitable, until in the final seconds we turned again.

We skimmed a ridge. 'One hundred per cent flaps', demanded the captain, and suddenly we were dropping. Down we went, down, down, losing a thousand feet in twenty seconds as we hurtled towards a thin, brown strip of runway that struck straight through the green of the valley floor. We were falling like a stone – down to 250 feet ... 150 ... 100. In seconds we were skimming over the end of the runway at 50 feet and 120 mph.

Warnings, commands and acknowledgements snapped through the head-sets.

'Fifteen seconds,' called the captain.

'Your line,' said the co-pilot. 'Your line ... steady ... your line ... steady.'

'Ten seconds.'

A searing blast from an alarm klaxon. *'Action stations!'*

'Action stations,' came the echo from the back.

'Red on!'

'Red on.'

'Green on!'

'Load moving ... load gone.'

Suddenly a ton lighter, the aircraft jumped several feet. The village flashed past below us, and the captain climbed away under maximum power towards the jagged sky-line way above. 'I hope I'm aiming for the right gap in the horizon,' he said calmly, 'because if I'm not, it's the last mistake anyone on this aircraft will ever make.'

We cleared a ridge, only a few feet above rocks and snow. As we came round for a second pass, I went down into the cargo bay, where the despatch crew were manoeuvring the next loaded base-board along rollers towards the tail. With the ten-foot tail-gate open, the noise was so ferocious that speech was impossible, and the load-master, in touch with the flight deck by head-set intercom, had to give commands by hand-signals.

As the aircraft swung round to run in again, glittering snow-peaks, waterfalls, blue sky, green hills, brown hills, rock faces rushed crazily past the huge, square window of the open tail. Then the floor levelled off, and again we were dropping fast, with tiny, terraced fields whipping past, hair-raisingly close beneath our belly.

In a few seconds we levelled off at fifty feet. The despatchers stood tensely, shoulders jammed against the load. The load-master's fist was up. By his head a red light went on, then a green. Down came his hand. *Heave!* and out went the pallet-load of sacks, which hit the ground like a bomb-burst in a cloud of dust. Many of them came hurtling after us, jumping and vaulting. Several burst, sending jets of golden maize flying up into the air. As we pulled away I caught a glimpse of small, dark people moving quickly forward from where they had been waiting by the tower. Their eagerness to get their hands on the manna from heaven was painfully obvious. Perhaps they would keep some of it for themselves, but most would be carried away to remote villages by human porters, each man bent beneath a sack weighing nearly ninety pounds and walking for maybe a fortnight to reach his destination.

I was lucky enough to join at least one Hercules sortie every day; but between the heavyweight missions I had another memorable trip – with Hardy Führer, a Swiss pilot who took to the air in a white silk shirt and lemon-coloured bell-bottom trousers. Flying a single-engined Pilatus Porter, he had been reconnoitring landing strips on behalf of the RAF, testing to see if they would bear the weight of a Hercules. One morning, as he was about to take off for Jumla, a village away to north-west, he suddenly said, 'Why not come along?'

Minutes later, as his tiny plane climbed towards ramparts of snow and ice, I felt as if I was in a dinghy, swimming out into a mighty ocean of sky. I wasn't frightened, but it was slightly alarming to see that Hardy apparently had no maps. When I mentioned the matter, he brushed it aside with an airy wave. 'Maps?' he said. 'What for? Obviously this is Annapurna' – he flapped a languid hand half right – 'and this is Dhaulagiri.'

'Where's Jumla, then.'

'Straight ahead.'

Soon it became clear that he could name almost every peak, every valley, every *khola* (river) that we passed over. Our destination was more than 8,000 feet above sea-level, and formidably remote. There was no road to the small town, set in a valley along the banks of the Tila river: only a short airstrip gave it some connection with the outside world. At that altitude I expected to find snow still lying – but no: although on the way in we skimmed over snow-laden ridges, the valley itself was dark and sodden.

Evidently Hardy was expected, for people were waiting by the control tower. He landed without fuss, taxied a short distance, shut down the engine and went off to walk the strip with a couple of locals, leaving me with a crowd of curious onlookers. I was struck by the utter poverty of those little mountain people and their ragged children. They looked cold and thin and wretched, and they were of a dirtiness not easily described – black from head to foot, pickled with soot from their fires, their legs encased in torn-up strips of hessian sacking, wound round and round like puttees. I was afraid they had hoped we would bring them something, and I struggled to explain that we were merely scouting. It was a relief when Hardy returned; but he said there was no question of a Herc landing, so that, as elsewhere, the emergency supplies would have to be dropped from low level.

Short as our visit was, it brought home to me the urgency of the humanitarian role that the RAF had undertaken. Back at Bhairawa, spirits were high, first because senior Nepali officials had visited the camp and praised the RAF's efforts effusively, and second because it had been decided that the airstrip at Surkhet – the same distance out as Jumla, but further south – was by then fit for use, and the first-ever landing by a Hercules in the Himalayas was planned for next day.

That trip is graven in my memory – not so much for the flight, or for the approach to the target, as for the intensely moving reception which the plane received after landing. When the tail-gate was lowered, a line of porters queued up to carry off the sacks. Their clothes were ragged beyond description, their shoes in ruins, their faces crumpled and creased by sun and wind; but as each one stepped on to the loading ramp, he stopped, stood upright and raised both hands together before his face in the traditional greeting, *Namaste*, paying homage not to humans, but to the great steel giant which had brought salvation from the sky.

Next morning, full of my exclusive – most of which I still had to write – I set out for home. It was a Friday, and I hoped that if I reached London on Saturday morning, I could get an article into that weekend's edition of the *Sunday Telegraph*. Hardy gave me a flying start with a lift to Kathmandu, and from there I managed to put a call through to my office in Fleet Street – no easy task in those days. 'I'm on my way back,' I shouted through howling interference. 'I've got a great story.' I started telling it, but was rapidly shot down.

'Keep it short, old boy,' said my colleague Desmond Albrow. 'The paper's very tight.'

'How many words can I have?'

'Eight hundred.'

'Christ! That's impossible. I need far more than that.'

'Keep it short,' he repeated.

Why the hell didn't he show more interest? Had he no imagination? Seething with indignation, I caught the short flight to Delhi and then the nine-hour haul to London. I slept for part of the night, but for most of the time I was scribbling sentences in my note book or in my head, so that when I reached Fleet Street I was able to type the piece straight out. In mid-morning I handed Desmond a thousand words and went out for a late breakfast. When I came back, he was full of enthusiasm. 'This is marvellous stuff,' he said. 'Can't you do any more?'

Curses! I stifled a scream of frustration. 'You said eight hundred, and I've done a thousand already.'

'I know – but this is really good.'

So I sat down and rattled out another 800 words. The article took up most of a page, and it cemented my relations with the RAF. Infinitely more important, Operation Khana Cascade brought relief to thousands of mountain families, and strengthened even further the bonds of friendship and goodwill which had existed for more than 150 years between Britain and the Kingdom of Nepal.

CHAPTER EIGHT

Among the Snow Giants
1974

Back in England, I felt I had been in another world, and hastened to share my excitement with a lifelong friend, Val Fleming, nephew of Peter, and a keen outdoors man. 'The country's unbelievable,' I told him. 'We've simply got to go and walk there.'

So it was that October 1974 found us – a party nine friends – flying out to Kathmandu and on by small aircraft to Pokhara, 200 miles further into the mountains, for a twenty-three day trek in the Annapurna region. Our team consisted of Val (of the merchant banking family) and his wife Elizabeth, myself and my wife Phylla, her brother Gerry Barstow (a solicitor), Nigel Buchanan (known from his great height as 'Lofty'), Eileen Strathnaver (an American friend who needed support and distraction, as she was in the process of separating from her husband), Sarah Matheson, a lively friend of the Flemings, and Mary Taylor, ditto.

We went under the auspices of Mountain Travel, the firm founded by Colonel Jimmy Roberts. A retired Indian Army officer, and a pioneer of Himalayan trekking, he had unparalleled knowledge of the terrain, as he himself had walked all the trails in the region. We found him settled in his modest house outside Pokhara, deeply tanned but rather battered-looking, and not nearly as positive as he had sounded in his letters. Surrounded by pheasants in pens, with a springer spaniel and a golden retriever on the lawn, he regaled us with tomato juice and the story of a German party who had arrived a few days earlier – among them a woman who fired off volley after volley of complaints. Everything about Nepal was wrong, she said. The hotels in Kathmandu were *schrecklich*:

the lavatories were unspeakable, the food disgusting, the people filthy – and she finished her tirade with a blast at the weather. '*Ent*,' she wound up, '*it is CLOUDY!*'

She had a point. The monsoon had been late that year, and with the sky still heavily overcast, there was no view of the big mountains. Only dark foothills were in sight. More worrying was Roberts's news about the Khampas – armed exiles from Tibet, who had set up bases along Nepal's northern borders and had become a danger to tourists. Because of that threat, he warned us that we might have to change or curtail the route he had planned for us, which was through the foothills and outliers of Dhaulagiri.

I think we were all nervous – not about bandits, but about the physical challenge we had set ourselves. None of us had tackled the Himalayas before, and we knew that punishing climbs and descents lay ahead. Whatever the challenges, Roberts had furnished us with a strong support team: Nima Tsering, our head sherpa, his four assistants and twenty-three porters, two of whom were women.

It was slightly depressing to find that our first camp site could be reached by road – and off went our kitbags in an ancient lorry, while we set out on foot by a winding route, and, as I wrote in my diary, 'got our first taste of hot sun, huge trees and the point-blank stares of locals.' A three-hour walk brought us to the village of Seti, where we found our tents already pitched in a meadow beside a rushing, opaque turquoise river. Most of us immediately plunged in – and after our sticky walk, the warm, fast-flowing water was pure delight.

The outlook was dull. We were surrounded by scrub-covered hills of maybe 6,000 feet, but still the clouds were down and the light began to fade early in the evening. Then, as I was sorting out clothes in our tent, one of the sherpas stuck his head round the flap and said quietly, 'Sair – the mountain.' A moment later someone shouted, 'My God! Look at that!' I dodged outside, and there, riding in a cloud-gap at an unimaginable height, was a triangular peak of ice and snow, blazing in the last of the sun – the summit of Macchapucchare, the Fish-Tail. I stood transfixed, so incandescent and ethereal was it, its magic increased by the drift of the clouds, which gave the illusion that the mountain itself was moving. All too soon it disappeared, swallowed by grey fog; but we had caught a glimpse of the world that towered above us, and got some warning of what lay in store.

My diary, scribbled in pencil, took up the story next morning:

> Tea, biscuits and porridge at 6.30 am. Porters move in on tents and fell them with terrific speed and precision. One of the *sherpanis* [women porters] loads up, to everyone's embarrassment, with two kitbags and her own belongings all lashed together in an 80 lb burden. Camp disappears as if devoured by locusts. Move off at 7.10, sun already fierce on our backs.

So our trek began, and a routine was quickly established. Before first light the sherpas would bring us what they called 'wassing wattair,' warm in bowls. Some of us shaved, some didn't bother. After an early start we would walk for several hours, sometimes stopping for brunch, sometimes keeping on until midday. Then, after lunch and a short siesta in the open, we would tramp on for two or three more hours until Nima chose a site for the next night's camp.

We soon saw that he was a star among sherpas: thirtyish, friendly, always cheerful, quick moving and quick witted, with passable English and a ready sense of humour, he managed the whole unwieldy party with the greatest skill. His choice of camp sites was faultless, and every time we moved on, he insisted that every scrap of litter be collected, so that we left no sign of our occupation. His second-in-command, Bakhta Bahadur – easily identified by his red hat – was less communicative though equally efficient; but Nima's most valuable lieutenant was Artendi, an older man, whom we nick-named 'The Chairman'. He always brought up the rear of the party, acting as a sweeper, nursing stragglers, and singing gently to himself in a mournful falsetto as he guarded the camp at night.

At first we were worried by the way the porters wheezed and whistled as they struggled uphill. Then Nima explained that the noises were not signs of distress, but made deliberately because they somehow helped with breathing. He himself let out prodigiously powerful whistles, usually to recall porters who had taken a wrong turn, but often to converse with the eagles and lammergeyers which circled high overhead. He could imitate the birds' calls to the life, and often they answered, their cries ringing back off precipitous rock faces.

After heat and ferocious gradients, the worst hazard of the trails was leeches, which were ubiquitous. Most of them were small – no more than two inches long – but they could climb rapidly, end over end, up the sides of boots and legs, hanging on by suckers at both their extremities. We had patent jelly, allegedly repellent, to smear round the tops of our boots, but this did little to deter them, and we kept finding them with their jaws sunk into our legs. Salt, or a touch from a lighted cigarette, would force them to drop off, but the anticoagulant in their spit made blood pour from their bite-marks, and everyone hated them. One morning Sarah was bitten seven times and reacted vociferously (as I noted), 'much of the Western Himalayas hearing the news of each arrival.' We quickly learned to spot the little beasts undulating upright on the track, waving back and forth in search of a contact. After a few days we thought we detected a pattern in the attacks. The fact that the leading walker got fewer bites than anyone else seemed to indicate that the leeches were stirred up by the vibration of footsteps, and roused themselves in time to assault targets further back in the column.

Our motto was the same as that of St Andrew's, Pangbourne, the prep school at which Val and I had been: *Altiora Petimus* – we seek higher things. Our ambition was to go as high as possible on our route through the foothills of Dhaulagiri; but for the first few days we were relatively low down, between 3,000 and 5,000 feet, always climbing or descending steeply, sometimes in rhododendron forests or woods of feathery pines alive with monkeys, whose babies parachuted among the canopy, using springy branches to slow their descent. More often we were passing between brilliant green rice paddies or through villages of small, well-built rock houses, and climbing through the hundreds of narrow fields into which the hillsides had been terraced. It was odd to reflect that in visiting Nepal we had landed among people sustained by medieval methods of agriculture and simultaneously jumped ahead to the year 2033.

The heat was punishing, but there was always solace at hand in the form of cold water – freshly melted snow and ice – which raced downhill in streams and rivers, splashed over waterfalls or gushed from the hillside in jets. After big storms the rivers turned grey with silt, but usually they were the glorious, inviting turquoise which I had seen from the air a year earlier; and even if a torrent was only a couple of feet deep, to lie down in it after a hot walk was magnificently refreshing. I had one extraordinary bit of luck when, as I wallowed in the Kali Gandaki, my gold Rolex (left me by a grandfather) came undone and disappeared in the rushing water. By some miracle, as I made a desperate, blind, downward swipe with one hand, my fingers caught the strap and saved it.

Of many exhilarating natural showers, the most sensational was a cataract in which a stream coming down a hundred feet of steep rock was bouncing out into space so that gouts of water weighing maybe ten pounds each were falling the last fifteen feet clear of the rocks: down they came, *thump, thump, thump,* exploding over our heads, shoulders and backs with such force as almost to knock us over. As I remarked to Gerry, in the West you could pay thousands at a spa and not get a hydraulic pummelling half as powerful.

With tourists still rare birds of passage, our arrival in any village excited intense curiosity, and whenever our sherpas pitched camp near habitations, an audience of thirty or forty spectators would assemble to watch the performance. At first this was amusing, but later it became tiresome – as when, one morning I awoke to find a man staring into our tent from a distance of about four feet with an air of intense concentration, hands on knees, flexed forward, as if obeying a stage instruction to look alert. Nigel, however, was wonderfully patient with the children, playing games and entertaining them with tunes on his tin whistle. Since they were very small, and he, at 6′ 5″, towered over them, they must have thought him a real giant of a pied piper.

Somehow the poverty of the villages did not worry us. It was obvious that the people lived a very primitive life, but our consciences were eased by the knowledge that we were bringing money – in the form of the porters' and sherpas' wages – into their communities.

On yet another glorious morning we started by climbing a horribly steep face through terraced pastures, with the sun hot on our backs. Every time we stopped for a rest, someone complained to Nima about the heat and the lack of any attractive outlook; but he just smiled happily and said, 'Very nice at top' – to which I muttered, 'It had better be.'

On we went, gasping and sweating, until at last we reached a ridge – to be confronted with a thrilling panorama of snow peaks – an absolute knock-out of a view. As each of the party struggled on to the top, he or she cried out, and Nima, making the most of the moment, struck a heroic stance as he called the names, flinging out his right arm, palm upwards, in a separate grand gesture for every summit: 'Dhaulagiri One! Nilgiri! Annapurna Fang! Annapurna South! Gangapurna! Macchapucchare!'

After a long halt, spent gazing in wonder, we went on up, and from that evening's camp, securely lodged on grassy ledges at 8,200 feet, watched a most glorious sunset:

> High pillars of cloud coming from the west are lit by a pink and yellow glow as they pile onto Dhaulagiri, obscuring the summit. From the valleys below us other wraiths rise and float up into the sun's dying rays. To our right, Annapurna South, Fang and Nilgiri blaze up ruddy pink and orange. Then, just before the sunset is extinguished, the shoulders and peak of Dhaulagiri ride clear of the clouds, magnificently gilded for the dying moments of the day. At the last moment the clouds dissolve off Annapurna, and the two great peaks are left glowing against the darkening sky. The glow fades as we watch: the fire goes out of it; until only a soft pink is left. Then that goes too, and suddenly the mountains are cold and dead again, white and black instead of alive with flame.

As usual, we lit an amateurish fire, but two of the sherpas, spotting the huge, hollow root of some long-dead tree, heaved it downhill and crashed it onto our smouldering heap. Ninety-nine out of a hundred fires would have been extinguished by such brutal treatment, but this one flared up inside the hollow trunk, ignited it, and produced such a blaze that no one could go near it. Basking in its heat from a distance, we had a great feast of Tibetan meat balls, potato cakes, spinach, cucumber and a special cake baked by Nima.

Fire-making was one of the sherpas' and porters' special skills. Once, as we tried in vain to coax flames out of a wigwam of sodden twigs, the huskier of the two sherpanis, who habitually went barefoot, stood watching us with a mixture of amusement and pity on her face. Losing patience with our farcical incompetence, she stepped forward and scattered our little structure with a single, rousing kick from her bare toes. Then she reassembled the pieces, bent down, sucked in a huge volume of air and with an incredibly powerful blast from her pursed lips blew the fire into instant life – whereupon she moved off shaking with laughter.

After supper the talk turned to that inescapable Himalayan subject, the yeti. None of our supporters claimed to have seen one, but Artendi, through Nima, recounted how a girl herding yaks at 14,000 feet in the east of the country had been attacked by an ape-like creature earlier in the year. Four yaks had been killed – apparently by being flung bodily about – and the girl, who had had all her hair torn out, had been paid compensation by the government. According to Nima, a yeti is brown, stands upright, and a female has human-shaped breasts. When going downhill the animal is obliged to move slowly because its long hair falls over its eyes, limiting its vision; going up, on the other hand, it can travel like the wind because the hair falls back off its forehead.

Purely in terms of altitude, the high point of our tour came on Day Ten. We had camped at 10,400 feet, and the summit party set out at 6.55 am, aiming to reach our target pass at 15,000 feet before midday. The weather was disappointing, except for one short spell when the cloud parted, to give us a thrilling glimpse of Gurja Himal – a silvery ghost shining through the mist on our right. But, as we soon realised, the absence of sun was a blessing, for the ascent was severe. First we twisted upwards through woods; then we came out onto scrubby pastures, and next, at 13,000 feet, on to coarse grass like that on ridges in the Scottish Highlands. With the temperature dropping sharply, everyone donned sweaters or anoraks, except Val, who sported his perennial tweed jacket.

By 13,500 feet we all had tight foreheads or backs of heads, and by 14,000 every step demanded a fierce effort. My heart was hammering, and forty steps were all that I could do between rests.

The porter deputed to lead us was going much too fast, and either did not understand or ignored our requests to slow down. At 14,900 feet, when he and I were far ahead of everyone else, I told him we had better wait – at which he lit off uphill like a chamois and vanished into the mist. Nima, appearing with the rest of the party, announced that we would have brunch where we were, and eventually, after tremendous whistling, ho-ing and cho-ing, re-established contact with the guide – whereupon we had a sumptuous picnic.

Thus fortified, we made a final push to the pass, which turned out to be a long, level ridge at 15,100 feet. The mist was ice-cold, and so thick that we abandoned our attempt to set eyes on Lala lake, claimed by our map to be on our right, but said by the guide to be below us to the left. Soon we were on our way down, with headaches shifting from front to back or vice versa. Ours was no great achievement – there were plenty of higher passes not far away – but a shower-cum-bath in a water-spout, an issue of Gurkha rum and a five-star supper of vegetable soup, Tibetan meat dumplings and potato cake balls assuaged any disappointment.

Every day brought something different. One morning, as we climbed through forest, an apparition suddenly came flying down the track to meet us: our cook, wild-haired and wild-eyed, in frantic pursuit of a sheep which he had recently bought but of which he had foolishly lost control. Nima mocked him as he hurtled past – but the cook had the last laugh, for later he caught the runaway, and that evening he slaughtered it, skinned it and cooked it for our supper – and amazingly good it was.

Another morning, and another apparition: a tall, willowy peroxide blonde, maybe in her early forties, came swinging up the track in a brilliant scarlet shirt and very short navy shorts, preceded by a single Sherpa and followed by three porters carrying heavy loads. 'You British?' she called in an American accent as she went past. 'You all look British.' Eileen, who is American, ground her teeth and kept silent, while the rest of us mumbled some kind of response; as we watched her legs – which were amazing – disappear up the hill, we speculated agreeably about her relationship with the Sherpa.

Alas, our trek was coming to an end. For three weeks we escaped from the real world and travelled in a magical kingdom, freed from all responsibility. We had lived like royalty, with every want supplied: wonderful meals provided, our tents pitched and beds made every evening, no need to plan or worry. We had seen no wheeled vehicle, no telephone wires, no other Europeans. We had heard no radio and seen no newspapers. We knew that a general election must have taken place in England, but we did not know who had won it, and we did not care.

Imagine our chagrin, therefore, when, we found the last camp-site already occupied by a party of middle-aged fell-walkers from Yorkshire. They were friendly enough, dispensing whisky and invitations to play bridge, which Nigel accepted; but already, on the first evening of their trek, there was dissent in their party, fomented by a tiresome younger man whom we instantly christened The Outward Bounder. Shouts erupted during a game of Scrabble, when one of the senior players claimed that *troot* was a valid word – the Scottish equivalent of *trout.* This was too much for the Outward Bounder, who yelled, 'If that's the way you're going to carry on for the next two weeks, *I'm not coming any further!*'

After three weeks of freedom, re-entry to civilisation was a strain. For more than twenty days we had had no chance to read a newspaper, hear the news on radio, use a vehicle of any kind or even enter a building. Coming down to earth therefore gave us a jolt. At the Panorama Hotel in Kathmandu, where we stayed one night, we ordered dinner and quickly demolished the dishes that appeared. Assuming they were *hors d'oeuvre,* we asked for the main courses, only to be told we had already had them. Such were our appetites that we had to call for a second round.

Worse occurred the next evening as we prepared to catch the evening flight to Delhi. As I knew from the year before, Kathmandu airport was then primitive and dimly lit, but we checked in and boarded the aircraft without difficulty, only to find at the last moment that Gerry was not with us. Luckily we had seats right at the front, by the door, and before the hostess could stop me I ran back down the steps in search of him. It took only a minute to find out what had happened. Thinking that the girl in the money exchange had cheated him, he had struck the glass panel in the front of her tiny kiosk and cracked it from top to bottom. When the girl gave a scream, two policemen had moved in and frog-marched him off.

A superintendent told me he was already in custody, and could not come with us. 'In that case,' I said, 'I need to get his kit off the flight.' Back on the tarmac, I ducked under the belly of the aircraft and stood up in the luggage hold, surrounded by ranks of suitcases and back-packs, three or four deep. If Gerry's had been in the front row, I could have dragged it out – but it was not in sight. By then people were shouting, and I had no option but to duck out, nip back up the steps and into the plane, just as the hostess was closing the door.

So we flew to Delhi, and then to London, one short. Gerry had the ignominy of spending a night in the cooler and paying a fine of eighty U.S. dollars. He was released next morning, and recovered his kit in Delhi; but for him it was the inglorious end of a glorious holiday. The rest of us came back elated, and a great deal fitter than before, enchanted with Nepal, and with images of those superlative mountains graven in our minds.

CHAPTER NINE

Phantom Encounter
1973

In 1973 the Russians were doing their best to irritate us by probing our air defences – just as they are today. Long-range TU 95 bombers, known to NATO as 'Bears', were taking off from their base at Murmansk, coming round the North Cape of Norway and heading south-west towards the Atlantic. Most were going through the gap between Iceland and the Faroes, or between the Faroes and Shetland, and on to Cuba, but some were turning due south and flying down the North Sea, provocatively close to British airspace. Although many of the flights were probably just training sorties, some were clearly designed to gather information or shadow NATO ships, and it was the RAF's task to challenge the intruders and escort them away.

'Trade', as the RAF calls it, was unpredictable. Sometimes there were no flights for weeks on end, sometimes several during the same day. The irregularity was no doubt deliberate, and maintained as a further annoyance; but when a call came from my public-relations contacts, saying 'Get to Scotland immediately,' I reacted sharply, flying to Edinburgh, hiring a car and setting off at high speed for 43 Squadron at RAF Leuchars, on the coast of Fife.

There I was quickly kitted-out for a sortie in a Phantom fighter-bomber: woolly underwear, G-suit, thick, olive-green immersion-suit, bone-dome helmet – all much the same as for the Lightning, but with refinements.

In the crew-room of 43 Squadron I found the pilots and navigators of the I.A.F. (Interceptor Alert Force) awaiting a summons to scramble.

Out on the apron a row of Phantoms was lined up on ten-minute state, ready to take off on receipt of an alarm signal.

The crew-room was pervaded by the hypnotic beat of an electronic metronome, relayed by direct link from the master radar station at Buchan, on the north-east corner of Aberdeenshire. *Tock, tock, tock, tock* it went, showing that the vital communication link was open. Earlier in the day radars on the coast of Norway had reported trade coming down from the north, but now the intruders had vanished from the screens. That meant one of two things: either they had turned back, or they had dived to low level, below the radar, and would reappear suddenly when they climbed again, presenting what were known as pop-up targets.

Tock, tock, tock, tock went the metronome, all through that day and the next. On the second afternoon, still without action, my kind hosts proposed – as compensation for the boring wait – that I should go for a tail-chase. Foolishly I accepted the offer without realising how violent the flight would be. A few minutes later I was in the navigator's seat of a Phantom, directly behind the pilot, pursuing another aircraft which was doing its best to throw us off its tail. Over the North Sea we climbed, dived and put in one hard turn after another. I cannot remember how many G we pulled – six, anyway – but the experience was shattering, and soon I was fervently wishing it to end.

Next day, having recovered, I felt I must get back to the office, and reluctantly set off for the south. Three or four more days passed, and then suddenly the call from the north came again: 'Trade!' Again I hastened to Leuchars, only to learn that the Russians had done their usual trick of shearing off and had never come within range. Nevertheless I was issued with a full set of kit, and introduced to the pilot who would fly me – if the chance arose. He was the genial Major Skip Yohe, of the United States Air Force, on an exchange tour with the RAF; and as he had recently completed a year's combat missions in Vietnam, I had every confidence in his ability.

That night someone threw a party in the Officers' Mess, and I went to bed late, having drunk more than was sensible. The next thing I knew, footsteps came clattering down the passage and someone banged on the door of my room shouting, 'Get down the Squadron! Now!'

It was 5.45 am. In a flash I was up, dressed and running. Just as I arrived in the crew room, the *tock, tock, tock* of the telebrief stopped and a voice took over. 'Buchan for Wing Ops and I.A.F. We have contacts in November Lima Lima Kilo, designated track number zero-zero-seven, strength three, heading two-seven-five, flight level two-eight-zero, speed three hundred, expected penetration time one-one, one-five zulu.'

Everyone was wide awake. The radars had picked up a group of three aircraft in grid square NLLK, 800 miles to the north east. They were heading south-west at 28,000 feet and 300 knots, and were expected to penetrate our defence area at mid-morning. The report put everyone on edge, and a few minutes later the telebrief opened up again with the galvanic message: 'Buchan for Wing Ops and I.A.F. Alert one Phantom.'

Someone punched a button. Hooters howled for action. Skip and I trotted out to our Phantom – a much bigger aircraft than the Lightning, and deadly-looking, with its long, pointed nose, elegant body and heavy tail. As I settled into the navigator's seat, behind the pilot and separated from him by a bulkhead, a helper plugged in the leads for oxygen, radio and personal survival pack. To a professional crewman the space was luxurious, but to me it was claustrophobically small.

Now we were on two-minute state. Our call-sign was Six-Three, our partner Phantom's One-Six.

There was Buchan again, now in our headphones: 'One-Six and Six-Three – scramble, scramble, scramble. Acknowledge.'

'One-Six answered our partner. 'Scramble.'

As Skip started our engines, a white Victor tanker took off across our nose and climbed away. We began to roll, with our partner just ahead of us. Then his reheats blasted out fire and away he went. 'Burners coming in,' said Skip calmly. 'Two good burns – and here we go.' Seconds later we were flung bodily into the air, and in less than a minute we were at 25,000 feet, heading due north, with our partner lifting and dipping in the brilliant sunshine, graceful as a swallow on our left wing-tip.

Soon we caught up with the tanker and flew beside it, one on either wing of the big, white-bellied whale. After an hour we went on C.A.P.

(Combat Air Patrol), taking a long sweep to the east and then, on orders from the ground, one to the west, searching immense areas for the intruders. But Skip was also keeping a close eye on our fuel state: we were already a long way north, and unless we could refuel from the tanker, we would soon have to turn back,

Control, at Pitreavie in Fife, did not seem to take his first request very seriously – whereupon he erupted, and shouted back: 'I've got this goddam journalist on board. If we don't get gas, he's not going to see a fucking thing!' That did the trick. Permission was granted immediately, and Skip told me: 'Find the tanker.'

Struggling to remember my instructions, I fiddled with the radar screen between my knees. On it was a thin red outline, roughly the shape of a rugger goal post, and I knew I had to get it positioned so that it framed the white dot in the centre. Somehow I achieved a lock, and we homed in on the tanker, which had fallen twenty miles behind.

Now from the belly of the whale a long hose was trailing, with a basket-shaped drogue on the end. As we swam up towards it, the Phantom's refuelling probe went out from the side of the fuselage beside my right knee with a heavy thump and flutter. With beautiful precision Skip took us up to the drogue – I could see he had done this many times before – and we coupled at the first attempt. Fuel started flowing at once – but then, as we hung there lifting and falling, with the huge white V of the tanker's tail a few feet above our heads, Ground Control came on the air again, telling One-Six he had a target.

One spurt of fuel flew out of the hose as Skip eased back to break the connection, 5,000 lbs the richer. Then he pulled round in a tight turn. My G-suit clamped tight onto stomach and thighs, but I was too busy to worry, as I had the task of working the radar in search of our partner as we hustled after him.

'Zero Six,' Control told us, 'we have contact with two bogies ten miles apart. Bearing two-five-zero, range sixty miles ... bearing two-five-five, range fifty miles. Bogey No 1 is turning slightly starboard ... both bogies are heading zero-one-zero.'

'Judy! Judy!' called the pilot of One-Six, telling Control he was taking over the intercept. The next few minutes were intensely exciting. The hunt was on. We were closing in on our targets. But where the hell were they? I scanned the sky for other aircraft. Nothing. Then suddenly Skip cried, 'There he is – one great big, ugly bear!'

'Where?'

'Straight above us.'

Staring up through the canopy, I could see nothing but sky. Then I realised that, in the middle of the blue, one tiny white smudge of condensation trail was showing, 3,000 feet above us and twenty miles ahead. 'Going up,' Skip announced laconically – with which he fired the re-heats and stood the Phantom on its tail. As we rocketed up, the white smudge expanded miraculously, as if we had a telephoto lens pulling it towards us. First it was the size of a model aircraft; then within seconds it had become a TU-95, a silvery four-engined bomber, with a long, slim fuselage and swept-back wings, leaving behind it a con-trail which stretched half across the sky.

We saw One-Six – a little black dart in comparison – go speeding up to its level and draw alongside on its left. For a couple of minutes the Phantom held station; then we took its place. From close quarters the Russian plane didn't look anything like a bear: it was ugly, all right, but more like a fish than an animal, slender as a cigar tube, its nose extended by a refuelling probe and its fuselage swollen here and there by bulges holding radar apparatus. There were no markings on its flanks, and only a big red star on the tail fin, but the shape alone enabled Skip to identify it as a Bear F.

The bomber was cruising at 300 knots – a speed at which, in the thin atmosphere at 28,000 feet, the Phantom could only just hold its position. After a minute or two Skip dived away and came up on the other side of the bomber. Now faces were visible in one of the blister ports towards the back of the fuselage: they looked friendly enough, and when we waved, they replied with cheerful, two-finger gestures, which we returned. Their captain, however, was less generously inclined. Suddenly the near wing tipped down as the huge aircraft turned heavily towards us. 'Bastard!' Skip muttered. He evaded the clumsy manoeuvre easily enough, slipping away and down; but next time we came up to the Bear's level he stood off a greater distance.

'Now then,' he muttered. 'I need to get his number.'

Since this was painted on the nose-wheel housing, he had to make a pass close beneath the Bear's fuselage, and for a few breath-taking moments we floated across under the belly of the bomber, so close that our whole upward view was filled with white-painted metal, and I felt sure our tail fin must make contact with the lumbering giant.

On the ground I had been told that interceptor aircraft were not allowed to approach intruders closer than 200 metres. As we pulled up level again, I said, 'Skip - if that was 200 metres, I'm a Dutchman.'

'Well ...' he drawled, 'more or less'.

By then the second Bear had closed up on its partner, and we repeated our manoeuvres. Soon we had completed our task: we had identified both bombers and reported their track. They had come up out of the Atlantic – whether or not all the way from Cuba, or whether they had turned round after an outward journey, we couldn't tell – and they were heading north-east for home.

Control gave us our bearing for Leuchars, 450 miles to the south-east: 'Your pigeons-to-base are one-five-eight.' Back we came at 40,000 feet. The day had turned brilliantly fine, and when we reached the north of Scotland, the whole country was laid out beneath us like a gigantic map, the mountains showing brown and the coastline sharply etched against the blue sea, with every firth, every loch, every mountain clearly visible.

I recognised many stretches of country that I knew from the ground, and I conceived a sudden plan – that when we reached Sutherland, Skip should descend to low level, fly up the line of the little Mallart river and then, as we crossed the dam at the bottom end of Loch Choire, switch in the re-heats, to liven up the estate's head stalker, Jock Cairney, with a thunderous roar. Alas, we had no clearance for low flying in that area, on that day, and my plan was still-born.

Our return to Leuchars was exciting enough. A 35-knot wind was slanting across the runway, and Skip took the Phantom in crab-wise, with the nose pointing way off to the right. At the last moment he straightened up and made a perfect touch-down – and so ended a three-and-a-half hour sortie, during which I had never been bored for a second, or noticed the slightest discomfort.

Fifty years on, the Russians are still playing the same dangerous game, probing our defences and testing our alertness with irregular flights around the edge of British airspace. The intruders are still Bears, still powered by turboprop engines, and basically the same long-range bombers. The RAF respond in much the same way, now with Eurofighter Typhoons rather than with Phantoms. There has never been a fatal clash – but who knows what catastrophic repercussions one mistake might set off?

Going East

My supersonic career peaked in 1979 with a flight to Bahrain on Concorde. In the past three years British Airways and Air France – partners in the enterprise – had established transatlantic flights, from London and Paris to various destinations in America, which took half the time of conventional jet crossings. Air France also flew Concorde to Rio de Janeiro, and now British Airways were hoping to open a route to Singapore. This inaugural flight to the Gulf was part of the planning.

How I managed to wangle a seat on the flight deck, behind the second pilot, I cannot remember – but there I was in the cockpit as the crew prepared for take-off from Heathrow. There were only thirty or forty passengers in the cabin – capacity was about 100 – but they included several important-looking sheikhly figures in Arab dress.

Having flown in RAF fighters, I was prepared for the acceleration of the take-off run, but not for what happened next. As the pilots exchanged brief messages – 'Airspeed building ... 100 knots ... Power checked' – the long, pointed droop snout lifted clear of the runway and the aircraft was tilting upwards, putting the flight deck high off the ground, when suddenly the second pilot called 'Engine failure! Abandon!' Instead of four green lights spread across the instrument panel, he had three greens and a red. Instantly the captain cut the power: the plane tipped downwards and the nose-wheel hit the tarmac with three or four tremendous crashes – *BANG! BANG! BANG!*

As we turned and came bumping back along a perimeter track, I greatly feared that the landing gear must have been damaged by that alarming impact, and that my Concorde trip was over. But no – the captain seemed unperturbed, and once back at the terminal he remarked jovially, 'You've now had your free tour of Heathrow airport.'

On the stand again, the passengers' nerves were calmed with champagne, while up front we waited for the duty engineer. I did not feel very hopeful when he appeared – a shambling, Yeti-like figure in filthy overalls, with straggles of red hair hanging down over his face. What did this creature know about the innards of the multi-million pound aircraft?

Answer: everything. For a couple of minutes he moved along the wall between flight-deck and passenger cabin, pulling out one steel box after another, inspecting it critically and pushing it back in. These (I think) were amplifier circuits, and in about the fifth he discerned a fault. 'Ah,' he exclaimed in a strong French accent, 'I think zis is ze problem.' Reappearing with a replacement, he slotted it into position, rammed it home with a well-placed kick and declared that all was well.

So it was: the second attempt at take-off was faultless. As the nose lifted, four greens lit up on the instrument panel. At 200 mph we were airborne, and we roared away above Hounslow, no doubt giving hell to people beneath us – for I had noticed out in the country that whenever Concorde went over, the noise far exceeded that of any other commercial jet.

After that excitement I retired for a while to the passenger cabin, which I remember as small, cramped and noisy. What matter, when an indicator on the bulkhead at the front was flickering between Mach 2.0 and 2.01? It was amazing to think that we were travelling at twice the speed of sound – about 1,330 mph. I was not altogether reassured by the fact that, from a seat at the back, I could see the wings flexing gently, or by the information that at this velocity the temperature on the skin of the plane was so high that the whole body had stretched, and was eight inches longer than on the ground. Worries receded when stewards brought round caviar and champagne.

By the time we were over Saudi Arabia, 56,000 feet above the desert, travelling faster than a rifle bullet, I was back on the flight deck, and I was thrilled when the co-pilot offered me his comfortable seat, on the right of the cockpit. I had barely settled when the captain said, 'If you'd like to have a go, I'll switch off the autopilot for a minute.' Gingerly I took hold of the handles which stuck downwards from the forked control stick, like the handlebars on a bicycle. My mind shot back to the sortie in the Lightning when I had inadvertently done two complete rolls before Brian, the pilot, corrected. Even one roll in Concorde would not please the sheikhs. When the captain said, 'She's all yours,' I therefore reacted with extreme caution. Not daring to move a muscle, I sat fascinated by the feel of the stick – which had a heavy, hydraulic resistance, stiffer than I had expected, as if a great weight was pulling against my hands.

For a minute or two I tried to analyse the strange sensation. Then suddenly a brilliant white light appeared beyond the windshield. 'Hey!' I exclaimed. 'What's that?'

'Relax,' said the captain. 'It's the moon.'

'But it's moving!'

'Looks like it – but that's because we're going so fast.'

He explained that, as we were travelling eastwards at 1,300 mph, in the same direction as the rotation of the earth, we appeared to be accelerating the moon's ascent. Half-mesmerised, I handed back control.

In Bahrain Concorde's arrival caused enormous interest, and because the aircraft was due to continue pioneering further afield, I came home on an ordinary flight. But plans to establish a route to Singapore never came to fruition, and I felt fortunate to have caught that exhilarating, experimental thrust to the east.

CHAPTER TEN

Across the Water
1978

One afternoon early in 1978 I was sitting at my desk in Fleet Street, wrestling with some difficult article, when my telephone rang. On the line was Phylla, sounding very odd, and for a moment I was irritated at having my train of thought disturbed.

'What is it?' I asked.

'It's two hundred' she replied in a squeaky voice.

'Two hundred what?'

'Two hundred thousand dollars.'

'My God!'

A miracle had occurred. Six hard-bitten New York editors had sat up half the night bidding for the American rights in her historical novel, provisionally entitled *Distant Thunder.* No matter that the book was by an author they had never heard of: they had gone for it like tigers, and in the end Berkeley had secured the American rights. The news threw us into a frenzy of speculation. What would we do with all that money – over a million dollars in today's terms?

Phylla's mighty hit derived indirectly from our long-range drive home from Delhi. An editor who had enjoyed one of her short stories commissioned her to write a novel, and, inspired by wide historical reading, she came up with *The Queen Bee,* the story of a girl who goes out to India to buy fabrics for her boutique in England, and is swept into the kingdom, or hive, of a mysterious female dominatrix in the Himalayas.

The advance on that first book was a modest £200, but the author's potential was spotted by another editor, the brilliant Rosie de Courcy, then working with her partner Anthony Cheetham (whom she later married), in their firm Futura. Fed up with seeing American women earn huge advances for historical novels, Rosie commissioned three of her own – and one of them was Phylla's rip-roaring saga, *Distant Thunder*. Again, it was about a girl – Lady Caroline March – going out to India 'to forget her past'. But this time the date is 1857, and as the Mutiny rages, Caro – 'headstrong, courageous, exquisite' – is caught up in rollicking adventures and threatened with one ghastly fate after another .

Rosie first tried the book on the New York firm Fawcett, who offered an advance of $25,000; but then Anthony flew to the States in pursuit of another novel, *The Thorn Birds,* by the Australian author Colleen McCullough, and by skilled advocacy pushed the bid for *Distant Thunder* to $35,000. When we heard that he had rejected this, too, we thought he had taken leave of his senses. But then, the next we knew, Fawcett had dropped out and put the rights up for auction – in which Berkeley eventually triumphed with a bid of $200,000.

We were temporarily stunned – and so was our agent Richard Simon; but as the top rate of income tax in England was then 83 per cent, we engaged the services of Anton Felton, an accountant who specialised in authors' affairs and positively enjoyed the odd bout of fisticuffs with the Inland Revenue. His recommendation was succinct. He could arrange various reverse trusts to our children and nephews, but these would bring only small relief, and we would still lose most of the money to the Government. By far the best thing to do was to emigrate. 'Go and live in Ireland,' he told us. 'In Eire, bona fide creative artists pay no tax at all.'

The idea seemed preposterous. '*I* can't emigrate,' I told him. 'I'm ... I'm Chairman of the Nettlebed cricket club!' Other equally ridiculous objections rose to the surface of the mind, only for us to realise how easily they could be overcome. The most serious problem was that I had a good job, with excellent prospects: as Assistant Editor in charge of features on the *Sunday Telegraph,* I was right-hand man to the Editor, John Thompson, with whom I got on very well. Another consideration was that both our children were by then at boarding school, and, if we went, would have to fly out and back for holidays.

After a week of dithering, we pulled ourselves together and took the big decision: throw up everything and go. We needed to move fast, because, to be sure of obtaining full tax relief we had to be out of the country one clear week before the beginning of the new financial year on 6 April 1978. Moreover, once we had left, we would not be able to set foot in England for 365 days: if we so much as touched down, we would lose all our advantage. (When my father heard this, he announced to the family that if or when he died, I was not going to come to his funeral. He lived for another twenty-two years.)

Our first essential was to find somewhere to live in Ireland, and we were fortunate in that an old friend of my father's, the distinguished Irish writer and editor Terence de Vere White, put us in touch with Denis Bergin, an estate agent in Dublin. Denis turned out an absolute godsend. A man of immense charm, knowledgeable on forestry, shooting, archaeology, sheila-na-gigs and many other arcane subjects, he had (and has) innumerable contacts in the property world, and he soon identified three houses that might suit us.

Over we went on a reconnaissance, flying to Dublin and hiring a car to drive out west. The first possibility, in Kildare, was a rather plain house in absolutely flat country, and did not appeal. The second was more promising: a cottage in the grounds of Emo Court, a vast, neo-classical mansion standing on a wooded hill in Co Laois. My spirits rose when, as we drove up to it, a fallow pricket bounded away through the trees. But although we liked many aspects of the place, we decided it would be too small and claustrophobic.

The third candidate, Kilboy, near the town of Nenagh in Co. Tipperary, was in effect an enormous bungalow – all that remained of a house burnt down in the Troubles. Although no beauty, it was set in a lovely park, a few fields out from the foot of the Silvermine mountains, which made a splendid, 2,000-foot backdrop. The whole building was on a plinth, and the part offered to us was clearly the old front, approached by a flight of stone steps. That bit of the bungalow alone contained five bedrooms, two bathrooms, sitting-room, dining-room and large hall – all the space we could want – and we decided to take the place for a year.

Back in England, Olivia, again the heroine, agreed to occupy our house – even though, this time, we could not tell how long we would be away. Still more generously, she also undertook to do all the necessary school runs. After a week of frantic sorting and packing, I drove off after breakfast one morning, with Alice (then fourteen) as navigator, in our little horse lorry, dangerously overloaded with furniture, clothes, bed-clothes and sundry equipment without which we thought we could not exist. It was a long, slow trip – to the ferry at Fishguard, by sea to Cork, and then for three hours along tortuous roads up to Kilboy, where Phylla and Guy, who brought our car, joined us next day.

At first everything went well. Once we had been into Nenagh and bought a load of furniture (most of it made in East Germany), the house became comfortable, and the environs were definitely attractive. In the grounds was a lake that held sizeable trout, and the mountains offered stiff walking. Friends who came out to stay were delighted with our situation, among them Tim and Susie Keown, with whom we climbed to the summit of Slieve Kimalta on a lovely summer's day. We were particularly pleased with our telephone number, Silvermines 9. The owner of the property, Tony Ryan, founder of the airline Ryanair, welcomed us civilly and took us to his favourite pub, where he claimed (and we agreed) the Guinness was second to none. He also introduced us to hurling – an exceedingly violent game – in a match in Thurles, a few miles to the south.

There was, however, one major snag: he refused to allow our two Labradors, Pumpkin and her daughter Pepper, into the house. To us this was totally unreasonable. The dogs were part of the family, had always lived indoors at home, and were fully house-trained. At Kilboy there was only one good carpet, in the sitting room, and I guaranteed that if the dogs should spoil it, I would buy a replacement. None of this made any impression on Ryan. The dogs were banned from the house – which meant that they had to spend the day outside (if it was fine) or in the car (if it was wet), and that they had to sleep in one of the old stables, which was a 500-yard walk from our front door, round the outside of the long courtyard. They hated being dumped out there, and putting them to bed on a rainy night was thoroughly depressing.

Any guilt we felt about becoming tax-exiles was assuaged by a splendid letter from Rebecca West. 'I am strongly in favour of all forms of tax evasion,' she wrote:

> That taxation is an evil in itself is proved by the fact that the beautiful Aztec civilisation was destroyed not because the Aztecs were frightened by Cortes's horses, but because they were so heavily taxed they would not take any change of government. I regard you not exactly as saints and martyrs, but getting on that way.

For a few weeks we made the best of things. When friends from Oxfordshire came out for a weekend, we climbed the Silvermines on a rare fine day and had a picnic on the summit. I even dug out a patch of waste ground to start a vegetable garden, and soon we had our first crop of spinach, which seemed quite a triumph, as potatoes and turnips were almost the only vegetables available in the shops. (A friend, to his amazement, once found some avocados in a greengrocer's: he bought four, and as he was leaving the shop, the lady behind the counter said, 'Tell me now. How long do you boil them things for?')

Then one day Alan McClintock, a delightful estate agent who lived and worked in the area, mentioned that a house called Rathenny, about ten miles away, was up for let. One visit was enough to make our minds up. Here was a beautiful, 18th-century building, not too big, with harmonious proportions and huge windows, set on rising ground in its own park at the end of an avenue. Its rooms were large and light, and in about 1790 itinerant Italian plasterers had come past, leaving their mark in the form of bunches of grapes and sheaves of corn moulded onto the end-wall of the sitting room. It was wonderful to think that they might have been working in the room while Mozart was composing *The Magic Flute.*

For us a further attraction was the stable yard at the back of the house, which would be perfect for keeping our own horses. The fields around were gently undulating, with great stretches of gorse-infested bog beyond; but the dominant feature of the landscape, ten miles to the south, was an obvious nick in the skyline known as the Devil's Bit – the legend being that the Devil, angered by shortage of conquests as he flew southward, took a gnash out of the mountain, but then spat out the chunk, which became the Rock of Cashel.

Kilboy versus Rathenny was no contest. Apologising to Tony Ryan, we packed up and moved. He, not surprisingly annoyed by our desertion, held us to a full year's rent.

Our new home had certain drawbacks. There were rats in the cellar, and the roof leaked in so many places that whenever it rained – i.e. almost every day – we had to set out half a dozen buckets on the landing. The Aga (in local parlance 'de-agga') was supposed to heat the water, but it was so ineffective that we called in the local plumber, whose name, needless to say, was Looney. 'God!' he exclaimed. 'It (de-agga) should put dat fella (the hot water tank) hopping.' In fact the system was so feeble that Looney resorted to the fearful expedient of connecting up a vacuum cleaner backwards into the pipes – which produced one of the biggest air-locks ever known in Tipperary.

These, however, were minor problems, and we soon grew to love Rathenny. One major asset was our house man, Tom Boyd, who came with the property and did all sorts of odd jobs. At first we had some trouble understanding him, for he spoke very fast, with a cracking country accent. He talked of pairking the cair, described the Government's economic policy as 'a fairce', and stumped me completely when I mentioned the trunk of an old beech tree which had fallen in the park. In return for my suggestion that I should cut it up for firewood, he replied, 'I'd say it's hairdasairn.' Baffled, I asked again, and again he said, 'Hairdasairn.' It took me some time to work out that he meant that the wood must be hard as iron. We cut it up and burnt it, nonetheless.

Sean Cawley, who managed the farm, was constantly helpful, and endlessly cheerful, no matter how foul the weather. Stories told in his high-pitched voice took us into the heart of the country – as when he described a farmer who came to grief in a point-to-point race. 'He was a mile in front. Going the finest, he was. Then what? God, didn't there have to be a *pig* in the grass! And didn't the bloody pig have to run out between the harse's feet! And sure, that was the finish of him.'

We soon realised that we had landed not only in another country, but also in another time, half way back to the halcyon years conjured up in the novels of Somerville and Ross. Our neighbours were perhaps not quite as eccentric as those with whom the Irish RM hunted, but they were odd enough – witness Sonia Duxbury, who introduced herself to us by unrolling a great length of lavatory paper, scrawling on it an illegible message with crimson lipstick, and hanging it over a step-ladder in our hall.

A fearful story was told of Sonia's prowess as a cook. Wanting to make a steak and kidney pie, she diced up a large quantity of meat and put it in a bowl. Then, however, some urgent summons took her away to Dublin, and when she returned, the meat had gone green with mould.

'Throw it out!' her son told her. 'For God's sake - it'll kill us all.' 'Never,' she said. 'It's perfect.' To stop his mother proceeding further, the boy tipped the whole lot into the lavatory – which of course it blocked. Water would gradually drain through, but the meat would not move. What to do? 'Meat'll burn!' someone cried. 'Burn it out!'– so they poured in petrol and struck a match. *Whoosh!*, and the curtains were on fire. Having soothed their nerves with bumpers of Jameson's, they had a new idea: fetch the hunt terriers, which were half-starved, small, agile and trained to go down holes. In went the dogs, which attacked the blockage with gusto ... but then they disappeared round the bend, never to be seen again.

It was horses that got us into local society. Almost everyone around owned, bred, bought, sold, trained, raced and above all hunted horses, and soon we acquired mounts of our own. Phylla had ridden since childhood, and found a beautiful dark bay mare called Abba; I, pretty much a beginner, started on Billy, a borrowed grey Irish Draft, and as I learnt, gradually moved up the scale. Around the 130 acres of the farm we built a few practice jumps, which were ideal for a learner.

We soon joined the Ormond Hunt, which was about to celebrate its 200th anniversary. The kennels were on the edge of Cloughjordan, a small town north of Rathenny, and we were recruited by the Master, the irrepressibly cheerful and enthusiastic Donald Swan, a former captain in the 1st Queen's Dragoon Guards who had moved to live in Ireland in 1965. When he and his wife Theresa found Modreeny, their fine house just outside the town, it had been uninhabited for fifteen years, except by chickens upstairs and sheep on the ground floor; but they had made it into a comfortable family home and opened a restaurant, the Fox's Den, in the basement. Dinners there were riotous affairs, often ending at four in the morning.

Hunting with Donald and the Ormond was immense fun. On weekdays the field might amount to no more than eight or ten farmers; the meet was often outside a pub, where we would stiffen the sinews with bumpers of port and brandy, mixed in equal measure, before moving off – and away we would go, over walls, ditches, banks, fences, fields and bogs in whatever direction hounds took. Once in the autumn we invited Donald to a cub-hunting meet at Rathenny, and after a rousing run-around we entertained the field to a breakfast of kedgeree and vodka.

My finest hunt lasted no more than half an hour – yet every detail of it is etched in my memory. Phylla had been invited elsewhere, so I went alone to the meet at the village of Ardcroney, taking Dominic, by far the best horse I had ever owned. Donald was riding Patrick, a favourite hunter who had been laid up for weeks with tendon trouble, but now was back in action for the first time.

As a dozen farmers gathered outside the pub, lowering copious drafts, I heard one say to another, 'You're not treatening me' – to which his neighbour replied, 'I'm treatening nobody.' Then he concentrated on the task in hand, and said, 'If he goes over that drop at the top of the hill, I'm not following. I am not. I'm going round.'

Hardly had we moved off when hounds found and started running. Away we all went, once round a small cover and then up a long slope. Looking ahead, I saw, to my horror, the leading horses go over a hedge on the skyline and fall out of sight like stones. 'My God!' I thought. 'It's the drop!' It was too late to take evasive action: all I could do was sit right back in the saddle and hope. Dominic landed like a feather, and was off. Fences, walls, ditches – he flew the lot. For once I was flying with him, in perfect harmony. Instead of my usual struggle to do the right thing, everything seemed easy, and the feeling was incredibly exhilarating.

Over one more fence, we landed in a rough field full of ponies – and there was Donald, on his feet, holding his horse's bridle. After that one short burst, Patrick had pulled up lame. It was essential that Donald carried on somehow, to control the day. Almost without thinking, I rode over and said, 'Here – have my horse. I'll take Patrick home.' Without hesitation Donald thanked me, scrambled up and made off, leaving me to lead poor Patrick along a lane, back to his box at the pub. As we walked, I was in tears – not because I had deprived myself of further excitement, but in let-down from the high tension of the past half-hour, and sadness for the veteran clopping along beside me.

Another inveterate horse-coper was Peter Anderton, a wiry and wily old Englishman of huge experience who had come to Ireland in 1931, lured by the prospect of unlimited hunting, and had stayed ever since. Jockey, trainer, instructor, stud manager, dealer, he knew every horse for miles around, and was for ever in search of the perfect mount for me. On one unforgettable occasion, together with his wife Sheila, we drove up country to try out a dark bay of which he had had good reports. When we reached the yard, after some prevarication it became clear that the horse in question was no longer there; but presently the owner had another brought down the road from a different farm, and swore it was the very one, telling me to try it.

From the front, the creature looked alarmingly narrow. I got up, as bidden, feeling very nervous. Before I was even settled, the owner, already mounted, took off across his garden with a cry of 'Dat harse'll kill yer! Follow me!' and jumped the wall into a field. I followed, finishing up round my horse's neck, but hung on as we galloped down a slope. At the bottom was another hedge, hairier than the first. Again the owner put his horse at it, with a cry of 'Dat harse'll be the death of you! Follow me!'

Again I just about hung on, and we arrived back in the garden with me all over the place. Peter, seeing that the horse was entirely unsuitable, shepherded us away, and the next I knew, we were washing down oysters with Guinness in a hostelry on the banks of the Shannon, congratulating ourselves on having *not* spent £5,000 – the outrageous price which the dealer had demanded. When he said 'Dat harse'll be the death of you,' he was nearer the truth than he imagined, for he pronounced 'death' as 'debt' – and even if I had survived it physically, the animal would have certainly done severe damage to my bank balance.

Also prominent on the hunting scene was David Rudd, a jovial Englishman who farmed pigs at Moneygall, just down the road from Rathenny, and lived in a large, dilapidated house with his splendid wife Prue and their brood of nine children – two of his from an earlier marriage, and seven with her. Like everyone in the area, the Rudds were immensely kind to us, and helped us settle in.

A bit to the north at Ballingarry were the Kennys, a powerful farming and hunting family. It was Johnny – youngest of three brothers – who heard that I had played cricket in England, and lured me into the only local team, the Ballyeighan Gentlemen.

There were certain differences from cricket in England. One was the fact that villages are so far apart that we often had to drive for more than an hour to reach our rendezvous. Having stopped at least once *en route* to refresh ourselves at some hostelry, we would arrive in combative mood, unworried by finding that the ground had been mown only by sheep, and that there was no pavilion. On one field we could not dislodge the resident donkey: when we tried to drive him off, he galloped in circles with his tail stuck straight out behind him, braying furiously. In the end, when he came to a halt, someone said, 'Ah – carry on, Jack. Leave him: de ass will stand for umpire' – and we would have been better off if he had, for the home umpire was grossly biased.

At one point, when I was bowling, the batsman took a terrific swing at the ball; as it passed his bat there was a noise like a rat-trap going off, and it was caught head-high by the wicket-keeper; but when all we roared 'HOWZAT?' the official blandly said, 'Not out. Not at all. Play on!' And then as I walked back past him he muttered, 'Sure the ball jumped. But there was no timber in it. Play on!' Latter I heard that in an earlier match, after rejecting two appeals for LBW, the same umpire suddenly cried out at the batsman, 'You're out, and away witcha. You've three lives, and that was the last of them.'

Unlike in England, there was no opposition to hunting. Almost everyone took part, and it was a fact of life. Shooting was different. In theory I had the rights on Rathenny land, but sometimes when I walked one of the rough hedges with our labradors, in the hope of putting up the odd cock pheasant, a spaniel would pop out in front of me, and I would find some armed interloper working the hedge in the opposite direction. I should have tried to join one of the local gun clubs, which seemed to control the shooting in our area; but I did not want to seem intrusive, and restricted myself to solitary forays, taking care to observe the rule that one spared hen pheasants and hares.

One enthusiast, apparently licenced to shoot anywhere, was the Anglican priest who held services in several parishes round about. Permanently on the lookout for vermin, he drove between parishes like Jehu with a loaded shotgun laid across the back seat, looking to left and right, and stopping suddenly to engage any target he saw. On his way to church one Sunday morning he spotted a magpie in a field and braked so violently that he was rammed by a BMW following behind.

In the summer we took the children to America, staying with our cousins in Maine, to which I and my sister had been evacuated during the war. Having bought tickets from a travel agent in Limerick, we boarded the Aer Lingus plane at Shannon and flew to Boston comfortably enough. There, however, trouble set in. The immigration officer took one look at our passports and said, 'Where are your visas?'

'We don't have any visas.'

'Then how in hell did you get on the goddamned aircraft?'

'We walked on.'

The man shot me a filthy look and said we had two alternatives: either go straight back to Shannon on the same aircraft, or go to Canada for the weekend. I remonstrated, arguing that nobody had told us we needed visas. '*You* don't need a visa to come to Ireland,' I told the immigration chief. 'Why do we need visas to come this way?' The officer was far from pleased, but in the end he agreed to parole the family for twenty-eight days, and let us go. Later I heard that the authorities fined Aer Lingus $1,000 dollars per head of the Hart-Davis family for not scrutinising our documents properly.

Up in Maine we had a grand time, re-establishing relations with my cousin Mary Bok and her family, who were still living at Hillside Farm near Camden, where my sister and I had spent two years during the war. I was amazed to find how everything seemed to have shrunk. I thought that the white clapboard house, which stands on a slope above the road, was approached by a long drive – but what I remembered as a substantial avenue turned out to be only a few yards long.

The highlight of our trip was a deep-sea fishing expedition, for which we joined a party of other holiday-makers on an ocean-going boat. Out in the deep water we were thrilled to see whales surfacing, but there was a big swell, and Guy (then twelve) soon felt horribly sea-sick. To cheer him up, the skipper (who sported a dummy seagull on the peak of his cap) waited until he himself had hooked a fish and then handed the rod to Guy, saying 'Give it to him, Boy!' After a dire struggle Guy landed a 40 lb pollock, the biggest fish of the day, and felt a whole lot better. We returned to base with 200 lbs of cod and pollock in the trunk of the car, and because the temperature was about 90 F, we had to move fast to distribute the catch among friends.

That winter an unprecedented snap of cold weather hit Co. Tipperary. The temperature dived below zero; great sheets of flood water froze on the fields, and for three or four days we had wonderful skating. We managed to assemble enough players for rough games of ice hockey, astonishing locals who had never seen anything like it.

What drove us home in the end was the telephone system. At first we had found trying to make calls an agreeable joke. Our instrument had a crank handle for rousing the exchange, but when turned it also rang a bell in the house, so that anyone in earshot shouted 'Telephone!' 'No, no,' I would call, 'It's me ringing out.' As I waited for the exchange in the village to come on the line, I got a clear image of Mrs O'Flaherty sitting in front of her little board, into which she plugged the appropriate cable leads.

'Good morning,' I would begin.

'Good morning to you as well,' she would answer.

'Hardy weather still.'

'Oh, fierce. Tis desperate altogether. What can I do for you?'

'Will you get me Moneygall 5, please?'

'I will of course. Hold on now.'

Sundry clicks and beeps would follow before the Moneygall exchange answered. Then, through a roar of interference (even though the village was less than ten miles away) I would hear Mrs O'Flaherty swap further meteorological observations before asking her counterpart, 'Will you get me Five?' Through the blizzard came the answer: 'Tis no use calling Five. Five's gone shopping. Back at one o'clock.'

'Nine, then,' I would say, breaking in.

'Nine's on holiday. Back next week.'

'Oh well ... Thank you.' And that was the end of it. In a way the switchboard ladies were very useful: acting as a local intelligence service, they knew where everybody was, and were a good source of information. Dealing with them was always amusing – but long-distance calls were another matter. One morning I began trying to get an urgent message through to my publisher in London at about 9.30 – and proceedings began with the usual skirmish.

'Telephone!' shouted voices in the house.

'No. It's me. I'm calling out ... Good morning, Mrs O'Flaherty ...'

The battle lasted for more than three hours, frequently interrupted by misplaced incoming calls. Again and again the phone would ring, and there would be a man asking 'Are you Boris-in-Ossory Nine?'

'I am not.'

'Ah glory!'

More often, as I hung on, it was a man with a ghost voice saying 'Finished? Finished?' and me yelling 'No!' The struggle ended at 12.45 when I heard a girl with a wonderfully soft Dublin accent exclaim, 'Divine praises – I've given the man the wrong number!' By then my whole morning had been wasted, and my publisher had gone to lunch.

When such frustrations were compounded by the Oifig an Phoist, the Irish postal service, going on strike, communication with England became almost impossible, and we feared we would lose contacts and commissions. By the autumn of 1978 the pressure had become too great – and we were further unsettled by the fact that, in England, Christopher and Olivia had bought a farmhouse of their own, and were keen to go and occupy it. We had never had any clear idea of how long we would stay in Ireland, but now with enormous regret we decided to return home. Leaving Rathenny was a wrench, for it was the most elegant and welcoming house in which we had ever lived.

Altogether we had had a wonderful time across the water. We had made many new lasting friendships, learnt a different language and seen a different way of life. Our financial manoeuvres had proved successful, and although we had blown a good deal of Phylla's unexpected bonanza – on horses, rent, champagne, travel to America and flying the children back and forth to school – we had enjoyed spending it, and at least we had not meekly handed it to the Inland Revenue. Moreover, the episode had jolted me out of a full-time career in Fleet Street, to which I never returned.

CHAPTER ELEVEN

Animal Man
1973-1990

I first met Jimmy Chipperfield in the spring of 1973. I had written an article about the British safari parks – which he invented – and because he liked the piece, he invited me to accompany him on a tour of his projects. By then he was enjoying runaway success with parks at Longleat in Wiltshire (established in 1966), Woburn in Buckinghamshire (1967) and Knowsley, near Liverpool (1971). A fourth park was about to open at Bewdley, near Kidderminster in Worcestershire.

My instructions were to present myself at Heathersett, his large, modern house on the expensive northern fringes of Southampton, at five to nine – and because I had heard in advance that he was a devil for punctuality, I was there a minute early. Out he came, wearing a smart brown suit, and greeted me with a broad smile; but before we left he had to say goodbye to the baby chimpanzee which his wife Rosie was rearing on a bottle. The tiny creature lay in state in a spare bedroom, swaddled in a pink, knitted jumpsuit. 'Lovely, isn't she?' he said softly, chucking her gently under the chin – and with that we were off.

From the start of our trip he made no secret of the fact that he was showing off – to impress me. He wanted me to know how well he had done, how far he had come – and he was so straightforward about it that what from other people might have sounded boastful, from him seemed a straight recital of fact. I warmed to him immediately, and we quickly became friends.

I could see he was a tough customer. A short, dark-haired man, then sixty-two, he still had the powerful, broad-shouldered physique gained from working as a trapeze artist in the family circus, and his hard, dark eyes quickly assessed everyone he met. His accent was neutral, but it still carried traces of his childhood haunts in Wiltshire and Hampshire, and his speech was enlivened by echoes of circus life: he spoke, for instance, of being 'bitten with a lion' or 'kicked with a giraffe.'

John, his younger son, drove us to Southampton airport in the Bristol. 'Marvellous car, this,' said Jimmy as we purred along. 'I got it because I wanted something fast and reliable to use whenever the Rolls is being serviced.'

At the airport we were met by his private pilot, James Harrison, who had already warmed up the eight-seater cabin of the Piper Navajo. Within a couple of minutes of boarding, we took off, heading north for Halfpenny Green and the West Midlands Safari Park at Bewdley, Jimmy's latest project, still under construction. In the air he talked animals and parks continuously, but also reached back to the start of his own life, when he was born in the top bunk of what he called 'a me'ogany wagon,' in a field on the outskirts of the Wiltshire village of Corsham.

His family, who had been circus people for generations, then had a small travelling show which moved around the south of England to different pitches every summer. When he was a few days old, another family made a bid for him. 'I could do with that boy,' said the man, who had no sons, and offered £100 – worth perhaps £5,000 today – but Jimmy's father was not interested: to him, the family was the most important asset in the world.

That was as far as he got with the story before we were coming in to land, and he switched back to the present. 'It's amazing, the estates I'm being offered now,' he said. 'Every week somebody's asking me to put in a park. I had a letter yesterday from Buenos Aires. Remind me to ring the girl and send them an answer.'

On the ground we were met by Richard Luck, manager of the embryonic West Midlands park, and as we drove to the site Jimmy quizzed him ceaselessly about details. Apart from the price of the land, which Jimmy himself had paid, the establishment of the park was costing £600,000 – about £8 million in today's terms. From his experience with earlier ventures, he knew exactly what the capacity of the new set-up would be. Every mile of serpentine road within the park could accommodate a thousand cars a day: Bewdley, with four miles, would take 4,000.

From the office Jimmy rang home and asked his secretary to tell Buenos Aires he was interested. Then he settled a dozen points of fine detail. When we toured the park, he was displeased by the siting of one lion shelter, but delighted by the progress on the artificial pool and waterfall in which the bears would disport themselves. Could the fish not have been left for the sea-lions, I asked? 'No – because all they do is kill them, and leave them to float about and rot.'

As we bundled back into the car after a hectic tour, Jimmy said, 'One of these days I'm going to get a clicker, to count the questions I'm asked. I bet it's a thousand a day, at least.'

Lunch, in the plane, was coffee and sandwiches, after which we dropped down into Liverpool airport, where we were met by Lawrence Tennent, manager of the Knowsley park. From his office Jimmy rang Scotland, then Longleat. Mock-ups for the season's publicity campaign displeased him. 'I don't like that,' he told the trendy youth who had designed them. 'I don't like that at all.' Out went the whole batch of art-work. In quarter of an hour he authorised and re-directed the expenditure of £20,000.

In the park he pointed out how – as in all his projects – the lions had worked out their own territorial system. 'It's fascinating. As long as the cars stay on the road, they don't give a damn. But if anyone drives off the road, they go mad, because they think their space is being invaded. Watch this fellow: he's not going to look at us, even.'

As he spoke, a huge male ambled into the road ahead of us and stood there gazing into the distance. We crawled past, inches from his whiskers, and the great amber eyes did not flicker in our direction.

In the previous year the Knowsley park had taken £500,000, confirming the popularity of Jimmy's invention. Three times it had been jammed from entrance to exit, and the gates had had to be closed. For the present season two new reserves had been added, with an extra mile-

and-a-half of road. 'Eighteen thousand a mile, this road costs,' Jimmy groaned. 'That sort of figure gives me a pain.'

The baboons were having a terrific onion-eating party, all lined up with their backs to the wind. 'Look how happy they are,' said their proprietor. 'We've got more than 500 monkeys now, and not one of them's had a cold. If we'd heated their houses, like people said we'd have to, half of them would be dead.' Acclimatisation was one of the practices which Jimmy strongly advocated, in the face of much criticism – and by then his methods had been vindicated, not only by the monkeys, but by chimpanzees, lions, cheetahs, zebras and hippos. All had shown themselves perfectly able to survive the rigours of the British winter.

Back at the airport, we took off for Glasgow and the Loch Lomond Bear Park. Having landed in the dark, we were met by Gerald Anthony, manager of the park, and put up for the night in the luxurious Cameron House Hotel, a multi-turreted Victorian castle on the shore of the loch. At dinner Jimmy proved a generous host, at ease in these sybaritic surroundings; but he himself was abstemious – a small glass of sherry beforehand, and then one of white wine.

Service in the restaurant was leisurely – which gave him plenty of time to talk about his background. What emerged most vividly was the tremendous strength of the work ethic which his father – an outstanding clown and acrobat – had instilled in him.

The family show was still on the road when Jimmy was born in 1912, but on the outbreak of the First World War his father settled down in the village of Amesbury, where he eked a living by running a primitive cinema. Then, with peace restored, the urge to travel returned, and the family set out on the road again with a travelling fun-fair.

Because they were always on the move from one town or village to another, living in their fine mahogany wagon, pulled by a traction engine, Jimmy hardly went to school. In those days the children of travelling families could simply walk into a school and be accepted; but after one term in Newbury (which he enjoyed) and one in Woolston, outside Southampton (which he hated) his formal education came to an end.

As he grew up, he took on every role in the family show, training animals, performing on the trapeze, wrestling with Bruni, the 250 lb Russian bear. But the guise he liked most was that of the clown, because, as he said, behind the grotesque make-up he felt anonymous and safe. Animals played a large part in the show: Black Spangle, the fortune-telling pony able to predict which girl in the audience was going to be married first; Barney the man-eating donkey, who attacked the clown with his teeth; the pig who could tell the time. All were conditioned by endless, patient training to respond to minute signals, undetectable by the audience.

When Jimmy told the story of Rosie the elephant, his eyes lit up.

'My brother Dicky and I went mad and bought this young elephant. Four hundred pounds, she cost us. That seemed a terrific amount – it was all the money we had. We hadn't a clue about elephants, but we knew she'd be a powerful draw, and we did our best to train her. The trouble was, she was nervous, and inclined to bolt when startled by something new.

'One of our worst days was in Monmouth, where we'd gone for the May Fair. We stabled Rosie in the yard of a pub, and on the morning of the show we walked her into town as a publicity gimmick. Everything was OK until we came on some cows being taken into market. At the sight of them she panicked and set off, screaming and trumpeting, back the way we'd come.

'At that moment a man with a terrible hangover was stumbling across the bridge over the river. When he saw an elephant coming at him with ears and trunk raised, he wasn't sure if it was real or part of his hangover, so he leapt over the parapet, landing in the shallow water, hurting his leg quite badly.

'Back at the pub, Rosie mistook the roofless gents' urinal for her stable and rushed into it, forcing herself through the narrow doorway. You know how an elephant's stomach bulges – well, once she was through the opening, she bulged outwards, and that was her stuck. The brick walls began flexing in and out as she breathed.

'People started collecting. Out came the landlord, yelling 'Get that bloody elephant out of there!' But there was nothing we could do to shift her, and she began to amuse herself by wrenching off the taps, throwing them out over the wall and squirting water back over her head. In the end, with me pulling her tail and Dick urging her from in front, we got her out; but we were so frightened that we cancelled the show and disappeared up-country before anyone could sue us for injury or damage ...'

Jimmy could have gone on telling stories all night; but we had to be away early in the morning, to fly south and visit the scene of his first safari park – Longleat. As we drove towards it, he recalled some of the hazards that had beset its creation.

The idea of letting lions loose had come to him in Africa during one of his animal-catching safaris; having seen the wild life of Uganda, he thought how marvellous lions would look against the background of a green English park. He chose Longleat as his first target because he had watched the proprietor, the Marquess of Bath, on television, and, seeing that he had a broken nose, 'reckoned that he must be a sportsman, the sort of man I could talk to.'

The venture was nearly sunk at the outset because at their first meeting Bath turned up half an hour late. Mastering his irritation, Jimmy managed to engineer a useful preliminary discussion, but then said bluntly: 'There's just one thing. Our date was for eleven o'clock, and you came at half-past. Normally I leave after ten minutes. I don't care what time you suggest for another meeting. I'll come at midnight if you like. But I don't wait.' As Jimmy later remarked, during this mild tirade two retainers 'were trying to disappear behind the curtains or jump out of the window'– but Bath was never late again. He *was* extremely doubtful about the project, and several friends told him, 'Don't touch it'; yet after a fortnight he decided to go ahead. He and Jimmy had no further spats: on the contrary, the landed aristocrat and the clown-cum-trapeze artist-cum-bear-wrestler soon became firm friends.

With agreement reached, Jimmy travelled from one country to another, including Kenya and Israel, in search of lions. None came from the wild – all from circuses or zoos. At Longleat 12-foot fences went up and a serpentine road was laid out, curling back and forth through the park so that motorists could have numerous close encounters with the big cats.

Seven years on, as we drove down to the great Elizabethan house in its wide valley, he recalled the day he let the lions loose. The moment they came out of their travelling wagons, they fought like fiends and raced wildly in all directions, lashing out at tussocks of grass with their paws, then hid under any cover they could find. Jimmy wondered whether he had made a terrible mistake, but he was tremendously excited and thought, 'People are going to go mad when they see this.' Soon he realised that the lions, having spent their lives under roofs, were terrified of the sky, so high and wide open above them; but he reckoned they would quickly get used to it – which they did.

His revolutionary project drew fierce opposition, not least from Frome District Council, which maintained that the park would be a menace to the public. The most vociferous protest came from *The Times,* which ran a fatuous Fourth Leader calling on the Government to have the 'dangerous folly' suppressed. 'This', roared the Thunderer, 'is one of the most fantastically unsuitable uses for a stretch of England's green and pleasant land that can ever have entered the head of a noble proprietor.' No amount of soothing assurance, it said, 'could persuade sensible people that a quite gratuitous and unnecessary risk to life is not contemplated.'

For Jimmy and the marquess, this tirade had precisely the opposite result of that intended: far from stifling the embryonic park, it proved splendid publicity – with the result that when the Lions of Longleat opened at Easter 1966, the place was over-run by customers. Half Somerset became jammed solid with traffic. Bath himself took the first driver's £1 note at the gate, and during the holiday weekend some 3,000 cars crawled through. During its first season the park attracted over 100,000 private cars and 2,000 coaches, and it was clear that Jimmy had struck gold. By September the park had paid off the entire capital cost of the enterprise.

I was eager to see how he and Bath interacted. I might have guessed.

They were completely at ease with each other: there was no false deference, no condescension. They chatted and joked like the good friends they had become.

It was the same at Woburn Abbey, the Duke of Bedford's palatial home in Buckinghamshire, where we called next; but before we met our host, Jimmy rushed to the estate house in which his daughter Mary was nursing a baby hippo called Esme, born that week. We found Mary on her knees, sponging water over the creature's head (to persuade it that it was under water, where it would normally feed) and administering bottles of water, glucose and egg-yolk. When she was suddenly called away to stop a dog-fight, Jimmy went down on all fours in his natty suit and kept going with the bottle, encouraging me to stroke the creature. When I headed for the bathroom to wash the hippo off my hands, he called 'Watch out! There may be something in there.' Sure enough, a very small lion was staggering about the floor.

In the big house, as at Longleat, the atmosphere was relaxed and cordial – and that was hardly surprising, for it was the Duke himself who had initiated proceedings by inviting Jimmy to set up a park on his estate. But, unlike Longleat, Woburn had got off to a sluggish start when it opened at Easter in 1968, and for the first few weeks trade had been poor. Then a single accident precipitated a miraculous surge in business. A family crammed into a Mini persistently ignored the rangers' orders to keep the car closed, and they were careless enough to allow their small daughter to wriggle about so much that she stuck her behind out of an open window. In a flash a lion called Twiggy spotted a target and took a swipe at it with her paw, inflicting severe lacerations, before one of the guards drove her off. Even though the park staff were in no way to blame, the incident made headlines in the national newspapers and drew thousands of eager voyeurs, all demanding to see the lion which had attacked the child. In fact they had no chance of doing so, for Twiggy had immediately been moved to another reserve; but the accident put the park on its feet, and soon it was attracting 350,000 visitors a year.

In the five days I spent with Jimmy we visited two parks in Scotland, five in England, one in Holland and one in Germany. We took nine flights and travelled in twenty-two different cars; never did we use any form of public transport. We talked to dozens of people, many of whom addressed the Boss as 'Mr Jim' and some as 'Mr Chip'. To all of them, whether an elephant boy or the Marquess of Bath, he spoke in exactly the same voice. It was as if we had been moving around in an enormous family.

Back in Fleet Street, I had more than enough material for an article, and in April my report appeared in the *Sunday Telegraph,* which gave it most of a page – in those days of small newspapers, a lavish display. Jimmy was delighted, and very soon came back with an attractive proposition: that I should write the story of his life. Jumping at the chance, I had the good luck to fall in with Alan Maclean, most engaging of editors, who was then head of the publishers Macmillan, and we arranged a contract whereby Jimmy would get an advance against royalties, and I would get a percentage of the take. The book would come out under his name, and mine would not appear.

When I presented myself at Hethersett for the first of many recording sessions, Jimmy handed me a battered foolscap envelope, saying 'That's to start you off – and there'll be the same again when you finish.' In the envelope – which I opened after I had left – I found £1,000 in used notes, worth perhaps £12,000 today.

Calling frequently at Hethersett, I soon got to know other members of the family. Jimmy's wife Rosie, daughter of 'Captain' Tom Purchase, came from another family steeped in age-old circus traditions. Her father had been killed by a lion, and she herself – strikingly attractive as a girl – was famous for having danced in the lions' cage. No wonder she attracted Jimmy so strongly that they eloped when they were both twenty-two, scandalising their clans. When I met her, just turned sixty, I found her a wonderfully calm and capable person, able to hold her family together through all vicissitudes, one of which had been the loss of their first son, Jimmy, who died of tetanus when only six.

In due course I met their second son, Richard, of whom she and Jimmy were extremely proud. Then thirty-one, tall, strong, good-looking, fearless and highly-skilled at handling animals, Richard was all his parents could wish for. When catching elephants and giraffes in Africa, he had learnt fluent Swahili and somehow endeared himself to the tyrannical President of Uganda, Idi Amin. In England he not only trained lions, tigers and elephants, but also, starting from scratch, devised and perfected the layout of the safari parks. Further, he was a knockout with the ladies. My abiding memory of him stems from a photograph which showed him lying on his back in a huge bath, with only his head above water, a big grin on his face, and a luscious mermaid of a girl similarly all-but submerged, belly-up, on either side of him.

In the course of many further visits to Heathersett and the parks, I gradually collected much fascinating information about Jimmy's life, not least his account of how, in the 1950s, the family built up the biggest circus in England, with a tent that could seat 8,000 spectators. Yet the feat which I found most impressive of all was his extraordinary achievement in becoming a fighter pilot in the RAF.

Having been to school for no more than a few scattered months, and learnt only basic maths, he had no academic qualification. Another handicap was that he had only one kidney – the other having been pulped by Bruni the bear – which made him, in official terms, medically unfit for service. But by sheer persistence and bloody-minded harassment of the authorities he put himself into the village school in Stockbridge, learnt trigonometry, qualified as a pilot and ended up flying Mosquitoes, the latest type of fighter-bomber, over Germany. That, to me, was evidence of quite exceptional determination.

We were still working on the book in April 1975 when the family was hit by a dreadful tragedy. Richard, on another animal-catching trip in Uganda, was killed when his Range Rover ran off the road at night. President Amin sent his personal helicopter to recover the body, and Richard was flown home in a charter aircraft carrying the elephants which he had captured. He was buried in the churchyard at Great Wishford, the village five miles north of Salisbury where his grandparents had lived for years in their wagon.

Although shocked and greatly saddened, Jimmy fought back, reorganising his work force to fill the gaps that Richard's disappearance created. Together we finished the book, and on the last day of our collaboration the author handed over another large brown envelope. Macmillan liked the story, and when they brought it out under the title *My Wild Life,* Jimmy went on a successful promotional tour.

Later he left Heathersett and moved to a farmhouse in Wiltshire, which he did up in style, installing a swimming pool that came in under the floor. Whenever I called on him there, I found the place alive with exotic creatures. Even when progressively weakened by leukaemia, he retained his fascination with animals, and he acquired a new hobby in the form of expensive cameras, with which he equipped himself lavishly. He died in 1990, aged 77, and was buried at Great Wishford, alongside his father, his first son Jimmy, and Richard.

He made enemies, of course. He was always a tough negotiator, and proprietors of conventional zoos were jealous of his success, none more implacably so than Lord Zuckerman, who became President of the Zoological Society of London in 1977 and persistently denigrated the safari parks, claiming they were of no value to science or conservation. Jimmy defended himself vigorously, pointing out that he was breeding far larger numbers of threatened species such as tigers than could ever be achieved in Regent's Park, and that he was helping to educate thousands of people about the nature and habits of wild animals.

Critics could not deny that his imagination and energy introduced a major innovation to the British countryside. He also (I believe) saved several noble proprietors of country seats from ruin and gave their properties a new lease of life. For a boy born in the top bunk of a mahogany wagon, that seems to me no small achievement.

CHAPTER TWELVE

Three Men in a Boat
1984

During the winter of 1983-84 I got a call from John Ridgway's wife Marie Christine, ringing from Ardmore, their home on the north-west corner of Scotland. John, she said, was sailing round the world in his 57-foot ketch *English Rose VI*, attempting the fastest-ever, non-stop circumnavigation, with only one other crewman on board. In a radio call from somewhere in the Southern Ocean, sent via New Zealand, he had included a message for me saying 'Get off your arse and meet me for the last leg of the voyage.'

Was it a joke, a tease? There was no means of telling. I knew John fairly well, but equally, he knew that I was no sailor, and I couldn't imagine I would be any use to him. Nevertheless, I agreed to stand by.

Weeks passed, and I more or less forgot about the call. Then suddenly, early in March, another came. By then he was in the Bay of Biscay, within a few days of home. My instructions, relayed via Marie Christine, were to proceed at once to Barra, the island in the Outer Hebrides, where he would pick me up as he came past for the last stage of his journey. John is not the sort of person you would want to let down – so I threw a few clothes into a duffel bag and flew to Glasgow. There I caught the tiny plane that goes out to the islands, and at Barra – there being no runway – lands on the beach.

Expecting my onward transport to arrive within a day or two, I booked into the Castlebay Hotel, overlooking the harbour at the south end of the island. This proved an excellent institution, with delicious food and good wine, which for some reason was ridiculously cheap. Outdoors, there was not much entertainment except walking and bird-watching, and I tried to keep fit by climbing Heaval, at 1,200 feet the island's highest mountain, which has a curious white marble statue of the Madonna and child set prominently on a ridge. I also went jogging on the only road, which circles the island. Once as I returned to base after covering a mile out and a mile back, a cheeky boy called out 'Been right round?' – to which I instantly answered, 'Twice'. As a single circuit was seventeen miles, he looked astonished.

One day passed, then two, then three, four. Luckily I had brought with me the draft of a novel I was writing, and I worked profitably on that. In the bar there was still talk of *Whisky Galore,* the novel by Compton Mackenzie and the later film, based on the wreck of the S.S. *Politician,* which sank off Eriskay, just to the north, in February 1941 with 240,000 bottles of Scotch on board. Men from Barra certainly took part in the unofficial salvage operations that followed.

On the third evening I rang Marie Christine to ask about John's progress, only to hear that he was still the Bay of Biscay, becalmed. No one could tell how long it might be before the wind picked up. Should I sit tight or go home? I decided to give it another day, and next morning, in the harbour, I engaged the services of John Alan Maclean, the lifeboat coxswain, who agreed to take me out to meet the yacht when the time came.

Another day passed, and another. At least the delay gave me time to think about John's remarkable career. As his daughter Rebecca once remarked, 'Dad has made a few waves', and I knew from dealings with him that he was a tough, uncompromising character, always pushing himself to physical limits. In cities or towns he was liable to be chippy and aggressive, but in the mountains or at sea he settled down.

In 1966, while still a Captain in the Parachute Regiment, he had rowed the Atlantic with Sergeant Chay Blyth in a twenty-foot open dory. Two years later he sailed alone to Brazil. In 1964 he and Marie Christine had gone to live at Ardmore, one of the remotest hamlets in the British Isles, in a house without piped water or electricity, to which there was no road. To reach it, one either had to walk two miles up a stony track, or wait for a boat across the loch. There, in 1969, he had founded his own adventure school in the rugged mountain environment, where he had given countless young men and women the shock of their lives, usually beneficial; and in 1977-78 he had sailed the school's *English Rose VI* in the Whitbread round-the-world race.

Always on the lookout for new challenges, he kept ferociously fit by pounding the hill tracks around his home, but once, in a lyrical passage about his love of Ardmore and its wild surroundings, he wrote that he 'still had this need to get away sometimes and find a different challenge, just to make sure I was still able to cut the mustard.' For him the sea was 'a magic carpet which stretches right round the planet,' and its lure was always there on his doorstep.

I had already had direct experience of his teaching methods, for I was at Ardmore one day when a bus-load of junior executives from United Biscuits arrived for an adventure course. It was summer, but the sky was overcast and a cold wind was blowing. In the evening, as they tottered out of their coach, whey-faced after a long drive from Inverness, John lined them up on a beach and addressed them briskly: 'You'll be spending the night on an uninhabited island. So get changed into suitable clothes, and put what you need for the night in one bag. The rest of your kit will go to the school in the lorry.'

The girls were allowed into a hut to change, but the men had to strip off in the open. With their night kit tied into black polythene bin-liners, the whole lot were herded on board the school's big trawler and taken fishing. 'Make sure you catch something,' said John as he handed out lines and bait, 'because that's all you're going to have to eat tonight.'

First he took the boat to a place where he knew there would be no fish, and morale fell lower and lower as the sea loch yielded nothing. Then he moved to a more fruitful area, and the air began to ring with whoops and yells as lines went taut. Soon office girls, who would have screamed if they had had to touch a live fish before, were spattered with blood, knackering mackerel and pollock like Neanderthals and shouting with excitement.

As the trawler drew near the island on which the visitors were to spend the night, John called a halt and announced, 'There's an instructor over there who'll look after you. When I say "Jump", take your bin-liner as a float, jump overboard and swim ashore. First, though, I want you to hand over all the food you've hoarded about your persons.'

Holding a bucket, he went from one shivering management trainee to another. One by one they sheepishly yielded up their hidden treasures: out came half-eaten sandwiches, Mars bars, pieces of cake, boiled sweets. With his round completed, John tipped the contents of the bucket overboard with a flourish, and called out, 'There you go – Jump!'

To my amazement, everybody obeyed. We watched the swimmers struggle to the island, then went back to his croft, where Marie Christine had cooked a delicious supper – and when I asked *why* the youngsters had all jumped when he told them, he replied, 'I don't know. But they always do.'

Now he was on the last leg of his latest marathon. His final radio message had said that he would pick me up off Muldoanich Island, two miles off Barra's south-east coast, at 6 am. For the past few days the weather had been quiet, but during the night a storm blew up, and by the time I got down to the harbour at five o'clock, a Force 8 gale was roaring. John Alan was standing by, engine running, and I carefully handed down a supermarket bag of the food that Marie Christine had predicted the sailors would be craving: fresh milk, bread, meat, fruit and a bottle of wine.

Hardly had we left the quay when an incoming ship bore down on us, lights blazing. In the dark it looked the size of the *Queen Mary,* but in fact it was only the Caledonian MacBrayne ferry coming in. When the captain radioed John Alan 'You're not showing any lights', the answer was, 'I don't *have* any lights.'

Out we plunged, into the raging sea. The roar of the wind was deafening. The little boat was flung about by the waves, and spray repeatedly burst over our heads. Visibility was minimal, but as the light came up we began to see further ahead into the leaping white crests, with Muldoanich showing like a black lump to our right. Suddenly John Alan cried, 'There he is!' For a few moments I could discern nothing but angry sky and water. Then, way out in the distance, I spotted a yacht, though only for a few seconds. As it went up on a wave I caught a thrilling glimpse of a white hull heeling over, and two tiny figures in crimson oilskins clinging like crabs to the blue deck. Then it vanished into a trough.

'Do you think that's him?' I shouted.

'Must be!' John Alan yelled back. 'No other bugger would be out in this.'

English Rose VI it was. As we closed to within fifty yards John bellowed through a loud hailer, 'For Christ's sake keep clear of me! I don't want to be damaged at this stage.'

With that he let go of a rubber dinghy on the end of a rope, but the wind was so strong that for a few seconds the little craft stayed airborne, spinning like a leaf on the end of its tether, several feet above the waves. Then it dropped into the water upside-down. When it came alongside, John Alan managed to right it, half full of water, and while he held it against the side, I slid down into it, nursing my precious bag of provisions. Seconds later John had reeled in the line and was hauling me aboard.

'Another human being!' he cried. He seemed delighted to see me – as I was to see him. But the yacht's movement was so violent that after no more than two or three minutes I was comprehensively sick, throwing up all over the cabin floor. I thought he would be furious. Not at all – he made a joke of it as he cleared up the mess, and soon I felt well enough to take in his companion of the past 202 days – Andy Briggs, a young, red-bearded Yorkshireman 6′3″ tall. In spite of the rough weather, both were in high spirits, for they had already beaten the record for a non-stop circumnavigation by the huge margin of ninety-three days.

For the rest of that day and all night we sailed northwards – and for the whole of that time (it seemed to me afterwards) John *never stopped talking*. Andy put in the odd remark now and then, but it was the skipper who held sway with a loquacity that amazed me, for I knew him as a man of few words, not given to chatter. It was as if he and his crewman had run out of conversation weeks or months before, and now he had to let rip.

Physically, John did not in the least resemble the Ancient Mariner:

he had no long grey beard or glittering eye – for he had made a point of shaving on every day of the voyage, and his blue eyes had their usual steady look. But his narrative was wild and far-ranging. He spoke of whales and wandering albatrosses, of gigantic seas that knocked the boat down, of thunderstorms during which lightning flashed twenty times a minute, of how the deep therapy of the Southern Ocean had banished a nervous rash from his hands and restored hearing to his left ear. He described how he had reduced himself to tears by reciting Shakespeare *fortissimo* to the elements. For him the climax of the voyage had been rounding Cape Horn in a Force Ten snowstorm, the captain of his ship, the master of his soul. More mundanely, he told how he and Andy had taken turns to cook supper. When Ridgway was chef, 'it was curry, curry, and curry again. Think of that – a hundred curries! But I must say, I can turn out damn good rice by now.'

All day we sailed on to the north; the storm abated, and by evening the sea was quite calm, with the peaks of Skye showing finely to starboard. Andy cooked a special supper – *not* curry – and I fell asleep with John still holding forth. By first light we were well up the Minch, and the day of homecoming dawned bright and clear. As we turned into Loch Laxford, the rocks on the shore were glistening with the night's rain, and ahead, inland, the summits of Foinavon and Arkle stood out sharp against a blue sky. Suddenly hearing an engine, we looked round, and there was the BBC helicopter (about which Marie Christine had warned us) coming in for a low overhead pass. Since I was not supposed to be on board, I had to drop down swiftly into the cabin and stay out of sight until the cameramen had flown on.

The final strait, Loch a' Chadh-Fi, was alive with excitement. Sunlight flashed off the wet rocks. Children ran shouting along the shore, and their shrill voices rang out over the water. A sizeable crowd had gathered at the landing. Men were firing guns. Pipes were playing. Tethered balloons were swinging in the wind. Rockets were going up. The helicopter kept making low passes. Everything was combining to build up a tremendous emotional charge. There were tears in John's eyes, and in mine.

As we approached the jetty, I had to stay below, but I could covertly watch the heroes totter ashore, walking unsteadily with feet wide apart; and once the crowd had absorbed them, I too slipped onto dry land, to take part anonymously in the celebrations on that brave and brilliant morning.

CHAPTER THIRTEEN

He Came, He Saw, He Ran
1984

One afternoon in December 1983 the telephone rang on my desk at the *Sunday Telegraph.* On the line was Hilary Rubinstein, a seasoned and wily literary agent, then Managing Director of the A.P. Watt agency. I knew him as a driver of hard bargains, but also as a true book-man and someone who represented numerous successful authors; so when he said 'I have someone you might like to meet,' I was immediately interested.

'Who is it?'

'A Russian who's just come across.'

'Not Bitov?

'Yes. Bitov.'

'Where is he?'

'Here. In my flat.'

'My God! Shall I come round?'

For weeks London had been humming with rumours about Oleg Bitov, a Soviet journalist and translator, and a senior editor of the Moscow *Literaturnaya Gazeta,* who was said to be in London. He had apparently defected to the West in Italy three months earlier, during the Venice film festival, which he had been covering for his journal; but no one had been able to explain how he reached England. Surely there was a good newspaper story here – especially as East-West relations were particularly tense at that moment. In September Soviet fighters had shot down a Korean jet liner carrying 269 people, and the Kremlin, under the ailing, hard-line Yuri Andropov, had become obsessed with the belief that the NATO powers and the United States were planning a pre-emptive nuclear strike against the Soviet Union.

After a quick consultation with my editor, John Thompson, I jumped into a taxi and headed west. Bitov was not, at first sight, very prepossessing. Then 52, but looking older, he had the heavy, dull complexion of a chain-smoker, and his appearance – which must once have been quite handsome – was spoilt by a prominent row of grey, ill-fitting metal front teeth, which (I learnt later) he had had ever since a hard landing in a plane at Sverdlovsk. When I arrived at Hilary's flat he was smoking a cigarette and drinking a strong-looking whisky, and although he seemed calm on the surface, I sensed that his nerves were on edge.

Hilary lost no time in explaining that Bitov wanted to write his story, first in newspaper articles, then in a book. Would the *Sunday Telegraph* be interested in buying the serial rights?

We talked for about an hour. Bitov spoke with a strong Russian accent – for instance pronouncing 'o' s almost as 'a's – 'prafessional', 'pravacation' and so on – but his English was excellent, and we had no difficulty understanding each other. The trouble was that he remained evasive, side-stepping questions about what he would say in any article he (or we) wrote. He could describe aspects of everyday life in Russia, of course – but when it came to subjects like censorship, freedom to travel abroad and his own sudden appearance in the West, he clammed up. After a while I began to feel that he was fairly dull, and either could not, or would not, make any sensational disclosures. When, therefore, I asked Hilary how much they wanted for his story, I was startled by the answer: '£40,000' (about £120,000 in today's values).

Back in Fleet Street, I passed on my doubts to John Thompson – a calm and clear-headed editor. In our budget £40,000 was a huge amount; but we felt certain that if we didn't buy the story, our deadly rival the *Sunday Times* would. So we decided to go ahead – and thereby slung a heavy weight about my shoulders, as I was deputed to help Bitov produce his story.

The British security forces assumed that the KGB might try to snatch him back, and for the first few weeks of his stay in England he was therefore under close protection. Later he told me how grateful he was to have such skilled officers looking after him, and he often remarked on how *prafessional* they were.

MI5 had provided him with a flat somewhere in West London, but although I was authorised to hold meetings with him, I never knew where it was. Nor did I know his telephone number, although he could, and often did, ring me on some undetectable equipment. Occasionally I met an MI5 official for the hand-over of background papers, always in a well-frequented public place. These furtive encounters were pure Le Carré. When my contact came on the line, with his clipped, military voice, to arrange a rendezvous, I would ask, 'Where shall we meet?'

'I suggest the steps of St Martin's in the Fields.'

'OK. What time?'

'Say five o'clock.' (By then it would be dark). 'I'll be wearing an Indian Army tie – brown and blue diagonal stripes, with white lines between. What tie will you be wearing?'

'I don't think I'll have a tie. But I'm tall and fair-haired – and I'll be on a bicycle.'

'Fair enough.'

So at 4.59 I would glide to a halt at the bottom of the steps. A man in an overcoat and trilby hat would move forward to the kerb, hand over a brown envelope, exchange a few words and disappear into the rush-hour crowd – without my catching a glimpse of his tie.

At every early meeting with Bitov I was reminded of the wonderful opening of Edgar Allen Poe's short story, *The Tell Tale Heart*: 'True! Nervous – very, very dreadfully nervous I had been and am.' Bitov was very, very dreadfully nervous, constantly fearful of being seized or poisoned by some KGB agent, and several times his anxiety caused him to abort our carefully-planned meetings. A typical instance was the time I arranged a rendezvous for 6 pm in a flat near Marble Arch belonging to my in-laws, which I knew would be uninhabited during the evening – the safest place I could imagine.

I made careful precautions, giving him the address and telephone number, drawing a map to show where the flat was, and also a sketch of the building's internal layout. Playing safe, I was outside the door of the block, on the street, a few minutes early. Six o'clock came – no Bitov. Six-thirty, the same – so I went up to the flat and waited by the telephone. At 6.50 he rang, his voice sharp with fear.

'What happened?' he cried. 'What happened?'

'Nothing happened. What d'you mean?'

'You compromised the rendezvous.'

'Nonsense.'

'You did - you tried to trick me.'

'Rubbish! I'm not interested in tricking you. You've messed things up. I've been waiting here for an hour.'

I had not mentioned the place or time of our meeting to anyone – not even to his minders – and I told him so. Nevertheless, he swore he had been followed by a woman whom he noticed watching him on the tube. She had been carrying a Bulgarian Airlines holdall, so, not liking the look of her, he had got off at an intermediate station, waited on the platform and caught the next train, only to find her still with him. Then he went two stops down a branch line and returned, all without shaking her off. Finally, when she followed him out onto the street, he panicked and took a taxi back to base.

The incident shook him badly. When we checked, his minders had no knowledge of the woman, as he described her; but they agreed that it would be safer, and less stressful for him, to meet at my home in the country – an isolated house in the Chilterns. He therefore began taking an early train to Henley, where I would collect him and drive him up to the farm.

His mood varied greatly from one day to another. Sometimes he was ebullient, cracking jokes, but on others he was gloomy and depressed. Much seemed to depend on the telephone conversations which he had with his wife Liudmila and fifteen-year-old daughter Xenia, whom he had abandoned in Moscow. The calls were often traumatic: the strain was much increased by the knowledge that the KGB would be listening-in, and Oleg would spend days minutely analysing Liudmila's every remark, in the hope of discerning cryptic messages. Whatever his feeling for her, he absolutely doted on Xenia, whom he described to me as 'the dearest creature in all the world.'

His life in England seemed to be full of what he called *pravacations* – people constantly pestering him. If somebody so much as bumped into him in the street, he considered it a deliberate attempt to annoy him and get him into trouble. Men in pubs kept eyeing him in a way he considered aggressive. He was so touchy that he put me in mind of Queen Victoria, whose diary frequently described some incident with the phrase 'by which I was greatly vexed and provoked.' Bitov seemed to be vexed and provoked almost every day.

Most of the alleged harassment was, I am sure, imagined; but on bad mornings he would arrive saying, 'I think I need a lot of bottles,' and during the day he would get through a bottle of whisky, alternating shots with cups of black coffee, but never getting in the least drunk. He ate very little, and scarcely noticed the delicious lunches that Phylla prepared for us.

He was extraordinarily un-practical – as evidenced by his failure to master the idiosyncracies of our old-fashioned back loo. 'Pull down on the chain, count two and then let go,' I told him time after time – but he never got the trick, letting go prematurely and failing to make the cistern flush. He was also amazingly unobservant: once, in an attempt to jolt him out of his self-absorption, I took him for a walk down into the wooded valley beneath the house. We had gone half a mile before he noticed that snow was lying. 'Oh look,' he eventually remarked. 'It's winter.' Perhaps he was preoccupied by fear that the walk was a provocation, and that I was leading him to a spot where assassins would be lurking among the spruce.

In spite of these difficulties, we worked together amicably enough, and sometimes positively enjoyed ourselves, when he drafted passages in English and I suggested ways of polishing them up. Soon it became clear that he had an exceptional facility for languages, and liked playing with words. Less attractive was a streak of vanity and bombast which gave him an inflated idea of his own importance, and led him to believe that he could single-handedly lower international tension by building a personal word-bridge, explaining to the West what Russia was really like.

If only he had done that! In the event, he shot himself in the foot by composing an Open Letter to President-Elect Chernenko, who had succeeded Andropov. This ill-advised document, published in the *Sunday Telegraph,* wheedled, cajoled and then threatened the new Soviet leader if the author's demands were not met.

In order to provide illustrations for his articles I took him round London with a camera-man, and we got good shots of him in Parliament Square and in the London Library, which sportingly granted us access. But, as I feared, the two major articles which we concocted turned out disappointingly dull. The first made frequent reference to George Orwell – this being 1984 – and was entitled 'The Man from the Ministry of Truth'; the second was called 'How We Live in Andropov's Closed World.' Neither contained any sensational revelations. Nevertheless, they aroused much interest, and were widely syndicated.

Requests for further pieces and broadcasts poured in from many countries, Japan and the United States among them. In England the publishers Hamish Hamilton commissioned a book about Bitov's life as a journalist in Russia, provisionally entitled *Tales I Could Not Tell,* guaranteeing an advance of £5,000, of which he was paid £1,500 on signature. A further advance of $15,000 – half paid on signature – was put up by the American publishers Morrow. These successes led him to thank me effusively for my help. He said how delighted he was to have hit upon a colleague who was both sensitive and (a favourite word) *prafessional,* and we became good friends, united by the satisfaction derived from wrestling words into the best possible shape.

Gradually he shook off some of the inhibitions produced by life under the Soviet Communist regime. Gaining confidence, he moved around London without regard to his personal safety. He began to enjoy the good things of the West, not least food, for when relieved of anxiety he was a bit of a glutton. Yet for him the greatest pleasure – what he repeatedly called 'the one unmatchable pleasure' – was that of simply being free

He moved into a comfortable flat, where he installed a hi-fi system and a video recorder. He planned to supplement his two typewriters – one with English keyboard, one with Cyrillic – with a word-processor, then an expensive novelty. He also bought a car – a red Toyota Tercel – in which he caused havoc with his convulsive driving. Friends who had one ride in it swore they would never have another, for he went far too fast and was inclined to stop so suddenly that he was twice rammed from behind when he stood on the brakes. Even so, he loved the car, and drove it all over England.

Furnished by MI5 with a passport, he was able to travel abroad, and in May and June he spent two weeks in the United States as a guest of *Readers' Digest,* which paid all the expenses of his stay in return for an article about the black market in Russia. Before leaving England, he hinted to friends that he would also visit the West Coast, to see San Francisco and Los Angeles, but in fact he came back as soon as the magazine's subvention ran out. . One dangerous illusion which he harboured was that his English had become so good that he could be taken for a native. This was nonsense: he still had a heavy accent, and a few words were enough to proclaim him a foreigner.

By mid-summer 1984 he was confident enough to criticise the Soviet system in terms which I would have loved him to use in our joint articles (which had come out in February). In a broadcast for the BBC he made a bitingly satirical attack on the censors, and then gave a half-hour interview to the anti-Communist Radio Liberty, which he knew was an unforgiveable sin in Soviet eyes. All his behaviour suggested that he had given up hope of returning to Moscow, and had decided to settle in the West.

Then suddenly, on Thursday, 16 August 1984, he disappeared. When the news broke that he had gone, the world seemed to descend on me – the only person in England who had both known him well and was prepared to talk about him. During the day I gave seventeen television, radio and press interviews, and the corridors of the *Telegraph* building were jammed with camera-laden journalists clamouring for my attention. I could, and did, describe our meetings *ad nauseam,* but of his sudden departure I knew practically nothing, save that after a pub lunch with his MI5 minder his car had been found illegally parked in Empress Gate, close to the Soviet Embassy in Kensington, and that it had been wheel-clamped by the police. His flat was undisturbed: nothing was missing – not even his razor and toothbrush.

Speculation raged in the media and among his friends, who were baffled by the abruptness of his departure. One, Anatoli Gladilin (another Russian émigré), had driven over from Paris the day before, and when the engine of his Peugeot began giving trouble, asked Bitov to lend him the £300 he needed for immediate repairs. 'Of course,' Bitov replied magnanimously, promising to bring the money round at 1 pm next day. He never came.

One fact, more than any other, suggested that he had been snatched. Always vain about his appearance, he had at last started a course of six dental appointments designed to replace his ugly metal teeth. At the first appointment the dentist had removed them, leaving him with bare gums. It seemed inconceivable that he had chosen that moment at which to bolt for home, before the repair was complete.

For a month the mystery remained unresolved. Then, on 18 September, he surfaced at a televised press conference in Moscow. This put down a new marker in the mendacity stakes, for almost everything he said was false.

He pretended that in Venice he had been coshed in his hotel room, and taken off drugged to the mountains, where he was held prisoner in a villa 'for several days'. He claimed that his seizure in Italy and subsequent detention in England were all part of a *pravacation* by British Secret Service agents. He said that in England his minders had drugged and tortured him; that when he refused to write anti-Soviet propaganda, the security people made him 'leave London and go into the country'; that his *Telegraph* articles were written under duress. Perhaps his most ludicrous assertion was that any tape-recording which purported to be of him talking had in fact been fabricated by an ingenious device which could produce a perfect imitation of his voice and delivery. His comments about me personally were not friendly: he said I had 'a loose, slobbering lower lip,' and described me as a kind of simian creature, walking with the backs of my fingers on the ground.

Observers in the West could see that this was all palpable rubbish. The Foreign Office denounced his claims as 'absurd and offensive,' and I was delighted when the *Sunday Telegraph* gave me a whole page on which to hit back. On 23 September, under the heading THE MAN WHO WENT BACK TO THE COLD, I told him a few home truths, leading off with a straight left to the jaw:

'My Dear Oleg, I am afraid you remind me of Hilaire Belloc's Matilda: you know – "the girl who told such dreadful lies, they made one gasp and stretch one's eyes." At your press conference in Moscow on Tuesday you told *such* dreadful lies that I was staggered ...

'As I was not in Venice with you last September, I would pass over the crazy details you invented about being hit over the head, kidnapped and imprisoned in a villa in the Italian mountains – were it not for one inescapable fact. This is that on September 10 you stayed at the Old Felbridge hotel at East Grinstead under the name of David Locke. The signature is there in the ledger, rather shaky, but recognisably in your handwriting. Since everyone knows that you were still in Venice on September 9, there is simply no time in which you could have suffered all the provocations which, according to you, went on for several days ...

'Of all the lies which came out at your recent Press conference, the one which I personally find most tiresome is the claim that the articles which you published were written under duress and at the dictation of the security services. *Absolute* balls, Oleg! As you would say in Russian, "*Yerunda!*"'

I reminded him of how he would come down to Henley on an early train, and how we would work all day with a tape recorder running. 'Being a humble writer [I went on] I am afraid I have never been able to afford one of those amazing phonetic synthesisers which you mentioned at the press conference: machines so crafty that they can simulate a person's voice perfectly and produce whole speeches apparently made by him but in fact invented ... What I do have, on the other hand, are simple tapes filled with hours of your narration. Often you say, "And now please switch off", when we came to a point which you did not want recorded – and switch off I did.'

I also reminded him of his inability to master the downstairs loo, and said that the strongest psychotropic drug I had managed to get down his throat was whisky, of which he had put away a good deal. I asked if he had forgotten his experience in Winchester cathedral, which he told me he thought 'the most beautiful in the world', and where he had 'experienced a moment of prayer, suddenly understanding what awe means.'

Whether or not he ever read my riposte, I have no idea. He never made contact again, but for some time he continued to write ludicrous articles about his experiences in the West – and even now, thirty years later, I am not sure that I know what happened to him.

The most likely explanation came from a senior KGB officer who was working in London at the time. He told me that Bitov did go to Venice to cover the film festival, but that he had also been given some minor assignment by the KGB. In Italy he panicked and defected to the British, who brought him to England. In the autumn of 1984 he lost his nerve again and decided to return to Russia – whether from homesickness and desire to see his daughter, or in response to some offer of amnesty from Moscow.

On 16 August, after his pub lunch, he drove to Empress Gate, parked the car and walked up to the gate of the main Soviet Embassy building at 13 Kensington Palace Gardens, announcing to the security guard, 'I'm Oleg Bitov. Let me in.' The guard, who had never heard of him, told him to clear off; but Bitov then threw his briefcase over the gate, into the drive. Roused into action, the guard summoned the duty diplomat, who did recognise the visitor, and admitted him.

The briefcase turned out to be full of cassette tapes containing a marathon account of Bitov's dealings with the security service. Urgent messages from the Embassy to the Centre, the KGB headquarters in Moscow, elicited instructions that he was to be kept under wraps pending further orders, so he was given a room in the basement until a temporary passport could be prepared. A few days later, lying on the back seat of a car, hidden under a blanket, he was driven to Heathrow and put on a plane for Sofia, whence he returned to Moscow. Considering this a great coup, the KGB commended the London officers for their effort; but at the same time they were amazed that British surveillance had not picked him up when he was dithering outside the Embassy.

So much for the mechanics of Bitov's extraction. But why did his nerve crack at that moment? Why did he abandon ship toothless, leaving behind his contracts, his beloved car, his freedom to do what he wanted, and more than £40,000 in his bank account? People speculated that he found separation from Xenia intolerable – but I shall never know for sure.

What I do know is that Moscow's grotesque over-reaction illustrated, as never before, the inability of the Communist regime to understand the West. How could Bitov's cronies in the KGB imagine that the card-house of lies which they built at the press conference would stand up for a second in London? Their stupidity and ignorance took me straight back to 1957, when the burghers of Minsk refused to believe that anyone in the West could own a private car. It seemed that in the quarter of a century since then the fog of Soviet disinformation, far from gradually dispersing, had grown even thicker.

CHAPTER FOURTEEN

Ace of Spies
1994

Of far greater intelligence, interest and importance than Bitov was another Oleg who came my way – Oleg Gordievsky, thought by many to be the most valuable double agent the West has ever had. Although I did not know it when dealing with Bitov in 1984, Gordievsky was already in England then, serving as a senior official in the Soviet Embassy in London, but at the same time making almost daily contact with members of the British secret service to hand over secret information.

Later I became aware that in 1985 his cover had been blown, that he had been summoned back to Moscow by the KGB, and that, under sentence of death, he had made a dramatic escape from the Soviet Union; but I knew very little else about him – except that he had gone to ground in England, where for the first few months, he had worn a wig and false beard, and was living under an assumed name.

Then one day in 1994 I was talking about book projects to a friend with secret service connections, who suddenly said, 'Why not do Gordievsky next?'

I was amazed. 'Do you mean to say that nobody's doing him already?'

'Not that I know of. He's looking for someone to write his life story.'

Several telephone calls were needed to clear security blocks; but soon I made contact, and, after dealing with many dour Russians in the past, I was delighted to find what a lively intelligence and ready sense of humour Oleg had. Working with him was easy, for even though he talked to me in his fifth language – English – and could not yet write it very well, he was fluent in speech, and a first-rate raconteur, with an exceptional ability to expound complicated ideas. (His first language, obviously, was Russian. He had learnt German at school and college; then he acquired Swedish, then Danish when the KGB sent him to Copenhagen, and finally English).

In 1994, when I met him, he was living in England under an assumed name, but he was still on the KGB's death list, and had to be discreet about his movements. When he came to stay for a few days at our home in the country, we told nobody who he was. Nine years after his escape, he felt relaxed enough to move around freely outside the house, yet his security training was still much in evidence: once when my wife drove him back to the train, as he got out of the car at the station he managed to lock the doors, with the key the inside, incarcerating an already overheated Labrador. Only by forcing one of the small front windows did Phylla manage to break back in.

In his youth he had been a good middle-distance runner, and now, in his mid-forties, he was still pretty fit: a stocky but trim figure, with fair hair receding from his forehead and going grey. I knew that he was a keen cyclist, and rode for miles around his home; but as I had no suitable bike, after our first day of recording sessions I suggested that he ran a circuit of about three miles round the lanes – down to the village, up one hill and back down another. He completed the loop, but returned complaining vigorously about the steepness of the hills, and next morning he was so stiff in the calves that at first he could hardly walk. All the same, he wanted exercise, so I suggested we go wooding.

'Wooding?' he said. 'What's that?'

I explained that a neighbouring farmer allowed me to collect fallen timber on the escarpment above the house, and that we could pick up a load with a tractor and trailer. 'When we find a trunk,' I told him, 'I'll cut it into lengths with the chain saw, if you'd like to drag the pieces down to the path.'

'Fine!' he said. 'Let's go.'

High in the wood he worked with tremendous energy and enthusiasm, scrambling about the slope, hauling lengths down to the track and heaving logs into the trailer – so much so that next morning he was again crippled, but this time in his arms, which were not used to such violent exertion. Yet when I asked what he would like to do for exercise that afternoon, he immediately said, 'Go wooding again!' As a result, my shed was filled with an impressive stack of KGB logs.

Recounting his early life was relatively simple, for he described people and events very well, and there were no worries about the security of what he was saying to impede the flow of his narrative. Born in Moscow in 1938, son of political lecturer (and member of the NKVD, predecessor of the KGB), he was just old enough to remember being taken down into an unused Metro station when German bombers raided the capital in the autumn of 1941. Later that year his family were evacuated to Przhevalsk, in Kirgizia, almost on the Chinese border, and there they lived until they returned to Moscow late in 1943. One of his most vivid childhood memories dated from the winter of 1944, when the authorities staged a huge parade of German prisoners, who marched through the city 'with expressions sad as death.'

By the age of ten he had become a keen reader, with a particular liking for political periodicals such as *Pravda*. In 1953, when he was not quite fourteen, came a 'shattering event' which gave him 'another push down the road to freedom' – the death of Stalin. This, for Oleg, was 'a great eye-opener', and the beginning of his disillusion with Soviet Communism.

From school he entered the Moscow Institute of International Relations, where, as he recalled, the academic standards varied 'from high in languages to rock-bottom in Marxist philosophy, which was utter nonsense ... Spartacus, the Roman gladiator who led a slave revolt, was, of course, tremendously progressive.' Specialising in German, doing his obligatory military training, and becoming a proficient middle-distance runner, he much enjoyed his time at the Institute; but when he was offered English, as a second foreign language, he declined, thinking that it looked too difficult. Instead he learnt Swedish.

As the end of his four years at the Institute approached, in spite of his gradual political awakening, he was increasingly drawn to the idea of going into the KGB. 'We all knew that the Soviet Union was a prison,' he told me, 'and that the only way to escape from it for any length of time was to join one of the organisations that worked in other countries.' Chief among these was the KGB – and so it was that Oleg arrived in East Berlin in the evening of 11 August 1961.

He saw immediately that some extraordinary event was about to take place. For the past few weeks the citizens of the German Democratic Republic had been fleeing westwards in their thousands before prison walls closed round them, and, now, as a senior KGB officer remarked, it was as if the whole of the GDR was 'sitting on its suitcase.' On the morning of the 13th the city was in a frenzy as barbed-wire barricades went up and Berlin was divided in two.

The Wall had a profound effect on Oleg, for it made him realise how repugnant Communism was to ordinary people. After a stay of six months he returned to Moscow, where he finished his course at the Institute and then went through intensive KGB training at School 101 – three wooden buildings standing in a forest 50 kilometres north of the city. In Moscow again for exercises, students learnt to maintain surveillance on buildings, meet agents, use dead-letter boxes, make brush-contacts, and above all to carry out *proverka,* or dry-cleaning, a combination of moves to make sure they were not being watched or followed.

As we discussed his career, it was amusing to hear Oleg describe these tricks of the trade, many of them very amateurish; as he said, he and his colleagues sometimes felt 'it was fairly ridiculous that intelligent people who had spent six years at college should now be playing barely-adult games of hide-and-seek.' But even more fascinating was to hear how quickly he became disillusioned with the typical KGB mentality. In talking of his life he never boasted about any success he had enjoyed; yet it soon became clear that he was far more intelligent and clear-sighted than most of his colleagues, and easily saw through the Communist propaganda in which aspiring members of the organisation were steeped.

He got his first real taste of the outside world in January 1966, when he was posted to Copenhagen, ostensibly as a member of the Consular Department in the Soviet Embassy, but in reality as a KGB agent, with a brief to find and cultivate local contacts. Having just acquired Swedish, he had to put that aside and rapidly learn Danish. By then he had married a beautiful, half-Armenian girl, Yelena Akopian, and she too worked in the KGB, in a listening station which eavesdropped on the Danish security service.

Living and working on the frontier between different ideologies, Oleg found himself very much at home in the free-thinking West, and when he became the official press attaché in the Soviet embassy, the post gave him excellent cover and the chance to form useful relationships with journalists, politicians and civil servants. The details of how the British recruited him as an agent, how he returned for a spell in Moscow, how he divorced Yelena and married Leila Aliyeva, before being posted to London as Counsellor at the Soviet Embassy – all this was fascinating, but easy enough to record.

Thereafter, things became trickier. In 1981, while still in Moscow, he was amazed to read a KGB file with a blue cover about a Briton code-named Boot – for this was none other than Michael Foot, leader of the Labour Party, and a potential Prime Minister. How would he react if we said, in our book, that during the 1960s the KGB had regarded him as one of their most useful agents of influence in London? Foot would not be able to deny that he had marched with the Campaign for Nuclear Disarmament, and spouted Soviet propaganda in speeches demanding the withdrawal of American forces from England – but if we named him as a Soviet agent, he would surely sue for libel.

Oleg had plenty of evidence: not only the blue-covered file, but conversations with Mikhail Lubimov, his superior in Copenhagen, who had cultivated Foot during the 1960s when he was working for the left-wing newspaper *Tribune.* Over lunch Lubimov had repeatedly slipped him £200 or £300 in used fivers, and Foot had always said that he did not want the money for himself, but would give it to *Tribune.* Naturally, I urged Oleg to reveal as much as possible – but for the moment we left details in abeyance.

The next section of his narrative was fast-moving, and covered a lot of ground. It described how, in 1984, he had been appointed Resident – head of the KGB in London; how, on some flimsy pretext, he had suddenly been summoned back to Moscow, only to find that his flat had been searched and left secured with a third lock, which he himself never used. Worse quickly followed: he was drugged with doctored brandy and interrogated by two senior KGB officials, but he could not remember what he might or might not have confessed. Becoming convinced that he would be arrested and condemned to death, he decided to activate the escape plan which he and his British contacts had evolved against such an emergency.

The bones of the plan were that he would travel by train to Leningrad, and go on by bus to a rendezvous in a forest near the border with Finland, where a car would pick him up and drive him through the frontier. First, to buy a ticket for the train, he had to make his way across Moscow to the Leningrad Station. There was no difficulty about describing the incredibly elaborate *proverka,* or dry cleaning – all the twists, turns, deliberate delays, retreats and sudden advances – which he used to disguise his movements around the city.

More difficult was to determine how much we could write about the help he received from members of the British Embassy, without giving away the means by which he had made contact with them. Again and again a draft of the hot chapter disappeared into the maw of Whitehall, to re-appear with details softened or removed. The repeated tinkering became thoroughly irritating, but could not be ignored. Then, with publication imminent, Michael Foot's lawyers began threatening to sue for libel, and passages about the Labour leader had to be scaled down. Eventually the text was cleared, and the book came out under the title *Next Stop Execution,* attracting huge press coverage. Years later Oleg wrote to me saying, 'I still hope we will be able to cooperate again when Michael Foot will die (if it will be before I do).'

The last section of the book described the start of Oleg's life in England: the KGB's rage at his escape, their clumsy overtures designed to lure him back to Russia, their attempts to poison his relationship with Leila by telling her that he had taken up with a secretary. Once settled in the West, he travelled prodigiously, briefing intelligence agencies and political leaders in West Germany (three visits), Sweden,

Denmark, Norway, the United States, Australia, New Zealand (four visits), Singapore, Malaysia, Thailand, South Africa, Kenya, Brazil, Saudi Arabia, Israel, Canada, the Netherlands and Spain.

In England he suffered Margaret Thatcher's unstoppable garrulity but managed to get in enough words during an interview to brief her before her visit to Moscow in March 1987. An even more important meeting was with President Ronald Reagan in Washington later that year.

His greatest value to the West lay in his ability to explain Communist mentality, and to show how dangerous it was to under-estimate the stupidity of Soviet officials. As an example of this crassness he cited Arkadi Guk, the Resident (or head) of the KGB in London – 'a huge, bloated lump of a man, with a mediocre brain but a large reserve of low cunning,' who spent most of his working day locked in his office with a colleague, smoking and drinking neat vodka. One morning he summoned members of his staff and told them – yet again – to use the Underground as little as possible. 'You know those illuminated panels along the walls of the stations,' he said. 'They're supposed to be advertisements, but many of them are really glass-fronted cubicles in which sit members of the British security service, spying on our people as they go about their business.'

If a senior official in the Soviet Embassy believed that, what other crazy ideas might he or his superiors in the KGB harbour? Trivial though the example was, it showed how dangerous larger misconceptions might be – for instance the belief, prevalent at that date in the Kremlin, that the West was preparing a pre-emptive nuclear strike against the Soviet Union.

Vindictive as ever, the KGB refused to release Leila and her daughters for six years after Oleg's defection. By the time the family was eventually released, and flew to London in September 1991, his daughters Maria and Anna were eleven and ten, and 'had changed out of all recognition'. Inevitably he and Leila had drifted apart, and to his great grief their relationship broke down.

Only in 1994 did he at last discover the identity of the man who had betrayed him. He had suspected three others, but in the end the traitor turned out to have been a seedy American intelligence officer, Aldrich Ames, who received a first payment of 10,000 dollars for putting the KGB on his trail. By the time Ames was arrested by the FBI, he had received over two million dollars in Soviet payments.

Oleg, in contrast, had never spied for money. From the start he had sided with the West for purely ideological reasons, making it one of his conditions that he would not be paid for the information he handed over. When he settled in England, the Government looked after him well, providing him with a house and a pension; but, as he said, what had driven him was his contempt for Communist tyranny.

I found working with him immensely interesting, and also good fun – for in spite of all the stress and danger he had come through, his constructive attitude to life had remained intact, and his keen sense of humour had never deserted him.

CHAPTER FIFTEEN

Honorary Tiger
1981-2006

One October afternoon in 1981 a call came through to Fleet Street from Tony Colwell, a senior editor at Jonathan Cape – publishers of several of my books. 'Are you busy?' he said.

'Well,' I countered. 'Not particularly. What is it?'

'Just that we've got a promising typescript about leopards. It's rather fascinating, but it needs a lot of re-writing. Could you have a look at it?'

I agreed to pick it up on my way to Paddington that evening – and as I was doing the London part of my commute on a bicycle, it was easy enough to ride via Bedford Square and collect the package. On the train to Henley I read the first half, and then, returning to London in the morning, the second. As Tony said, the style of the typescript was often too compressed and excessively scientific, but the story looked a potential winner, describing how the author, Arjan Singh, known as 'Billy', had raised leopards in and around his home in Northern India, and set them free in the jungle. The book immediately evoked memories of Joy Adamson's *Born Free,* her account of Elsa the lioness, published with enormous success twenty years earlier.

As soon as I reached my office, I rang Tony and told him I was interested. But how could I contact the author?

'Oh,' he said casually. 'It's easy. He happens to be here in London. I'll give you his phone number.'

The voice that answered was manifestly Indian, and rather creaky; from its owner's hesitant replies I got the impression that he was a bit at sea in the metropolis, but he said he would be glad to join me for lunch –

so I booked a table at an Italian restaurant in Soho. I found him waiting there – a short, stocky man with thinning hair and immensely powerful-looking arms and shoulders, which strained at a crumpled grey linen jacket. Foolishly supposing that he was a vegetarian, and not at home with Italian menus, I suggested he should have the meat-less spaghetti Napolitana, and it came soused in feeble tomato sauce, which he ate clumsily with spoon and fork.

His English was perfect, but he had some slight speech impediment that made him sound rather jungly. At first he was guarded, and asked edgily what was wrong with his typescript. Then, as I tried to explain why it needed expanding at various points, and he saw I was interested, he opened out and began telling stories about the leopards, and about his home, Tiger Haven. Several times he repeated, 'You should come out and see the place for yourself.'

'When are you going back?'

'Tomorrow.'

'My God! So I only just caught you.'

'So it seems.'

It turned out that he had made the long journey to London, and had been hanging around for three weeks, in a final attempt to exact some agreement from Jonathan Cape, who had sat on his typescript for months. Clearly, they had done nothing about it until the last moment, and Tony Colwell's call to me had been their final throw. Had I not reacted speedily, I should have missed one of the most rewarding friendships of my life.

If the nine-hour flight to Delhi was routine, the journey up-country was a novel experience. Finding the Lucknow Express in the pitch-dark central station at 10.30 pm was an adventure in itself, but after a frantic scuttle from one platform to another, I settled comfortably enough in the upper of two air-conditioned bunks, with a friendly Indian snoring below. Even so, I slept hardly at all, for I knew we were scheduled to reach my destination, Shahjahanpur, at four in the morning, and I feared that if I dropped off too deeply, I would overshoot. As the train clanked and clattered through the night, often slowing to a halt, my mind was full of leopards and tigers, of crocodiles and peacocks and snakes, and all the other creatures which apparently surrounded Billy's home.

At last, just after 4 am, the train came to yet another halt, and I stumbled out into surprisingly cold air. Only one lamp burnt faintly far down the station, but the starlight was bright enough to reveal that the platform was carpeted with prostrate, motionless human bodies, smothered under rugs or blankets. Were they asleep or dead? It was impossible to tell. They did not move as I wove my way between them until I came to the exit under the lamp.

The moment I appeared, there was a stir in the yard, and half a dozen men rushed forward crying 'Riksar! Riksar!' Wash-out gestures and exclamations of 'No thanks!' only increased their clamour, and they began plucking at my sleeves. How to get rid of them? Salvation appeared in the form of a short, stocky man who materialised beside me murmuring 'Arjan Singh? Arjan Singh?' 'Yes,' I replied, 'Tiger Haven'. Pointing at his chest, he several times repeated his name, Sri Ram (later in the day I learnt that he was Billy's factotum.) Seeing that he was wearing a thick, padded jacket and had a scarf wrapped several times round his neck, I got an extra sweater out of my haversack and pulled it on.

With a couple of shouts to scatter the rickshaw wallahs, he led me to an open-sided jeep, without doors or windows, and off we went , bouncing and jolting through the cold, damp darkness. Billy had warned me that the drive would be a testing one – and so it proved. For the first two hours the jeep's feeble headlights gave only the vaguest idea of what lay ahead, and we constantly crunched into potholes that the driver had not seen.

Sometimes trees crowded in on either side of the road, but at others we were in flat, open country, with tumbledown habitations along the verges, traces of wood smoke hanging in the air, and stars glittering above. When at last dawn began to lighten the sky, I spotted a pistol lying in the shelf at the bottom of the windscreen. I pointed at it, and Sri Ram gave a little smile as he replied 'For dacoit' – bandits. As the light came up, wooden-wheeled bullock carts began pulling erratically onto the road in front of us, causing us to swerve and weave. In a ditch a swarm of vultures tussled over the putrefying remains of a cow on which they were feasting. Pinnacled termite mounds stood sentinel beside the road.

Three hours out, and deeply chilled, we reached the ramshackle town of Palia Kalan, where a sluggish river of pedestrians, cyclists, carts, stray dogs and wandering cattle was already on the move. Beyond the last shacks the road ran on an embankment raised above level fields, but the land was shrouded in mist almost down to ground level, limiting the view. At last, after a couple of miles Sri Ram turned off the road, left-handed down a steep little pitch onto a sandy track which wound away through trees and emerged on to farm land.

Peacocks lifted off the ploughed fields. A twelve-foot marsh crocodile slid from a sandbank and plunged into the river. Beside a stand of sugar cane a solitary sentinel stood guarding the crop from monkeys. When the driver slowed to have a word, the watcher pointed his stick at a ring which he had drawn in the dust round the track of a tiger, fresh in the night. By the time we rounded the final bend, the mist had burned off enough to reveal our destination: a long, white building, or rather a line of joined-up buildings, two-storeyed in places, with dark green shutters, balconies and a pillared verandah, all backed by a great wall of jungle. As we pulled up in front of the house, Billy came forward to greet me, looking immensely muscular in khaki shirt and shorts, knee-length stockings and black, military boots. Close behind him came his plump younger brother Balram, and in the background hovered Balram's wife Mira, tiny, beautiful and slim as a reed.

'Welcome to Tiger Haven!' they all exclaimed. 'Good journey? You must be frozen! What would you like? Tea? Breakfast? A hot bath?'

'A bath would be wonderful.'

A volley of shouted orders sent servants scurrying. One carried my haversack up an outside concrete staircase to a room with white-washed walls, simple furniture and at the back an open doorway giving on to a small bathroom. From behind the house servants came labouring up another outside staircase with pails of scalding-hot water which they tipped into the bath – a big, galvanised tub. The only way I could fit into it was by doubling my knees up to my chin, but the heat of the water was delicious, and in no time I was presenting myself, shaved and washed, for breakfast.

I felt I had arrived if not at the end of the world, certainly at an enchanted corner of it. In front of the house peacocks paced about a flat field, and jungle fowl like gaudy bantams foraged among them. An elephant stood under a single tree, delicately picking choice items out of a heap of forage as it shifted from one foot to another. Occasional flights of green parrots hurtled screeching overhead. The only other sounds were the cooing of doves and the *thwack* of a man lackadaisically chopping wood with an axe. Immediately behind the house nothing but a small river separated the building from the jungle, which rose majestically from a low escarpment on the far bank.

'Do have some porridge,' said Mira, as yet another servant placed a bowl in front of me. 'And this is *gur* – unrefined sugar – to go with it. Then I expect you'd like scrambled eggs.'

I sensed that Billy, polite though he was, could not wait to start work on the leopard typescript; and so, fortified by that perfect breakfast, I sat down with him at a table in the dining room, which, with a front wall made of wire netting, was light, airy and in touch with the outside – a perfect place to work. We had a rather slow start, for I had so many details to pick up; but soon he was calling me 'Duffji' and playfully needling me for being so keen on killing harmless deer. As for me – I quickly came not only to admire his achievement, but also to be extremely fond of him.

Because his story of involvement with big cats was as contorted as his prose, I had to go right back to the beginning of his life to clear my own head. He had been born in 1917 in the state of Balrampur, scion of the princely Kapurthala family, and grew up in an environment in which big-game shooting was part of everyday life. He killed his first leopard at twelve, his first tiger at fourteen.

One strongly formative influence was his friendship with Jim Corbett. As a boy, he sat at the feet of the legendary hunter-naturalist at his home in Naini Tal, in the Himalayan foothills, and heard at first hand the hair-raising stories of encounters with man-eating tigers which later Corbett published in his classic memoir *Man-Eaters of Kumaon*.

Billy claimed that a sickly childhood and a lack of natural talent had made him try to prove himself in society by the indiscriminate slaughter of wildlife. Whether or not that was a true diagnosis, his family had strong English connections. His father was an undergraduate at Balliol, whence he was sent down for tripping up a bulldog (one of the university's private police), and he trained as a barrister at Gray's Inn in London. Billy, although educated in India, was encouraged by him to read voraciously in English, with the result that in later life he could (and did) quote Shakespeare, Wordsworth and Keats as often as Kipling.

In the Second World War he joined an Indian gunner regiment, but, after spending months becalmed in Persia, he was ejected from the army for insubordination. Returning to India, he decided to go farming, and rented a 750-acre block of virgin land in North Kheri, not far from the border with Nepal, drawn to the area by the fact that it still teemed with big game. There, for the next nine years, he lived alone in a grass hut, in discomfort that few men would have endured, without electricity (and so without air-conditioning) in the 110 degree heat of summer, battling to save his crops from deer, antelopes and wild boar, and also from the *gaddis,* the Muslim graziers whose cattle and buffaloes respected no boundaries.

In later life, when he lived on his own except for a small army of servants, friends assumed that he had always been a bachelor. In fact, as a young man, he pursued girls vigorously, and he proposed to three, at least. None of his relationships had lasted long, and he came to realise that he could not reasonably expect any woman to share his solitary existence or live in the kind of environment that appealed to him.

Every year, for a break, he went with a gang of family and friends to a hunting camp in the jungle. As he himself put it, 'the old urge for slaughter' still smouldered in him, and 'the destruction of the master predator – the tiger – dominated all desires.' Then suddenly he changed. One night a leopard was caught in the headlights of his jeep, and with a lucky shot he killed it; but all he felt as he watched it die was 'an awful confusion – futility at the destruction of beauty, and the taking of life for personal pleasure.' That single bullet changed him from hunter to keeper, and he dedicated the rest of his life to conservation.

One day in 1959, feeling hemmed-in by the other farmers who had come to settle round him, he set off in search of new territory. On his elephant Bhagwan Piari ('Chosen of God') he forged northwards for five miles through marshes and ten-foot grass, until he came to an enchanted spot where two small rivers flowed together in a long pool of pale green water, with kingfishers skimming over it. Beyond the stream rose an escarpment surmounted by majestic sal trees, through which he caught glimpses of distant, snow-clad Himalayan peaks.

This, he decided, was where he would make his last stand. This was where he would spend the rest of his life, as far from civilisation as he could go. Having rented some land, he again built himself a hut and lived in it for a year before starting to construct a more solid dwelling – the house in which he and I were now working. Idyllic as it was for much of the year, the place became uninhabitable during the summer monsoon, when the Neora river burst its banks and swamped the ground floor. This meant that all the furniture and books had to be moved to the upper storey for the duration, and Billy himself decamped to Jasbirnagar, a rather soul-less concrete house which he built on higher ground near Pallia. Often, in the flood season, the only way he could reach Tiger Haven was on elephant-back.

The new site put him in close touch with the denizens of the jungle. Tigers and leopards walked past the house at night; monkeys, bears and crocodiles lived on the doorstep. Prey species abounded: chital (spotted deer), the smaller hog deer and diminutive muntjac (barking deer) all came out after dark to ravage whatever crops he tried to grow. The variety of birds was phenomenal – from giant hornbills, vultures, crested serpent eagles and fishing owls down to pied kingfishers and minute bee-eaters.

It was deer on which Billy focused his first major attempt at conservation. An enormous herd of barasingha, or swamp deer, 1,500 strong – the largest concentration in India – was threatened when

Central Government proposed to split up their territory and give it to small-time cultivators. A successful campaign to preserve the herd, spear-headed by Billy, not only attracted the attention of the Prime Minister, Indira Gandhi, but led in 1965 to the creation of the Dudhwa National Park – an area of 82 square miles, or 55,000 acres, stretching twenty-five miles from east to west on either side of Tiger Haven and reaching three miles towards the Nepalese border in the north. The southern border of the park ran along the bank of the Neora, not twenty yards from Billy's home.

His first big cat was Prince, an orphaned leopard raised by Anne Wright, a well-known conservationist living in Calcutta, who brought the cub to Tiger Haven when he was three months old. Learning as he went along, Billy brought him up in and about the house, sometimes restraining him with a collar and lead, but never confining him in a cage, and sleeping beside him on the verandah at night. His aim was never to keep him as a pet, but to return him to the jungle and so augment the dwindling stock of leopards that remained in the wild.

There was one more key member of his extraordinary menagerie – the small mongrel called Eelie. Years earlier she had arrived unannounced and unwanted, trailing behind a string of forest workers who walked past the house one morning. When she hung about, Billy's mother ordered the staff to get rid of her by bombarding her with clods of earth, but she stayed – and became Billy's indispensable companion. Acting as a kind of governess, with astonishing fearlessness and strength of character she played endlessly with Prince and his successors, sparring, chasing, dashing in and out of the river, keeping them in order and teaching them to hunt.

The human being most nervous of the big cat was Billy's mother Mabel, who was very small and lightly built; he repeatedly assured her that she was in no danger, but to put her at ease he built her a circular summerhouse, with upper walls of netting, on the bank above the river. Soon this became known as 'Gran's Cage,' and in it the old lady sat, doing her knitting or the *Times of India* crossword, while the leopard wandered around outside.

At first Prince had been frightened of the jungle, preferring to stay around the house; but Billy gradually persuaded him to go further afield by walking with him in the jungle, shooting parrots with a .22 rifle and building machans – wooden platforms raised on stilts – deep in the forest, which the leopard could use as safe bases. His education was not without setbacks, the worst of which occurred when he bit the eight-year-old son of Billy's filwan (elephant-keeper) so severely that the boy died. Billy himself had a narrow escape when Prince panicked and attacked him in a closed-in machan. He was saved by his own exceptional strength, which enabled him to hold the leopard off at arm's length by the scruff of the neck. Even so, he returned to the house with his shirt in tatters and covered in blood from puncture wounds in his flank.

Undaunted by such incidents, he established a closer and closer rapport with his protégé, and convinced himself that a leopard is not, as Victorian and Edwardian sportsmen claimed, mean-spirited and 'a bounder', but a perfectly honourable character; and he was delighted when Prince finally took to the jungle, vindicating his belief that a predator trained by humans could be successfully returned to the wild.

He followed up that first experiment by acquiring two more leopard cubs – orphans given to Mrs Gandhi, who passed them on to him. Calling them Harriet and Juliette after two English girls he met in Delhi, he brought them to Tiger Haven and made them a base in one of the bedrooms, letting them run about the place as they liked. As with Prince, his purpose was to train them to fend for themselves. They arrived at Tiger Haven in the autumn of 1973: like Prince, they lived in and around the house, and with a devoted human and an exceptional dog to teach them, they gradually learnt the ways of the jungle. But then, to Billy's great distress, Juliette's life was cut cruelly short: one morning in early summer she was found dead in the river, apparently poisoned by some ill-wisher.

Harriet flourished, and Billy developed an intense relationship with her: he was as nearly in love with that leopard as any man could be. He was thrilled when Prince returned to mate with her, and immensely excited when she gave birth to two cubs in a raised den he had built for her just across the river. Disaster threatened when monsoon rain flooded the banks; but Harriet showed her amazing rapport with humans, first by demanding a lift across the swollen torrent in a boat, and then by carrying the cubs, one at a time, dangling by the neck from her teeth, to safety in Tiger Haven and installing them in a bedroom.

As if his leopard work was not ambitious enough, Billy then decided to take a personal role in Project Tiger – the Indian Government's attempt to save its most famous species, which he thought was failing. He therefore persuaded Mrs Gandhi that it would be a good idea to bring out a young tiger from a zoo in England, and see if he could return it to the wild.

In the autumn of 1975, he flew to England, collected a female cub from Twycross Zoo and brought her to Tiger Haven, covering the last stage of the journey on elephant-back. He called her Tara – Star – and a star she proved. Like the leopards, she grew up around the house, and like them, under his tuition she learned the ways of the jungle. To the amazement of everyone except Billy, she got on well with Harriet, and played endlessly with Eelie, often rolling her down the bank into the river in boisterous play, but never hurting her. No matter that Tara grew to six or seven times her weight, the little dog still dominated her huge adversary.

Visitors were astonished by the sight of Billy going off for a walk accompanied by a dog, a full-grown leopard and a young tigress. He, too, wrestled with Tara, and although she frequently charged him and knocked him down, she never hurt him. Their relationship (he was convinced) rested on the fact that he was never frightened, and that she could sense his confidence – and his love.

As with Prince, her primeval instincts gradually asserted themselves, and she took to the jungle more and more, returning to the house only for occasional meals. In the end, at the age of twenty months, she did what Billy had always hoped she would do, and answered the call of the wild.

When I first arrived at Tiger Haven, it was disappointing to find that all the big cats had departed; but it was fascinating to work with Billy on the story of their upbringing. Every morning he was up at about 5.30, lifting weights on the flat roof outside my window, and I took to running along the sandy roads in the jungle while the air was still cool (later in the day the temperature climbed to a delicious 75 F – perfect Indian winter weather). Billy assured me I was in no danger from the Big Tiger – Tara's mate – whose pug-marks often showed along my route; but thoughts of him certainly kept me moving.

One night I was smitten by a fearful stomach upset, probably brought on by excessive consumption of hot chillies, and could not face an early start. When Billy tapped on my window at six o'clock and asked, 'Why aren't you running, you lazy blighter?' I told him I'd been poisoned and would lie low for another hour. Later, when he teased me again, I said I couldn't face the idea of a confrontation with the Big Tiger, seeing the state I was in. 'No,' replied Billy, with one of his nipping jokes. 'But you could have shat in his face and run like hell.'

Life at Tiger Haven was extremely agreeable, not least because of the family atmosphere. Billy was indisputably in charge. There he sat on the verandah or in the dining room, letting out an occasional abrupt summons when he wanted a servant to bring tea, fetch his spectacles or lace up his boots. *'Eh! Sri Ram!'* he would shout, *'Eh, Bolta!' 'Eh! Haplu!'*, and within seconds a small man would appear at his elbow with a soft *'Ji, Sahib.'*

I think Balram – fat and indolent – was still missing his former life as a boxwallah (businessman) in Calcutta, but, being highly convivial, he was excellent at his main task, which was to entertain visiting tourists and take them for drives in the jungle. He had a most attractive, deep voice, and I kept thinking that if I heard him talking in the bar of the Garrick, I would assume it was an Englishman speaking. Mira, on the other hand, though educated at Heathfield, sounded definitely Indian, enunciating her perfectly grammatical English words with beautiful clarity. An expert on birds, she could identify almost every one of the 400-odd species in the park, and she managed the logistics of Tiger Haven – ordering supplies, organising the servants – with unobtrusive efficiency. The food – cooked over a coal fire in a tiny kitchen – was invariably delicious, and

I shall never forget Hanif's shredded carrot pudding, simmered for hours and laced with divine spices.

Evenings were particularly enjoyable. After a peg or two of whisky and a delicious dinner, we would gather before a blazing fire in the sitting room and watch films of the big cats taken by cameramen from Anglia Television. For me the most moving shots were of Harriet bringing her cubs to safety through the flood waters, one at a time, with a little bundle of spotted fur hanging from her mouth on each perilous journey. Almost more extraordinary was the way in which, whenever Harriet appeared on the screen, Eelie would get up and go behind it, as if in search of her former companion.

Billy and I worked long hours, and I soon became familiar with his characteristic habit of raising his right arm vertically, elbow on the table, and turning his separated thumb and forefinger back and forth, as if to emphasise some ambiguity of language or action. Every day we took time off for a walk in the jungle, which in most places was extremely thick, with dense vegetation crowding in on the paths. Often we were accompanied by Billy's tracker, whose real name was Charan but who looked so like Jackson Toad in Beatrix Potter's *The Tale of Mrs Tittlemouse* that everyone called him Jackson, and he answered to that name. Billy never carried any weapon except a stick, and he rather dismayed me by the clumsiness with which he moved: instead of creeping stealthily, he stomped along in his heavy boots, crunching dry leaves and sticks as he searched for pug-marks, scrapes or spray marks on tree trunks that betrayed the predators' presence.

His methods were uncompromising, to say the least. One day, walking in the forest, we came on two men illegally cutting firewood. Although they were much the same height as Billy, they were nothing like as powerfully built, and he knocked them both down flat with two terrific blows, right and left, before roaring abuse at them as they fled.

Shortage of money was always a problem, but support kept coming from powerful friends who admired Billy's work. One was Haik Sookias, an Armenian entrepreneur with businesses in the United States, Calcutta and elsewhere; another was John Aspinall, gambler and zoo proprietor, who sent a handsome cheque every year. He came to Tiger Haven himself and was so impressed that he sent his daughter Amanda out to work there for a year – an experiment which had alarming consequences. One day, as she was sitting in her room, Prince came silently up behind her and put his paws on her shoulders. When she screamed, he bit and scratched her – before Billy dragged him off by the scruff of his neck. In no way repentant, he told Amanda that the incident was entirely her fault, because, in spite of strict instructions, she had left the door of the room open. But after that, she could not trust the leopard, and went home early.

On my first visit I stayed for two weeks. I never set eyes on leopard or tiger, but and came away with my head full of jungle lore. In London production of the leopard book went ahead smoothly, and it was published in the autumn of 1982 under the title *Prince of Cats.* Unfortunately Billy had already taken the wind out of his own literary sails by bringing out two earlier books. The first, *Tiger Haven,* was about his establishment of the house, and the animals of the Dudhwa national park. The second – *Tara – a Tigress* – was a garishly-produced account of how he had acquired and raised the cub. The result of these disclosures was that *Prince of Cats* lacked the impact it might have commanded with a clear start. I felt sure he would have done better if he had not let so many felines out of the bag prematurely, but kept all his stories for one blockbuster.

Undaunted, he was determined to keep writing, and so I made several more pilgrimages to his den – seven in all. Next year Phylla and I preceded a visit to Tiger Haven with a foray into Nepal. This time I had another task – to help a young naturalist, K.K.Gurung (known to all just as 'K.K.'), polish up a book he was writing about the wildlife of Chitwan, the immense area of forest and savannah between the Himalayas in the north and India in the south, not far across the border from Tiger Haven. The book had been commissioned by André Deutsch, most tight-fisted of London publishers, who had bought me an air-ticket but declined to pay any fee.

We went out via Kathmandu, where we were greatly helped by Lisa van Gruisen, a tall, slender, fast-moving English girl who had come out on the hippy trail in 1970 and had never left, establishing herself as an indispensable organiser of travel, not only in Nepal but over much of the Far East. It was she who made all the arrangements for us and posted us down to the celebrated Tiger Tops lodge, of which K.K. was then manager. (Later, she scandalised Billy by arriving for a stay at Tiger Haven with one man and leaving with another – after which he habitually referred to her as 'the Man-Eater'.)

I liked K.K. from the start. He had been born in the Himalayas and had studied natural sciences in India. Now, in his late twenties, he was rather suspicious at first, and it took me a while to persuade him that, far from trying to usurp his story, I was aiming to act as midwife and bring his book, *Heart of the Jungle,* into being with only his name on it. When we got going, I saw that his knowledge of local wildlife was comprehensive, and that his account of it only needed shaping up. While we sorted out his text, Phylla joined other tourists riding on elephants in search of rhinos, and between work-sessions K.K. took us to a fascinating research station which was breeding gharials – a primitive form of crocodile, so-called because it has a protuberance like a *gharial,* or pitcher, on its snout.

After a successful week in Nepal we headed for Tiger Haven. As a lammergeyer might fly, our destination was not many miles from Tiger Tops, but lack of roads and border restrictions meant that we had to take a roundabout route and make many changes of transport: elephant to the airfield, light aircraft to Kathmandu, commercial jet to Delhi, train to Shajahanpur, and car for the final three-hour stage.

We reached Tiger Haven as dusk, and we had scarcely sat down to a cup of tea when the cry went up, '*Hatthiya!*' Elephants in the sugar cane! Roaring off in a jeep, we stopped in an open space between the ten-foot crop and the forest to wait and listen. Behind us a clear full moon was rising over the jungle, and mist hung in veils above the river. Billy's farm-hands had already set up an encircling beat, augmenting the noise of fire-crackers and thunderflashes with their own abrupt yells – 'HOO! WHA! AY!' – and howling like wolves. In the distance flaming brands held on tall poles moved erratically through the darkness.

After a few minutes, somewhere close in front of us heavy intruders began shifting through the cane, clearly ill-at-ease but not wanting to abandon their supper. Then suddenly, as pressure from the beaters became intolerable, they accelerated and burst into the open – an avalanche of pachyderms. Our driver snapped on a spotlight, and there they were – two huge, grey shapes speeding across the open ground, one a handsome tusker with a bunch of stalks protruding from either side of his mouth like a giant moustache. Into the river they went with a tremendous splash, and up the far bank into the cover of the trees.

As usual Billy was immersed in his attempts to monitor Tara's movements, and he had taken to tethering buffalos as baits in the jungle, with the twin objects of encouraging tigers to stay in a relatively safe area near his home, and at the same time increasing his chances of showing visitors a big carnivore in action. He defended the practice stoutly against all criticism, insisting that, for a buffalo, death from one scrunch in the jaws of a tiger was far preferable to the horrors of a Muslim halal butcher's rusty knives and thrice-repeated incantations.

One evening at dusk we walked quietly up the path beside the river to a small, two-storey machan, where Billy and Phylla went aloft, and I stayed on the ground, more than a little nervous, as the back of the hut was open to all comers. The baiting site was on the other bank of the stream, only twenty yards away, and above it Billy had fixed up a lamp in a tree, with a dimmer switch which he could operate from the machan.

The night before, a male tiger had killed a tethered buffalo and eaten part of it, and Billy felt sure he would return. As we sat waiting, daylight waned, dying by imperceptible stages. The sky remained bright, but darkness seemed to rise stealthily from the earth, gradually blacking-out the jungle floor. The calls of monkeys and birds faded into silence until all I could hear was my own breathing.

Again and again I scanned the baiting site with binoculars, willing the tiger to appear. I could see the heap of straw with which the kill had been covered during the day, and a patch of light-coloured sand showed up on the opposite bank of the river. 'If only he came and stood on that,' I thought, 'I'd have a fantastic view.'

Then suddenly I realised that he *was* there – not on the sandbank, but standing beside his kill. A 500-lb cat, he had arrived without a sound, and as he stood gazing down the river, the last of the daylight, seeping from the west, blazed back out of his eyes, the brightest eyes on earth. He really was a tiger burning bright, in the forest of the night.

Satisfied that all was well, he settled down to dine. A great scrunching and cracking of ribs broke out, and then a fierce rasping sound as his tongue got to work on the carcase. He paid no attention when a lamp glowed faintly into life in the tree above him and lit up the black and orange stripes of his coat, giving us a magnificent view of him as he lay beside his prey. But suddenly he jumped up, ran a few steps along the river bank, and stood staring into the darkness. Had he heard something? Whatever it was, he listened for a minute before returning to his meal, and the crunching started again. We watched spellbound for a little while longer. Then Billy dimmed the lamp down to nothing, and we silently withdrew from our vantage-point, to creep back to the house through the dark.

By that time Billy was fighting a war on three fronts. One campaign was against the *babus,* the bureaucrats of the Forestry Service in Delhi and provincial headquarters who persistently tried to stifle his initiatives. The second battle was against local farmers who were poisoning tigers and blowing them up when their cattle were attacked; and the third was against the poachers who were killing tigers for their skins and bones, and smuggling them over the border into Nepal for onward transmission to China, where the demand was insatiable.

One day we were just finishing lunch when there was a flurry of excitement. A white van swept up to the house in a cloud of dust, and out tumbled a dozen rough-looking men, one carrying an AK-47 rifle, another a sub-machine gun, and more hustling two prisoners. A banker from Lucknow, exasperated by the inertia and incompetence of forest officials and staff, had set up a private sting operation, in which, posing as a dealer, he had lured poachers to a rendezvous in the jungle. After a lot of bargaining, a suitcase full of fake rupee notes persuaded the villains to produce a freshly-flayed tiger skin, with paws still attached to the legs, and a sack containing 70 lbs of clean tiger bones – whereupon the sting force erupted from hiding and grabbed them.

Because the leader of the operation wanted to repeat the process at another rendezvous at first light next morning, he asked Billy to keep the two captives for the time being, and they were locked into a store-shed, with an armed man guarding the door. Needless to say, just before dawn they escaped – almost certainly by bribing the watchman. At 4.30 am shouts broke out as they raced away down the dirt track before plunging across the crocodile-infested river and disappearing into the forest on the other side. The only consolation was that they left behind the skin and bones, which would have been worth thousands of dollars if they had managed to spirit them across the border into Nepal; but Billy reckoned that the sack held bones from at least three tigers – sad evidence of the size of the task he had set himself.

During that visit I worked with him on his next book – a general account of tigers, and in particular a much fuller description of Tara's upbringing and introduction to the jungle. By then his problems had been substantially increased by a new phenomenon – an outbreak of man-eating in his own area. It had begun in 1978, and by the beginning of 1984 the number of people killed by tigers in Kheri (his district) had risen to 110. No one – not even he – could account for it, but it caused hysteria and panic. Every new death was blamed on Tara, 'that bloody tiger of yours', who, because she had been brought up by humans, was assumed to have no fear of them, and therefore saw them as easy prey.

Time and again Billy was called out to the scene of a kill, dreading to find that Tara was indeed the villain. In more than half the attacks he could prove straightaway that she was exonerated, for the pug-marks round the kill were those of a male. Yet several of the man-eaters were female, and to his great distress he himself had to shoot one or two. The worst scenario of all came when his arch-enemy R.L.Singh – by then Director of the Dudhwa national park – killed a tigress, loaded the body into an open trailer on a bed of greenery, and made a triumphal tour of nearby towns, proclaiming that he had slain the dreaded Tara. Billy knew he had done no such thing, because the markings on the face of the dead animal were quite different from the unique catapult-shape on Tara's left cheek, and in any case the man-eater had been accompanied by a two-year-old cub, which for Tara would have been a physical impossibility.

Billy remained convinced that Tara was alive and well. Several times in the jungle their paths crossed, and he longed for her to come and greet him. She never did; nor did she return to Tiger Haven. But whenever he saw her, he fancied that she stood and looked at him for longer than any other tiger would have held its ground.

The forest authorities steadily increased their pressure. They cut down his two-storey machan, forbade him to do any more baiting, and broke up the bridge over the river which gave him a short cut into the Park. Further recriminations erupted when the babus in Delhi belatedly discovered that Tara had Siberian genes in her ancestry. Immediately Billy was accused of having destroyed the integrity of the Bengal tiger gene pool, and there were renewed calls for the tigress's extermination. The bureaucrats were not merely 300 physical miles away: they were a million miles from reality, with no conception of how thick the jungle was, or of how impossible it would be to find a particular animal.

Billy's reply was characteristic: all modern tigers (he pointed out) were descended from the same original strain, and if Tara had revitalised the Dudhwa gene pool with a bit of Siberian blood, so much the better. Great was his delight when, between Tiger Haven and the main road, there appeared a young male with strongly Siberian characteristics – a big head, and much white about the cheeks. In all, Billy reckoned, Tara had four litters and raised fourteen cubs.

Our next literary production was *Tiger! Tiger!*, which Cape published handsomely in 1984. The book opened with an historical survey of tigers and tiger-shooting, and went on to describe many of Billy's own experiences. In effect, it was an impassioned plea on behalf of the species, and in an eloquent foreword John Aspinall suggested that 'the nobility of the animal has washed off on the man.' When Billy travelled to England for the book's launch, Aspers gave a private, fund-raising dinner on his behalf at the Curzon Club in Mayfair, twisting the arms of his guests so ruthlessly that he raised £11,000 for the Tiger Haven Trust. Grateful as Billy was, he hated London. He could manage New York (he said) because there the streets were straight, set out on a grid pattern, and logically numbered. In the higgledy-piggledy urban jungle of London he constantly got lost.

Again, reviews were respectful rather than wildly enthusiastic, and I sensed that Billy had almost written himself out. He was greatly saddened by the death of his beloved Eelie, who had been his constant companion for more than twelve years, and I suggested to him that we should together write a tribute in the form of an extended letter to her, summarising her career and her extraordinary relationships with the leopards and Tara. This came out in 1987, under the title *Eelie and the Big Cats* – a slim volume of ninety pages, illustrated with extraordinary photographs of dog-and-cat mock combat.

That was the last of my literary collaborations with Billy; but I made several more trips to Tiger Haven, and in 1994 Phylla and I followed a week there with a visit to the Corbett National Park, which I had always wanted to see, partly because of Billy's association with the legendary Jim, after whom it had been named. Bigger by far than Dudhwa, and blessed with more spectacular terrain, because it is set in the densely-forested foothills of the Himalayas, Corbett was the first tiger reserve established by the Indian Government (in 1936).

Perhaps we were unlucky not to see a tiger during a week there, but we had splendid elephant rides, and met an amusing fellow-traveller in the form of Jan Perceval, a six-foot blonde who ran a PR company in San Diego. Three years earlier (she told us) she had been married up a tree in the park, to a 6′ 4″, 280-lb basketball player,.and now she had come back to bless the spot. She did indeed spend some time on a tree platform in the main camp at Dikkhala, and when she came down, she confided that she was taking advice from an astrologist as to whether or not, in her mid-thirties, she should have a baby.

We never heard what the stars recommended; but Jan came with us to spend a night at Gairal, an old dak bungalow deep in the jungle, poised on a ledge above the Ramganga river, which hurtled past in an icy, blue-grey torrent. Well supplied with whisky, and waited on by six boys from

Dikkhala, we had an enjoyable evening and a comfortable night; but the star of the show was the *phanit* who took us for a ride on his elephant Shampa Kali.

He wore a strange white head-dress that fitted tightly round his forehead and skull and hung down the back of his neck, which at first we supposed must have some religious significance – until we heard his story.

He had gone into the jungle to cut fodder for his elephant, and was attacked by a tiger. At first the elephant could not help him, for she was tied to a tree, and he twice fought the tiger off single-handed, once by shoving his hand down its throat and twisting its tongue. He then managed to crawl back to his mount, who lifted him up with her trunk and put him on her head, out of the tiger's reach. His own head was badly lacerated, and he had lost the back of his scalp: hence, ten years later, the protective covering.

The other highlight of our trip was our visit to Jim Corbett's home at Kalahundi, now a museum. The modest house stands in a large, unkempt garden dotted with mango trees,; but what brought the former owner vividly to life were letters written from Africa in 1947. Fearing that after Independence no one would want him around his old haunts any more, he had made the awful mistake of moving from his beloved India to Kenya – and here in his letters was pathetic evidence of his homesickness: enquiries about the health of old friends, and careful instructions to ensure that welfare payments were bring properly made to the families he had known.

In his eighties Billy inevitably slowed down. Hampered by arthritis, he no longer prowled the jungle tracks; but his intellectual vigour was unimpaired, and he continued to batter out letters on his typewriter, bombarding the babus with his central contention – that commercial forestry and wildlife conservation must be run by separate Government departments, with trained specialists in each, instead of being lumped together, as they had been in the past. As always, he was at loggerheads with the establishment.

But then, in December 2003, recognition at last began to come his way when *Sanctuary Asia* magazine accorded him its Lifetime Achievement award, calling him 'a living legend, considered by some to be the godfather of the movement to save the Indian tiger.' A year later, in December 2004, he won a still more important honour – the J. Paul Getty Wildlife Conservation Prize, administered by the World Wildlife Fund. The citation saluted 'the passion and tireless devotion' which he had given to tiger preservation, and with the award came a cheque for 50,000 U.S. dollars. Less than a week later he heard that the Chief Minister of the United Provinces, Mulayam Singh Yadav, had conferred on him the Yash Bharati award for outstanding achievement.

At the beginning of February 2005 I went out to Tiger Haven for the last time, accompanied by Billy's sister Amar Commander, a Tibetan scholar of international repute. By then a certain melancholy had descended on the house, for Balram and Mira were both dead, and Billy was living alone with his servants, except when the occasional friend came to stay.

Amar and I arrived in time for the presentation of the Getty award, which was held at the headquarters of the Dudhwa National Park on the evening of 4 February. Park rangers in their dark olive uniforms, some with rifles slung on their shoulders, manned the open doorways, and 150 people packed into the interpretation centre. Billy, looking small and shrunken, but wearing a jaunty, baseball-type cap, sat at one end of a dais alongside a row of big-wigs.

In an affectionate speech Ravi Singh – head of the World Wildlife Fund in India – described him as a latter-day Jim Corbett, and praised the unparalleled dedication with which he had fought his 'marathon battle' for Dudhwa. He spoke mostly in English, but occasionally slid into Hindi. When Billy replied in Hindi, and other dignitaries were invited to have their say, ripples of applause kept running through the audience, and palpable surges of emotion swept the hall as speakers sang the Honorary Tiger's praises. Afterwards, the company sat down to supper in a marquee, while log fires blazed around the compound. I longed for a tiger to call out of the forest – a single, deep *a-oom* would

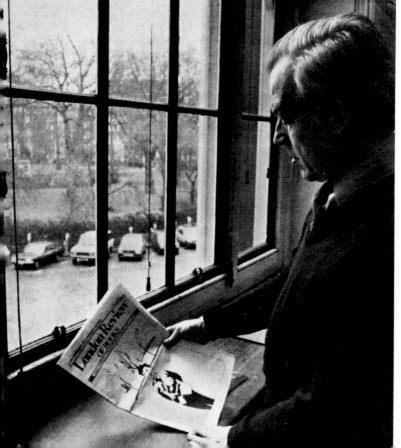

Above: Gulf War winners: General Sir Peter de la Billière with General Norman Schwarzkopf, 1990

Left: The Soviet defector Oleg Bitov in the London Library
Photo: The Sunday Telegraph

Left: Tiger Haven, Billy Arjan Singh's home in northern India

Below left: Billy's mongrel Eelie disciplines Harriet

Below: Billy with Harriet and Juliette *Photo: Anglia TV*

Above: Sir Alan (Tommy) Lascelles, Private Secretary to King George VI

Right: Lascelles with King George VI in World War II
Photo: Illustrated London News

Oleg Gordievsky advises President Reagan, 1980s *Photo: The Ronald Reagan Library*

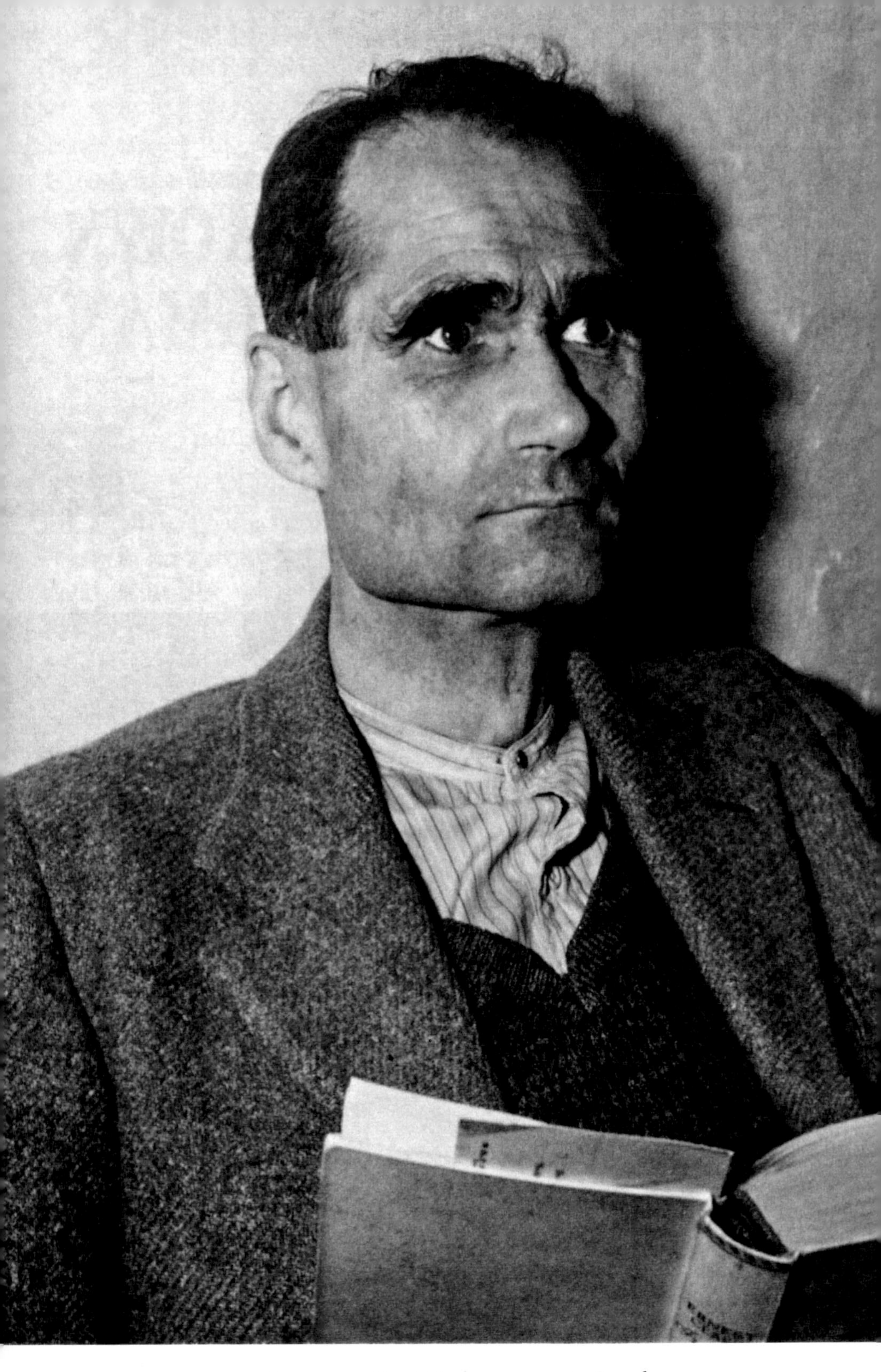

Hess or not Hess? The last prisoner in Spandau

Alan Hillgarth

Above: Eileen Soper closely monitored by her father, George, 1921

Below: Hedgehog painted by Eileen Soper
Pictures: Estate of Eileen Soper

have stood everyone's hair on end; but no sound came from the massed black trees, and it was left to humans to honour their local hero.

That was the last time I saw Billy. He died on New Year's Day, 2010, at Jasbirnagar, aged ninety-two. When the news spread, a huge crowd assembled. His body was washed by Seva Singh, a burly neighbouring Sikh farmer, helped by two sons, and laid in a trailer towed behind his ancient jeep. With Sri Ram driving and Billy's niece Brinda Dubey sitting beside him, the jeep set off for Tiger Haven followed by a train of cars and cross-country vehicles. At the junction of the Dudhwa road more people joined the cortege, and a lengthy procession trundled out to Tiger Haven. There, a gathering of Sikhs chanted passages from their holy book, the *Guru Granth Sahib*; Brinda read out a short prayer, and Billy's nephew Mukuljit Singh lit the pyre.

Afterwards the family scattered some of Billy's ashes on the river behind the house, and buried the rest among the graves of his beloved animals, as he had wished. Next day a Hindu priest came and conducted a short ceremony of closure. A marble gravestone, placed on the site, carries the following inscription:

'Billy' Arjan Singh lies here among the animals he
loved and for whom he battled.
A long and lonely crusade, fought with passion
and perseverance.
Few truly belong to the wild, but he was one.
R.I.P. Honorary Tiger.
I have fought the good fight. I have finished
the race.

CHAPTER SIXTEEN

Old or New?
1971

During the summer of 1971 there was much agitation in archaeological circles about the illegal trade in antiquities throughout Europe. The problem was two-fold: ancient objects were being smuggled out of Greece, Turkey and Italy in large quantities, and at the same time skilled forgers were creating artefacts so like originals that museums and individuals were buying fakes for huge sums in the belief that they were genuine.

Scenting an excuse for a trip to the Mediterranean, in August I persuaded the philistine powers at the *Sunday Telegraph* that a good story was waiting to be reported – and to my surprise they agreed. Moving swiftly, I brushed aside the fact that I had no contacts or positive leads, and got in touch with Sam Modiano, our veteran stringer in Athens, who encouraged me to drop by and see him.

When I did that, a couple of days later, he urged me to go on to Crete. 'That's the place for forgers,' he said. 'They're at it all the time. Go and see my lovely friend Katrina in Iraklion. She'll fix you up.'

On the short flight down from Athens I had visions of the beautiful Katrina: raven-haired (no doubt), lissom and in her twenties. For a few moments the reality rather took me aback: Katrina was on the wrong side of fifty, or maybe of sixty, with thinning, swept-back hair and pebble glasses. But what she lacked in glamour she more than made up in the warmth of her welcome and her readiness to help. She spoke some English, and went straight into action.

Hardly had I explained what I wanted when she said, 'Fthenakis.

He's the man for you.' She explained that he was a local craftsman who had recently been released from gaol, after doing time for forgery. She did not know where he lived, but recourse to the telephone directory soon solved the problem. Four people called Fthenakis were listed. Katrina ran her finger down the column and said, 'K. Konstantinos. This is him.'

She rang the number. A man answered. In a moment Katrina established that she had found the right person. She spoke in Greek, translating for my benefit between exchanges. 'A man has come from the English *Telegraph* newspaper. He wants to interview you. Will you see him?'

'Of course,' came the answer. 'Bring him round.'

'When can we come?'

'Now!'

'Do you speak English?'

'Unfortunately not.'

'Then we'll find someone.'

Within five minutes she had pounced on an English-speaking girl of about eighteen who was minding one of the tourist shops. When *Madame,* the owner, emerged from the back and saw that she was about to lose her interpreter for the day, she gave a prodigious shriek – but it was of no avail, and soon we were bowling out of town in a taxi.

We found the master-craftsman at work, sitting under a lemon tree in his garden, working with an old-fashioned dentist's drill, driven by whirring pulleys. Out of a lump of pumice he was fashioning what looked to me very like a Minoan owl – a neat, chunky little figure five or six inches high. As we arrived, he stopped the drill and stood up to welcome us – a man in his fifties (I guessed) with a high forehead and curly dark hair going back.

He greeted us warmly – and, far from being embarrassed by his recent release from gaol (where he had served 25 months of a 33-month sentence), he held forth indignantly about the ambivalent attitude of the authorities. During the trial (he explained) it emerged that he and 30-odd accomplices had been producing fake antiquities *with the active encouragement of the police* – the aim being to confuse the dealers and collectors who had begun to infest Crete in swarms, and so to staunch the outflow of genuine treasures from the island. He had thus been providing a service, rather than committing any crime.

In any case, he said, he never claimed that his artefacts were antique: he just made things that appealed to him and sold them to dealers. What the dealers did with them was their business, not his. If someone later claimed that the owl he was making at the moment was 3,000 years old, it was not his fault.

Certainly he was a highly skilled craftsman. His outdoor workshop was littered with fascinating objects, among them the shoulder-blade of some animal – probably a sheep – on which he had incised slender human figures moving in a ritual procession: a strange and somehow mysterious scene. He said he worked in wood, metal, stone and plaster with equal facility, and had secret formulas for ageing wood and bronze. He claimed that one of his small bronzes, of a man with a calf on his shoulder, had fetched five million drachmas (some £70,000) in Germany.

Aiding and abetting him was his nephew Aristotle Giannakoudakis, a cheerful, roguish-looking painter in his thirties who specialised in producing artificially-aged ikons. Like his uncle, he talked uninhibitedly about his methods, explaining how he aged olive wood with chemicals and used a drill with a fine bit to create fake worm-holes in the back of each panel. When I praised a small ikon of St Nicholas, he pressed it on me, even though it was not quite finished, and still had, in the middle of the forehead, the small hole made by the needle of the compass which Aristotle had used to prescribe the curve of the saint's halo.

So well did things go, so genial was the atmosphere, that someone suggested we all go for lunch to a little restaurant on the coast. There we had a wonderful meal. I do not recall how many kinds of fish we ate, but ouzo and retsina kept conversation flowing, and I have a lasting memory of waves booming as they burst beneath the floor, right under our feet. I had to withstand some ribbing about how were we, the Brits, to talk, as the English milord Elgin had stolen the marbles from the Parthenon?

But most of the talk was about the present, and revolved round the way in which antiquities, real or fake, seemed to go to ground for months or years but then turned up in Zurich or London or New York.

By the time lunch ended at 6pm, I had acquired such a magnificent haul of information and ideas that I felt I had enough for several articles, and might as well go straight home. Yet there had also been a good deal of gossip about the archaeological skulduggery rampant in Turkey, so I held to my original plan and went on there next day.

The journey was short, but in two hops. The first, to Izmir on the Aegean coast, took the ancient Dakota only forty-five minutes, but then a memorably infuriating delay set in. Through-passengers were told to stay on board while a few people disembarked, but others came crowding up the steps, and soon it was clear that more tickets had been sold than there were seats. As the aircraft sat there in baking heat, with the door open and no air-conditioning – the outdoor temperature was in the nineties F – tempers rose and arguments broke out. An official struggled on board, brandishing a list and calling out names as he tried to establish order. Even though he was speaking in Turkish, I could tell he was saying that some passengers would have to be left behind.

Luckily I happened to be in a corner seat right at the back, well away from the exit, and I decided to sit tight, come what may – if necessary, to feign disability. As voices rose, the temperature kept climbing, until it was barely tolerable: the cabin was like an oven, and the whole of my torso became drenched with sweat. In the end three or four passengers were bundled off and the door was slammed shut – but even then there were no seats for the two pretty air-hostesses, who had to perch on little, hinged flaps at the back, without seat-belts, for take-off and landing. Mercifully for all, the bumpy flight took little over an hour – and when I stepped out into the fresh, cool air of the Anatolian plateau, nearly 3,000 feet above sea-level, it was as delicious as diving into the sea.

I had no grass-roots contacts in Turkey, but information was available everywhere. The Minister of Culture, Talat Halman, assured me that during the past few years strenuous efforts had been made to suppress the illegal export of antiquities; sites were now better guarded, and the training of customs officers had been improved. But, he admitted, 'a vast smuggling operation is still going on.'

The size of the problem was immense. Turkey (he said) had 3,000 known sites from the classical era alone, and countless others dating from 7,000 BC onwards, when Neolithic art began to flourish in Central Anatolia. All over the country peasants were digging feverishly in the hope of making their fortune. 'Whenever they strike something big, word flashes to Izmir or Istanbul. There, dealers sit in wait, with big American cars and bundles of liras. Out they come in droves, to shift the finds to some convenient spot on the coast. Then one night a boat comes in, and the treasure next appears at one of the international dealers in Switzerland or Germany.'

A typical and most damaging incident had occurred nine years earlier near Antalya, in the south. When peasants unearthed a magnificent hoard of Byzantine silver dating from the 6th century AD, a dozen dealers sped out from Izmir, but the find was so dazzling that haggling over the price went on for a fortnight – with the result that only half the silver had been loaded onto a boat when the police arrived and intercepted the rest. Sure enough, the missing half reappeared in Zurich, where a dealer sold it to an American, who passed it on to the Dumbarton Oaks collection in Washington.

Pursuing the smugglers' trail to Istanbul, I called on Dr Nesih Firatli, Curator of Classical Antiquities in the Archaeological Museum, who confirmed that innumerable sites had been destroyed by illegal digging. 'They've been so heavily looted that they look like battlefields,' he told me – and he showed me photographs to prove it; but he did not want to be drawn on one of the most mysterious scandals – the Dorak affair.

This had started in 1961 when James Mellaart, an archaeologist of Dutch and Scottish descent, took the train from Istanbul to Izmir and found himself sitting opposite an attractive young woman who wore a striking gold bracelet. Her name, she said, was Anna Papastratis, and she offered to show him some antiquities which she had at home. Accepting her offer, he found that she did indeed have an astonishing collection, including a sheet of gold bearing Egyptian hieroglyphs and a date equivalent to 2473 BC. She claimed the treasure had been found at a place called Dorak; she would not let him take photographs, but she did allow him to draw the pieces. Having spent three days and nights with her, he departed with the promise that, when she sent him word, he might publicise the hoard. In due course she did make contact; he published his drawings in the *Illustrated London News* – and all archaeological hell descended on him.

Mellaart was already well-known for his excavation of Neolithic sites, notably Hacilar and Catalhöyük; but now he was damned from all sides, and banned from further excavation in Turkey. For one thing, experts declared that the collection he had drawn was not from a single hoard, but had been put together from different sites. Even worse, the address of the woman with whom he said he stayed in Izmir turned out not to exist.

The alleged hoard has never been seen again; and when, on my tour in 1972, I asked the leading collector Hoseyin Kocabas what he felt about it, he declared that he thought many of the pieces were modern fakes. He felt the same about another notorious collection of 137 gold objects which had surfaced in Switzerland and had been bought on behalf of the Boston Fine Arts Museum, becoming known as the Boston Gold Hoard. Ten years earlier, Kocabas told me, he had been offered several of the pieces, including a Mycenean-type gold mask, but he had seen at once that it was a fake.

His own collection, housed in a large flat next to the one in which he lived, was astonishing. Treasures from every era crowded the shelves in every room – Neolithic, Greek, Roman, Ottoman – and although by then he had more or less lost his sight, he could describe every one and give its provenance. His main passion was for seals – small cylinders like slender cotton reels, made of metal or carved from stone, and embossed or engraved with figures that leave an impression when rolled on clay or wax. He had drawers full of them, many of great antiquity and value, and he particularly wanted to show me one of Egyptian origin; but because he could no longer see clearly, the only way he could identify it was by rolling all the seals about the drawer, sensing their nature through his finger-tips. 'Ah!' he said at last. 'This it,' and he held up a beautiful little cylinder made of gold. It was awful to hear, later, that this kindly old enthusiast was being undermined by a younger member of his own family, who was stealing his treasures one by one and selling them in Switzerland.

CHAPTER SEVENTEEN

Artist Extraordinary
1989

In March 1989 the artist Eileen Soper, aged eighty-three, fell ill and was taken into hospital at Welwyn, in Hertfordshire, together with her elder sister Eva, who by then was too frail to live on her own. Anxious about Wildings, their house at Harmer Green, nearby, Eileen asked her solicitor Graham Field to go over and check that all was well. Although he had been in touch with her for some time, he had never seen the property – and when he did, he was astonished.

The four-acre garden had run riot. Six-foot saplings had grown up through the lawn. Vegetation was threatening to engulf the stuccoed building. A wooden trellis had collapsed under the weight of wisteria and clematis. Creepers had forced their way into the upper windows. Behind the house a tree had fallen and lay against the wall, half-blocking the door. Yet the chaotic nature of the surroundings gave Field less of a shock than did the scene inside.

Most of the rooms were so packed with furniture, apple boxes, cardboard cartons, carrier bags and shoulder-high piles of old newspapers and magazines that he could hardly squeeze in through the doors. The amount of paper was incredible: income-tax returns fifty years old, bank statements from the 1940s, copies of ancient correspondence with publishers, drafts of poems scribbled on the backs of torn-up cornflakes packets, share offers long obsolete, company reports and prospectuses – thousands of sheets carelessly folded and crumpled, stuffed down tight on each other in dense masses. There were also many pairs of shoes, carefully packed in plastic bags and stowed inside other bags.

One upstairs room contained boxes of jam-jars, which turned out to number 3,000. Mice were nesting not only in Eileen's slippers, but in a chest of drawers on the landing, and in other comfortable resorts. The high-ceilinged studio, at the back on the first floor, was also stuffed with books and papers – what caught Field's attention most sharply was the huge number of pictures. Several hung on the walls, but many more were stacked, and he saw at once that some were of value.

In search of expert advice, he approached the distinguished bird artist Robert Gillmor, Founder and later President of the Society of Wildlife Artists, with whom Eileeen had maintained intermittent contact for the past fifteen years. When Gillmor drove over to Harmer Green, he too was amazed by the decrepitude of the house – but he was positively astounded by what he found in the studio. There, half-buried in junk, stuffed into drawers, piled up behind pieces of furniture, was an immense treasure-trove of artwork. Some pictures had been foxed by damp or nibbled at the edges by mice, but most were in excellent condition, and many were of high quality. From the hand of George Soper, Eileen's father, there were 177 watercolours of horses working on the land, 71 wash-and-pencil drawings, 445 landscapes and 53 unfinished works, besides 3,500 prints and a large number of sketchbooks. Eileen herself had amassed hundreds of prints taken from her own early etchings, and more than 300 watercolours of the badgers, foxes, deer, squirrels, hedgehogs, stoats, otters and birds to whose study she had devoted herself in later years. Applying the most conservative judgement, Gillmor estimated the value of the unframed pictures at £900,000.

Eileen's burning wish, of course was to return to Wildings; but the local health authorities decreed that she and Eva could not possibly go back to the house in its present state – so, while they went into a nursing home for the time being, Field put in hand extensive renovations. With some of the contents removed to create space, workmen installed new plumbing, new bathrooms, an electric chair-lift on the steep stairs, a new kitchen, and new carpets of Eileen's favourite colour, cornflower blue. From a distance she herself took a quixotic view of the improvements. 'As long as they don't change anything,' she kept saying, and she issued one specific prohibition: the workmen were not, under any circumstances, to open the locked cupboard on the landing. In fact they had to, to put in new pipes – and found that it contained the old ladies' underwear.

Sad to relate, the sisters never went home. In March 1990 Eileen began to fail, and in less than a week she died. Eva met the news of her demise with an unanswerable observation. 'Of course she hasn't died,' she said. 'If she had, she would have told me.' Surviving for another six months, she too expired in September, aged 89, leaving £250,000. In their joint wills the sisters left Wildings and its garden to the Royal Society for the Protection of Birds, and the family's artwork went to the Artists' General Benvolent Institution.

How had the Sopers allowed the house and garden to fall into such a pitiful state of disrepair? How had their extraordinary hoard of artwork accumulated? What was it that had made them shut themselves away in the prison of their claustrophobic house? When the London publisher David Burnett suggested that I should write a short biography of Eileen, I was so fascinated by the mystery that I jumped at the chance.

My first step was to visit Wildings. The garden was exactly as Field had described it – a four-acre wilderness sloping gently down to a veritable jungle at the bottom. By the time I saw the house, building work had been completed, and fitted carpets had been installed, but the downstairs rooms were still so full of stacked paper that I had to wriggle between stacks to reach the far side. The studio was almost empty, yet in the middle, on an easel, stood a striking oil portrait – the head and shoulders of a young man, blue-eyed and already balding, wearing a grey jacket and waistcoat, holding an unfolded document in his hands. Who was this mysterious survivor?

From photographs and documents I gleaned details of Eileen's early life. Her father George was a countryman, born in Devon, who lived at various places in southern England. After a spell of military service, he became a talented artist, largely self-taught, with a particular skill in the depiction of working horses. Associating comfortably with ploughmen and foresters, he gained first-hand knowledge of rural occupations, and produced hundreds of fine etchings which captured the intensity of labour in the fields and woods. Later he went over to painting in watercolour, again with strong emphasis on the land.

His wife Ada (formerly Lehany) came from a more affluent background, and seems to have been a gentle creature, with kindly, deep-set eyes. After a prolonged courtship, he married her in 1897, and their first child, Eva, was born in 1901. Eileen arrived four years later. In 1907 their father heard through a friend that a plot of building-land was for sale at Harmer Green, out in the wilds of Hertfordshire. Enchanted by the open countryside, he bought a strip of sloping field in the hills above Welwyn and commissioned the building of a medium-sized, two-storey house at the head of the plot. The total cost of construction was £557-19-6. Being a keen conservationist (long before that term became fashionable), and also an enthusiastic botanist, he created a semi-wild garden which included a wide variety of species, none more spectacular than the ninety types of fern which were his favourites.

At first the house had no name; but later Eileen called it Wildings, and it was there that, from the age of five, she spent her entire life. Sepia photographs and paintings show that as a girl she had striking looks, with radiant, red-brown hair and a wide, intelligent face, slightly spoilt by some heaviness about the jaw, but definitely attractive. As she herself wrote, her earliest wish was to follow in her father's footsteps as an artist. Taught by him, she showed such precocity at etching that when she was still only fifteen two of her prints were hung at the Royal Academy, and she became the Academy's youngest-ever exhibitor.

The family were thrilled. But snapshots of pupil and teacher contain a disquieting element. In one, as Eileen sits working at some picture on a tilted board, her father stands behind her left shoulder, uncomfortably close, leaning over with pencil in hand, poised to make a correction. With his clipped moustache, stiff white collar, tie and heavy tweed suit, he appears rather intimidating – and in another photo, in the same clothes, he sits beside her with his right arm round her back, while she looks out with an air at least of resignation, if not of resentment.

Both photographs hint strongly at the control which the father exercised over his daughters. No doubt this seemed to them a normal part of family life; but George had one obsession which in the end proved profoundly damaging to both Eva and Eileen – his unreasoning fear of disease. So frightened was he of germs that he forbade the girls' nanny to make contact with other people when she took them for walks. She was not allowed to let anyone else approach the children, or touch them; still less might she take them into any strange house. George's dread of hospitals was such that, if he had to pass one while driving, he would make a detour to give it a wide berth. When Eileen fell ill with appendicitis, he got the gardener to scrub down a wooden table and insisted that the surgeon should perform the operation in the studio. Inevitably the girls inherited his phobia, which had a suffocating effect not only on their childhood, but on their entire lives.

In spite of it, Eileen was lively enough as a young woman. Although claiming to be handicapped by inherited gastric trouble, she had the energy to play tennis, go for bicycle rides and walk miles over the fields with her father. She learned to drive, and by 1924 had a Vauxhall Princeton tourer. She acted as chauffeur for her parents, driving a classic six-cylinder AC Ace, and later she bought a beautiful, low-slung Riley.

Her artistic ability advanced apace. Her success at the Royal Academy brought instant fame, and she began selling prints of her etchings in England and America. Then, more and more, she travelled with her father on excursions to new country – the Sussex Downs or the East Anglian coast – ever in search of new landscapes and rural scenes. She loved the age-old rituals of farming which he depicted so well, especially the heavy horses which were still ubiquitous, pulling plough, harrow, drill and roller, and hauling timber from the woods.

Did she ever fall in love? Searching through the mass of papers she left behind, I could find only one hint of romance, which seemed to refer – though the connection is by no means certain – to Eric Liddell, the Olympic sprinter who won a gold medal in the 400 metres and a bronze in the 200 metres at the Games in Paris in 1924 – feats commemorated in the film *Chariots of Fire*. Certainly he stayed with the Sopers as a child: his family was connected with theirs, and later – apparently in 1925 –

Eileen painted his portrait – the one left on the easel in the studio. Some time after that, in a nostalgic poem, she remembered sadly:

We walked the woods of June,
And in the tangled light
Where many names were carved
For lovers' past delight,
You wrote that Time might spell
The letters E and L,
Though loath to mar
The beauty of that tree
Engraved them but lichen-deep
With silver key.

Progress has cleared
The sunken way.
On fallen leaves
The beech is lying.
Nothing remains of that fair day
Save a lonely peewit crying.

Beyond that, I could discover no trace of any love life. Neither Eileen nor Eva married, and it was hard to escape the conclusion that their lives were rather joyless. When war came in 1939, the family stayed put at Wildings which, being twenty-five miles from London, was relatively safe from the threat of German bombs. But in August 1942 a thunderbolt hit them when George died of heart-failure, aged 70. Throughout the girls' lives he had lived and worked at home, and his sudden disappearance left Eileen in charge of the household – for her mother was already failing, and her sister was so passive as to offer little emotional help.

By then Eileen had become a prolific writer, pouring thousands of words into letters and poems. She was also earning good money as an illustrator of books, for she had struck up a fruitful partnership with the children's author Enid Blyton. Such was Blyton's output – seventeen books in 1943, twenty-two in 1944 – that several different artists were needed to keep up with her, but Eileen also worked fast, not least on the *Famous Five* adventure series, and several times contributed to half a dozen books a year.

Outside, the garden flourished eccentrically. Eileen loved flowers and knew a great deal about them, but at the same time waged a long-running campaign against Harold, the part-time gardener, whose instinct was naturally to maintain some sort of order. 'A patch of teasels must be left to go to seed for the goldfinches,' she wrote. 'Grass must remain uncut for the benefit of ground-nesting birds, stinging nettles left standing as cover for the blackcaps. How he [Harold] hates leaving those wild patches!'

Gradually she and Eva became enslaved to living creatures – mice, toads, deer, badgers, and above all birds. They fed the blue tits so liberally on windowsills that the birds invaded their bedroom and pecked holes in the book-bindings. 'You should have been here yesterday,' Eileen told a friend. 'I walked out into the garden with milled cheese on top of my head. Several long-tailed tits perched there feeding, also also blue tits and robins.'

Yet, without noticing it, the sisters were in the grip of a far more serious enslavement – to their fear of disease. Clearly, this had been started by their father, but by the time they were middle-aged, it had reached severely inhibiting proportions – for they believed that cancer, which they could not bring themselves to name, calling it 'the Dread Disease', could be spread by airborne germs as easily as a common cold.

This folly imposed crippling restrictions on their lives. It meant that they could not use public transport, frequent any public place, enter other people's houses, or even allow any stranger to enter theirs. The result was that they were confined more and more to base, becoming captives in their own home. Since it was too dangerous to enter a shop, food and writing materials had to be ordered by telephone – and if they needed to go anywhere, Eileen drove, rather than risk a bus or train. They boiled the clothes pegs with which they hung washing out to dry, and if a garment fell to the ground, they boiled it within inches of disintegration. When they took delivery of a new bath, they washed it down with Dettol 'in the interests of hygiene, as it had been handled by other people on the way.'

No one saw their predicament more clearly than Marguerite Roe, a neighbour whom I found after advertising for contacts. A social welfare worker, she got to know the sisters well, and was often invited to supper. After a year or so the invitations suddenly ceased, but it took Marguerite some time to find out why.

Then one morning an envelope fell through the Sopers' letter-box onto the doormat. Both sisters were immediately terrified, for they saw from the writing that the missive came from their cousin Muriel, who was suffering from the Dread Disease. Not daring to touch the envelope, they picked it up with the coal tongs and laid it on the stone hearth. Then, having burnt the doormat, they telephoned Marguerite for help. 'Open it!' they pleaded when she arrived, and they watched in horror as she slit the envelope. The letter turned out to be a courageous account of how the patient was faring; but when Marguerite began to praise the writer's fortitude, Eileen could not bear it, and told her to burn the letter in the boiler – which she did. Later she realised that the sisters had used her as cannon-fodder, supposing her to be already doomed by her contacts with cancer elsewhere.

A new phase of Eileen's life began in April 1951, when she saw her first badger. Having waited out for more than an hour on a cold spring evening, she stood 'in breathless excitement, feeling a sense of wonder I had not experienced for years,' when a badger came into view. From that moment she was hooked, and over the next three years she spent more than a thousand hours observing, sketching and making notes about badgers' behaviour.

Her main theatre of observation was a dell, or lightly-wooded hollow, lying on its own in a field. To this lonely spot she would creep evening after evening, sometimes with Eva or a friend, but usually on her own, and the sheer physical endurance which she displayed was extraordinary. Frozen and soaked in winter, tormented by midges and mosquitoes in summer, stung by nettles, harassed by rats running over her feet, she ignored every discomfort in her search for information and insights. She loved her expeditions, slipping off into the depths of the countryside to become a creature of the night.

By remaining immobile for hours on end, she gained the badgers' trust; but she also used artificial means to lure them, distributing peanuts liberally and smearing her boots with golden syrup, so that her subjects would come up to lick them. Cubs, especially, became so used to her that they would nuzzle her fingers.

Her passionate study of badgers lasted for nearly ten years, and during that time she also drew and painted numerous studies of foxes. But then in the summer of 1961 there appeared another animal which had a powerful influence on her life: muntjac, or barking deer. Standing only about 20 inches at the shoulder, these curious creatures descended from a breeding group imported by the eleventh Duke of Bedford and installed in his park at Woburn, and they were gradually spreading across the south of England.

Eileen was thrilled when a young buck appeared in the thicket at the bottom of the garden, and she set about studying the newcomer with her usual intensity, putting out apples and brown bread to lure him, and building little shelters thatched with bracken. Soon she increased the number of shelters to seven, and she would sit out all night with her binoculars, observing the buck's behaviour. When more deer appeared, she gave them all names – Darky, Tiny, Freckles – and in 1969 she poured her accumulated knowledge into a book, *Muntjac,* which was published by Longmans but attracted the enmity of another local deer-fancier, who dismissed it as 'amateurish and incompetent.'

By then the animals had established a paralysing domination over the author. She asked friends not to telephone after dark, for fear of disturbing her guests, and as she herself admitted, her own freedom of action was much restricted. 'No work could be done or fires lit where deer were liable to be harbouring in adjacent thickets. Scything was banned in the wild garden, as it deprived the deer of cover. Consequently stinging nettles and other weeds grew to rampant proportions.' She did accept help from one or two neighbours, among them Michael Clark, a young naturalist, author and artist who lived a few minutes away at Tewin and carried out essential tasks such as the removal, and release at some distant point, of captured yellow-necked mice.

The house had almost seized up. The plumbing system functioned so badly that it took an hour to run a bath, and because Eileen refused to switch on the night-store heaters which had recently been installed, the rooms were deathly cold, besides being stuffed with bric-a-brac.

One stranger who did gain access was John Lister-Kaye, a budding naturalist still at school, where he had reared a young weasel called Wilba. Along with his father, Sir John, Eileen invited him to lunch, and the boy reckoned that day an astonishing introduction to natural history. Eileen took an immediate fancy to Wilba, who arrived in John's pocket and ran up the sleeve of her smock and out the neck; and the visitors were amazed when a grey squirrel came in through the window to join them at table, and dormice kept popping out of the sofa. When they walked down the garden, birds flew out to settle on Eileen's head as she fed them with crumbs of cheese from the pocket of her smock, and a muntjac sauntered over to take a biscuit from her hand. She suggested that John should write, and she should illustrate, an article about Wilba for the quarterly journal *The Countryman,* and this duly appeared a year later – but the long-term effect of their meeting was incalculable, for it set John on the road to becoming a full-time naturalist and a leader in wildlife management.

A project with which Eileen struggled for years was a book of her father's engravings and etchings; in time this metamorphosed into an anthology of rural writing, but for various reasons she never managed to finish it. Although her own artistic ambition flickered on, it was gradually smothered by increasing infirmity, and by the weight of domestic chores – for Eva had been smitten by spinal arthritis, and Eileen had to look after her as well as run the house. She became querulous and unwelcoming, complaining that she was ill, but that the doctor would do nothing for her; in fact, she was so self-opinionated that she would never accept medical advice unless it coincided with her own ideas.

When she was finally taken into hospital in March 1989, she was much agitated by the slow progress of another project, master-minded by

Robert Gillmor, who was arranging publication of *George Soper's Horses* – a book of her father's watercolours. She died in September 1990, before this came out, but Eva, who survived her by a few months, was delighted by the dust-jacket, and claimed to remember the painting, of two horses ploughing, from which it was taken.

It was my misfortune that I never met Eileen. Yet as I spent a year burrowing through her mass of papers, and speaking to some of the few people whom she had allowed to know her, I became fascinated by the strange contradictions in her character. I felt sorry for her and Eva, whose lives were blighted by their father's obsession with disease. But I felt huge admiration for Eileen's physical and mental endurance, and above all for her skill and perseverance as an artist. Her watercolours are wonderful: the best of her badger paintings glow with a kind of *joie de vivre*. They suggest that the animals had a sense of humour, and confirm what otherwise might not be apparent – that she certainly had one too.

My biography came out in 1991 under the title *Wildings: the Secret Garden of Eileen Soper*, lavishly illustrated with her etchings, drawings and watercolours. Thanks largely to the attractive lay-out devised by David Burnett, the book sold extremely well; within months a second edition appeared, and then a large-format paperback. As if confirmation were needed of the Sopers' excellence as rural artists, father and daughter, an exhibition of their work at the Wildlife Art Gallery in Lavenham, held in September 1990 proved a huge success. People came from every corner of Britain – from Cornwall and Scotland – to see the watercolours and engravings, and with individual prices ranging almost up to £3,000, the sale raised over £100,000.

CHAPTER EIGHTEEN

Boot of the Indie
1986-2000

Towards the end of 1985 convulsions shook the *Daily Telegraph,* when Andreas Whittam-Smith, the City Editor, resigned and went off to found his own newspaper, the *Independent,* taking several colleagues with him. I was still loosely attached to the *Sunday Telegraph,* but had no definite job there; and perhaps it was because Phylla and I had recently moved into deeper country – from Oxfordshire to Gloucestershire – that I had the idea of writing to Andreas, asking if he planned to include a rural column in his new organ. He replied cautiously that he might, but he asked, if I wrote one, what sort of column it would be.

'I don't know,' I told him; but as a trial run I wrote a piece about the use, in our part of the world, of the words *bugger* and *buggery.* Neither, I hastened to explain, was often deployed in its physical sense, but both were constantly used in a variety of applications. *Bugger-all* and *bugger off* of course meant the same as anywhere else; but the cricket ball which had to be exhumed from the midriff of the square-leg umpire was said to have been *going like buggery;* the weather in summer was sometimes *hot as buggery,* and in winter *cold as buggery;* a golden retriever appearing on television at Cruft's was *spruced up to buggery.* A single *bugger!,* uttered in cracked tones, could mean 'Absolutely not' . . and so on. In the *Independent*'s new office an elderly sub-editor was seen carrying a copy of the article about with a face of thunder, and when someone asked what was displeasing him, he replied, 'This is the funniest thing I've ever read. I'm glowering so that I don't keep laughing.'

On the strength of it Andreas commissioned a column which,

in reference to the *double entendre* tried by Hamlet on Ophelia, we decided to call 'Country Matters'. For me the agreement proved the most astonishing stroke of good fortune. For the next fourteen years I contributed a weekly article, missing the odd issue only when I was on holiday. Looking back, it seems extraordinary that I must have written nearly 700 rural pieces. Never once did the editors of the paper suggest a subject; never once did they criticise what I had sent (except that, if I had done a realistic piece about culling deer, my charming female sub-editor might plead, 'No more killing for a month, please.')

Far from carping, Andreas and his successors were extraordinarily indulgent, and kept encouraging me to carry on. For months on end I occupied the same position in the paper, at the bottom of the leader page on Saturday morning, and this fixed abode meant that I could write exactly to length – 1190 words – without fear of the piece being cut. All outlying members of the staff were issued with Tandy 200 laptops, and with this primitive but excellent little computer I fired off my weekly article: as I pressed the Send key, I imagined the piece soaring up eastwards over the ridge like a mortar bomb and dropping neatly on to its target in London.

I had an absolutely free hand – so much so that I occasionally felt like pulling readers' legs with the trick played on William Boot in Evelyn Waugh's deathless novel *Scoop*. (In one of his rustic despatches sent from Boot Magna to the *Daily Beast,* William's sister Priscilla surreptitiously changes 'badger' to 'crested grebe' – with dire results.) Because the editors and readers of the *Independent* were predominantly urban, I often had an urge to try something similar and see if anyone noticed. Would they know that swallows do not bury themselves in mud during the winter (as Dr Johnson believed they did), or that ptarmigan do not go mad after gooseberries? In fact there was so much genuine material available that only once or twice did I resort to fantasy – and the column gave me a legitimate reason for moving around the country, visiting projects and meeting characters of every description.

Our new surroundings, on the Cotswold escarpment, were agreeably rustic, and locals spoke much as they had in the 1930s when Evelyn

Waugh, living nearby, made the boy in *Scoop* who crashes the lorry say, 'It be the corners do for I'. A latter-day grave-digger sounded just the same. After he had opened up an 18th-century tomb to inter an old lady with her ancestors, and I asked why he had not replaced the heavy stone slab above her, he replied, 'Er'll be all right. Nobody don't want she for stew, do 'um?'

One particularly fertile source of subjects was (and is) Chas Wright, who in 1984 re-started our village brewery, founded in 1833 but derelict since 1900. A Falstaffian figure, big and bearded, with a penchant for wearing a French-type beret at his office desk, he knows every pub and practically every beer in the south of England. Once a distributor of Theakston's Old Peculier, he is now the producer of his own fine ales, all named after breeds of pig: Hogshead Bitter, Pig's Ear, Old Spot, Severn Boar. His business took off when Old Spot, his five percent strong ale, won first prize at the Great Western Beer Festival. Little did the organisers know what it was that had given the brew its special tang. When Chas found that the malt (barley) store had been invaded by mice, he swept everything up and tipped the harvest into the mash tun, droppings, spiders and all.

Chas it was who introduced me to Jasper Ely, a robustly old-fashioned character who had a small farm and cider orchard at Priding, hard by the bank of the Severn. Never marrying, Jasper had been many things – merchant seaman, river bailiff, fisherman, farmer, cider-maker. You could see that he'd been a sailor from the yachting cap which he wore indoors and out, on top of a halo of snow-white hair and beard. His language was salty, too: whenever BBC Radio Gloucester sent someone out to record him, his discourse had to be heavily censored before it could be broadcast. It was said – though I never asked him about it – that on his back an extensive tattoo depicted hounds running downwards after a fox, which was about to disappear into its earth at the bottom.

Revering old things, he had covered the front of his house with ancient enamel signs rescued from railway stations and other public buildings: Typhoo Tea, Bovril, LNER and so on. Hygiene was *not* the name of Jasper's game. Once when I found him in his kitchen, peeling onions for pickling, he pointed out the mark reached by flood water the last time the river had burst its banks: the muddy streaks were level with the table-top, and no re-decoration had been attempted.

I shall never forget a dank, November afternoon spent in his cider shed – a long barn, lofty but narrow, Hogarthian in its dinginess and clutter. Inside the entrance, on the right, stood huge oak barrels of cider and perry – the previous year's vintage. Beyond them, also on the right, were pigsties, walled off by wooden partitions about four feet high. Up at the far end of the shed two fair-haired youths clad in yellow oilskins were toiling at an ancient press, cranking away to force apple juice out of a sack of pulp, down into a tub.

The shed was full of noise, most of it generated by pigs in the sties over the wooden wall, and the air was suffused by an overwhelming smell – a combination of apple juice and manure powerful enough to knock new arrivals back on their heels. The stone-flagged floor was running with juice, through which two multi-coloured dogs kept skating. Whenever some newcomer arrived, a little old man with only one eye, who appeared to have no other function, announced in a squeaky voice: 'Old Spot sow wi' thir-een on 'er.' Every utterance was greeted by a volley of grunts and squeals, silenced only when someone tipped yet another bucket of apple pulp over the wall into the sow's trough.

Jasper, tankard in hand, was directing proceedings from a vantage point in front of one of the casks. Through the hubbub, supping steadily, he kept up a running dissertation on cider orchards, varieties of apple, cider making, sheep, the Severn Bore, the lave fishermen in the river, the construction of putchers (wicker traps for catching salmon) and a dozen other local topics. The orchards, he remembered, used to stretch from here to Gloucester, ten miles away. Now almost all were gone. 'Same with plums,' he said. 'Plums used to make good money – cos knock 'em off, and that was near enough.' Then, creating a magnificent quintuple negative, 'Trouble is, nowadays nobody don't want plums for jam nor bugger-all no more.' Next he was on to 'they old perry pears'. 'Pears is for heirs,' he pronounced, meaning that if you plant a perry pear tree, you will have to wait a human generation before it bears fruit. 'When it comes to cider apples, course, you've got to know what variety you want – Bloody Bastard, Early Treacle, Merrylegs, Jug Rumbles, Stinking Bishop ...'

As he talked, the cider he had pressed on me began to take effect: the air in the shed seemed to grow thicker, the light dimmer, the porcine outcry louder, the smell even more overpowering. Again the one-eyed ancient piped up, 'Old Spot sow wi' thir'een on 'er!' Suddenly Jasper gave a shout at the young fellows labouring on the press: 'Don't fuck about up there! Keep winding!' Re-filling his own tankard he remarked, 'Eight per cent, this lot. Some of the ladies don't like it. They reckon it's a bit bread and cheesy. Bloody hard luck. Perry's the stuff for they.' He described how, in the old days, cider makers would drop chunks of meat into the barrel, where the maturing liquor would dissolve them and gain more body. One year, he said, a whole family of rats fell in. What did he do about it? 'Nothing. The cider did yut 'em and we did drink 'em. Came to the same thing.' When I asked how he had acquired his farm, he gave an explosive snort: '*Bought* the bugger! They don't give 'em away, do they?'

Jasper was always worth a visit – and when he died more than 200 people crowded into the church at Arlingham. Farmers, brewers, publicans, solicitors, poachers, writers, fishermen – all kinds came to say farewell. After the service we packed into the Red Lion, where he had been wont to hold court; but although the air was alive with Jasper jokes, I felt a strong undertow of sadness, for everyone sensed that his spirit had gone down the shining river, and we would never see the like of him again.

Other rustic characters float up from the past, none merrier than the Oxfordshire farmer Jack Hatt. Six foot three, heavily built, ruddy of countenance and instantly recognisable from his magnificent sideburns, on which a preservation order had long been in force, he generally wore an old deerstalker hat bristling with trout and salmon flies, and walked with a pronounced limp – the result of a motorbike accident in youth, which mangled his left ankle.

The injury did nothing to slow him down: he was always fizzing with energy, and talking with inimitable gusto in short, quick-fire sentences. 'At the end of the war we wanted to get rid of some tree stumps. Great big sods, they were. Even with a tractor the job would have taken weeks. Heard about this fellow who blew things up down Salisbury way. Phoned him. Up he comes – little old chap. Drills a few holes, puts charges in 'em. Connects 'em up. 'Stand back,' says he. Pushes the plunger. BOOM! Up goes the bloody lot. Job finished. "What do I owe you?" says I. "Ninety quid," says he. Ninety quid! Blimey. That was a lot of money in them days. But he'd done the job in just a couple of minutes. '

The result of that episode was that Jack continued to farm but also branched out into explosives, blowing stumps, demolishing redundant buildings and creating lakes and ponds, with his business slogan 'Dam and Blast.' He soon became an expert hydraulic engineer, advising landowners all over the country on water-works old and new. No matter how busy he grew, he never abandoned his twin passions of fishing and shooting, at both of which he excelled. It was said (though I never saw it) that he was so quick with a shotgun that during a pheasant drive, using only one gun and rapidly re-loading after the first two shots, he could have three birds dead in the air at once. On river or loch he always fished with a fly, casting elegantly, and he never tired of relating how, in two nights at Testwood, near Southampton, he had once caught forty-five sea trout, the biggest a fourteen-pounder. 'Didn't that bugger go! In the middle of the night!'

As a raconteur he was priceless, and in constant demand as a speaker on festive occasions. Appearances at our annual village cricket dinners were eagerly anticipated, but we were always slightly anxious that he might overstep the bounds of decency and send the vicar creeping ashen-faced for the exit. Having downed a bottle of port with his main course, he was impossible to stop, and when he rose to speak, we all held our breath – as with the story of the red-headed girl on top of the corn stack. 'There she was with her pitchfork. Chucking the sheaves down into the thresher. Gives a sudden shriek. Mouse has run up her trouser leg. But quick as a flash he's down her other leg and away. You know why he didn't stop, don't you? Course you do! It was cos he'd seen her ginger pussy!'

Few of the stories I came across were stranger than that of Arthur Strutt, laird of Kingairloch, the 26,000-acre deer-forest in the wilds of Ardnamurchan, and his wife Patricia, one of the most bloodthirsty female deer-stalkers who ever took to the hill. On an autumn morning in 1977 Arthur walked out of the lodge carrying a hand-saw, to do some pruning in a forestry plantation – and never came back. His staff stayed up all night, waiting for him, and at first light went out to search. Soon they were reinforced by police, soldiers, an RAF helicopter, and the mountain-rescue team from Glencoe, with dogs trained to find climbers and hikers overwhelmed by avalanches, whether alive or dead. No trace of the missing man was discovered. Six months later, when the winter snows had melted, another major hunt also drew blank.

Five years on, a memorial service was held for him one Sunday at the church in Kingairloch. On the very next morning forestry contractors, prospecting the route for a new road through a plantation, found his skeleton, fully clothed, sitting propped against the trunk of a young tree less than half a mile from the house. By then it was impossible for the coroner to determine the cause of death – but men who had helped in the original search remained convinced that the body had not been at that spot when they first went through the wood. Another inexplicable fact was that the bones were still in perfect formation, and had not been pulled about by foxes or badgers.

It was well known that the Strutts had not been on the best of terms with each other, and scandalous rumours circulated – for instance that Patricia had had Arthur poisoned and that his body had been stored in the deep-freeze until the hunt died down, whereupon it had been put out again. Whatever the truth, she stayed on at Kingairloch, and every autumn she continued to stalk with fanatical enthusiasm, crawling forwards and backwards about the floor of her bedroom before the season opened, to strengthen her stomach muscles for the fray. She was a deadly shot, and by the time she died at the age of eighty-nine, she had killed over 2,000 stags.

To my great disappointment, I never met her. But I heard so much about her from Iain Thornber, a local historian who had taken her to the hill innumerable times, that I came to feel I had known her. I'm not sure that I would have liked her, but I would have loved to watch her in action on that magnificent high ground above Loch Linnhe and the Sound of Mull.

On our small-holding, the animals made good subjects – and none more often than Agamemnon, our first Wiltshire Horn ram. Ever since, as a lamb, he won a gold medal at our local agricultural show, he had had a high opinion of his own importance, and the older he got, the more aggressive he grew.

The first sign of trouble came one morning when Phylla, looking up the hill from her desk, saw a man flying head-first through the air, downhill over a fence, with the ram licking his lips in the background. Thereafter, we could not put him in any field that had a footpath running through it, for, with his curling horns and huge weight (maybe 250 lbs), he was quite capable of crushing to death anyone he managed to knock over.

One of his hobbies was smashing fence-posts – an expensive pastime, as they cost £2.50 each, and replacing them meant a lot of work. He took particular exception to my rotary mower – though whether it was the noise that annoyed him, or the fact that I ignored him while cutting the grass, it was impossible to tell. For him the machine seemed to be a *bête noire* – or rather a *bête rouge.* As I worked back and forth on the lawn, he would pace along his side of the fence, charging one post after another, leaping the last two feet of every assault in a single bound.

His apogee of bad behaviour occurred when I took him down to the Severn, on loan to Jutta, a German woman who ran a small-holding with her partner, known as Pineapple Pete. She wanted to borrow the ram to cover her Cotswold ewes – but I warned her, 'Just be careful. Don't trust him. If you see him licking his lips, watch out. And if he starts wagging his tail, stand clear.'

On the first night she rang to report that he was entirely peaceful. 'I don't know what you're worried about,' she said. 'He's standing in the stable like a lamb.' 'Good,' I said, 'but watch yourself.'

A couple of evenings later she rang again, her tone a great deal more urgent. 'Will you please take your ram away?'

'Well – I could come tomorrow ...'

'No. Now!'

'What's the matter?'

'He's got our neighbour up a tree ...'

After I had mentioned him in dispatches a couple of times, a woman in Norfolk wrote to the paper declaring that Ags (as we called him) was her 'favourite thug in the English language' – but he became more and more difficult. When we bought a younger ram, Rivet, as a possible successor, the two proceeded to fight in ritual combat. Like rugger players taking a place-kick, they would square up, back off half a dozen paces, take one step to the left ... and charge. As long as they met head-on, no damage was done; both would reel away dazed, until they had recovered enough for another bout. But then Rivet was caught awkwardly and suffered a broken back leg, which the vet declared irreparable, and I had to shoot him.

Maddening though Agamemnon could be, we were fond of him, for in his youth he had often behaved in endearingly ridiculous fashion. In some of his antics – high skips performed by an exceedingly stout party – there was a kind of heroic buffoonery. In the end, though, we decided he had become too dangerous, so we summoned the man from the local hunt, who despatched him with a humane killer and took his carcase away for the hounds – a sad end to a career full of excitement.

Usually I wrote about individual incidents or people, but any major rural event that took place was fair game – and none more so than the so-called Peasants' Revolt of 1997, when columns of marchers from all over country converged on Hyde Park to protest against the threat to rural sports and traditions posed by a Labour MP's anti-hunting bill. Having taken the train north, I joined members of the Lakeland contingent at Caldbeck, where John Peel is buried, and in the morning of 14 June we set off to walk twenty miles over the fells on the first leg of their journey south. Next morning the second column set forth from Coldstream. On the 22nd the Cornish team started from Madron, outside Penzance, and on the 27th, the Welsh marchers walked out of Machynlleth.

Their departure was marked by a strange, almost supernatural, incident. David Jones, their leader, and huntsman of the David Davies hounds, had just explained to a television journalist how a ban on hunting would put paid to the red kite – because farmers would scatter poison in carrion to keep foxes down. Hardly had he led off when one of the majestic raptors appeared: coming in fast from the right, the bird dived to within a few feet of the straggling crocodile and flew the length of the column with its head turned to one side as it scrutinised the 220 humans. When it reached the front, it dipped one wing and lifted away like a fighter aircraft, vanishing into the sky. If that was an omen, what did it portend?

Having walked some distance with each of the columns, I was enormously impressed by the energy, endurance, practicality, commitment and sheer good nature of the marchers. Many of them were hunting people, it is true, but many were not, and all were prepared to make an exceptional physical effort – as well as to lose anything up to a month's earnings – to demonstrate their beliefs. Each column had a nucleus or core of maybe twenty marchers, who had guaranteed that they would go all the way to London, but a great many more supporters attached themselves every morning for that day's stretch.

Coordination of the whole demanded a high degree of organisation, which was master-minded by Charles and Chips Mann, who farmed in Gloucestershire. Much also depended on the owners of large houses along each route who agreed to put up, and put up with, the core marchers for a night, when they arrived sweaty, hungry, thirsty and exhausted. The northern contingent developed a running joke, whereby they politely enquired of any host whether he or she had any old whisky that was in danger of going off. Most of the walkers behaved impeccably, but there were occasional lapses brought on by excessive consumption – as when Shān Legge-Bourke, generous hostess of the Welsh team at Glanusk, her home near Abergavenny, recorded, 'Only one of them missed the lavatory.'

The peasants' positive attitude to life was no less evident at the culminating rally in Hyde Park on 10 July, when a vast crowd of 120,000 demonstrated against the hunting bill. The great gathering seethed with emotion and anger, yet everyone behaved with perfect decorum, incensed though they were by the fact that the Prime Minister, Tony Blair, had sent a message of goodwill to a Gay Pride rally a week earlier, yet had felt unable to do the same on this much larger occasion.

After the rally I felt that the events of the summer should be properly commemorated, and with the backing of David Burnett, the publishing friend who had left London to set up his own firm in Ludlow, I wrote a short book which we called *When the Country Went to Town*. For author and publisher it was a labour of love – but sales picked up smartly when Roddy Fleming, one of the banking family and a fanatical hunting man, ordered 600-odd copies and arranged for one to be placed on the desk of every Member of Parliament.

One year, spotting in advance that April 1 would fall on a Saturday, I wote a lyrical description of the annual rat-shoot in the cellars under Harrods. Remarking that I had unaccountably not been invited to this premier sporting event, I described how the seven hot-shots were greeted on arrival by the Head Cellarar, dressed in plum-coloured velvet britches, who handed them a glass of champagne and invited them to choose a weapon from the cabinet of double-barrelled 410s specially built by Holland & Holland for the event in 1912.

The rats (I revealed) were driven by electronic goads from beneath pallets in the storage cellars, which extended far under Hyde Park, and the culminating massacre took place in the muesli block, where the fugitives had been concentrated. Depending on the prowess of the guns, a bag of 200 was possible; but the ancient custom of delivering the victims to the Zoo in Regent's Park had recently been discontinued, for fear that the inmates of the reptile house might be poisoned by lead shot.

How all this was received by the Harrods publicity department, and in particular by Mohamed al-Fayed, who had recently bought the store, I never discovered. But no recrimination followed, and I know that quite a few readers took my account as gospel. The same happened on another April 1, when I invented a race for Argo eight-wheel-drive, all-terrain vehicles, from Mallaig, on the West Coast of Scotland right across the mountains to the Findhorn estuary in the east. I managed to make proceedings so realistic that even my brother-in-law Gerry – a seasoned deer-stalker and SAS volunteer – was taken in.

What finished my long stint as Boot of the *Independent* was the outbreak of foot-and-mouth disease in the spring and summer of 2001. Until then I had depended on being able to range freely around the country, visiting land-owners, farmers, foresters, gamekeepers and others in pursuit of stories; then suddenly movement was severely restricted by emergency regulations, and subjects were harder to find. Even walking the dogs became a problem, as one was forbidden to use footpaths or cross fields. At home, on top of the hill, it was particularly galling to have to stick to the metalled lane while a flock of a hundred or more seagulls lifted lazily off one field and settled on another, inevitably spreading whatever germs were lurking on the ground.

Sad as I was to lose the connection, I found it a relief not to have to produce an article every week. But I had had a wonderful innings, of which the most intoxicating period came in 1989, when the circulation of the *Indie* passed 400,000, and we were breathing down the neck of *The Times*. To have overtaken the *Thunderer* after only three years in being would have been a phenomenal achievement. Alas – the powers-that-were decided to start a Sunday paper as well, and the move proved over-ambitious. The *Independent on Sunday* drew off so much money and talent that the circulation of the original gradually declined, never regaining its highest level – but at least I had had the fun and satisfaction of working for the paper in its glory days.

CHAPTER NINETEEN

In the Camp of the Mountain King
1986

Nepal again – but this time with a quite different assignment: to interview King Birendra Bir Bikram Shah Dev, incarnation of the god Vishnu, the only Hindu monarch in the world. My chance came about through my friendship with Tommy Stonor, whose family had lived at Stonor Park, near Henley-on-Thames, since time immemorial. Tommy, himself an Etonian, was chosen by the Foreign Office as a mentor for Birendra when the young prince was sent to the school in 1959. With some difficulty Tommy persuaded his parents, Lord and Lady Camoys, to let Birendra use Stonor as his home whenever he could not return to Nepal for short holidays. The arrangement worked well, and Tommy had maintained amicable contact with the royal family ever since. Now, in 1985, he arranged for me to meet the King, who had succeeded to the throne of Nepal a dozen years earlier.

Thus I arrived in Kathmandu in January 1986 with, as it were, a royal warrant, and I landed in the safe hands of Hemanta Mishra, then Deputy Head of Conservation in Nepal. Stocky, ebullient and highly articulate, with five times the energy of most of his compatriots, and with his vocabulary startlingly embellished by expressions picked up during an autumn working as a ghillie on a Scottish Highland deer forest, Hemanta proved an ideal companion.

The King, he explained, was out of town on one of his annual expeditions, during which he set up camp in the wilds so that he could inspect important development areas, galvanise the locals and see for himself how much was being achieved. With him went most of the

Cabinet and a small army of civil servants, all of whom, to their acute distaste, were obliged to spend weeks living rough at some god-forsaken place out in the sticks.

Because the palace had not given me a precise date, Hemanta proposed that we should go down for a few days to the jungle station in Chitwan where he was conducting research into the behaviour of rhinos, and there await a royal summons. A five-hour drive in a jeep brought us to a small working camp with basic accommodation but top-class Gurkha rum cocktails, which gladdened every evening as Hemanta struggled to make radio contact with the King's A.D.C. Maddened by interference, and by the signal coming and going, he would gabble out a stream of words in Nepali, which sounded like curried Italian, punctuated by occasional explosions: *Wurrawurrawurra*oforfuckssake! ... *Wurrawurra wurra*obuggeration! as he lost contact yet again.

Since the King seemed in no hurry, Hemanta decided to go ahead and dart one of the rhinos he was studying. The animal had managed to divest itself of the radio collar which researchers had fitted to monitor its movements, and they wanted to replace it.

'You shoot deer, don't you?' said Hemanta one morning. 'You shoot this bloody rhino' – whereupon he handed me a CapChur dart gun – a clumsy weapon with an effective range of only about forty yards, of which I had no experience. Before I could remonstrate, I was sitting on the neck of an elephant, jammed up against the back of the *phanit* (the Nepali version of a *mahout),* who steered his mount by jabbing it behind the ears with his big toes, and occasionally giving it a whack over the head with his *ankus,* a short iron bar. Gripping with my knees, I clutched a rope in my left hand and held the loaded gun vertically in my right, as we set off on a drive through thick scrub: five elephants in a crescent, about fifty yards from each other.

Far away to our right on the horizon the eternal snows of Annapurna and Manaslu gleamed like gigantic white teeth through the heat-haze of a perfect winter day. Our heavyweight beat sent jungle fowl toddling forward ahead of us, and grenade-bursts of five or six peacocks exploded into the air, squawking with alarm. For such large birds they had an amazing rate of climb, and their long tails glittered brilliantly in the sun as they powered away. Wild boar scuttled off with their tails stuck straight up in the air.

It was some time before Hemanta and his colleagues spotted our target. Then they recognised him by a split in his left ear, probably gained in a fight. He was standing on his own, glowering suspiciously about, having obviously heard the noise of our approach, but, with his short sight, not having spotted what was causing the disturbance.

Elephants do not like rhinos: they tolerate them at a distance, but not at short range. As we closed in, several of our party began to play up. My mount, having behaved perfectly so far, started to heave and dance about, turning from side to side. For one thing, this was very uncomfortable; and for another it meant that I had to keep lifting the rifle over the *phanit*'s head, shifting it from one side to the other in attempts to line up for a shot as he disciplined his great beast by cracking it over the head with his *ankus*.

Eventually we were within range – about fifty yards – with the rhino facing away from us. 'Go on!' cried Hemanta from a neighbouring elephant. 'Shoot!'

Aiming for the rhino's backside, which must have been five feet wide, I pulled the trigger. At that split-second my elephant gave another twitch, with the result that the dart, with its four-inch needle, landed not in one of the target's mighty buttocks but in the root of his tail.

'Firkinell!' cried Hemanta.

'Will it work?' I shouted back.

'I don't know. I've never seen that happen before.'

The rhino started, evidently aware that something untoward had occurred, but not sure what. Then he took off on a fifty-yard sprint, crashing through the scrub at a speed astonishing for a two-ton animal. Coming to a halt, he stood still. Then, after ten minutes he began to sway gently backwards and forwards as the cocaine-based M99 drug took effect, until at last he lay down on his front, with legs folded neatly underneath his chest.

Having bombarded him with sticks and provoked no reaction,

Hemanta got down and, as a final safety precaution, pulled his tail. No response. The rest of us then descended from our elephants and went cautiously up to him – an incredible hulk, if ever there was one. When I punched him on the shoulder, I fully understood for the first time the meaning of the word 'pachyderm': his skin was like knobbly armour plate, so thick and hard that I could only just feel that living flesh lay underneath. Looking at his great bulk, I thought of the bizarre traditional rite whereby every new king of Nepal had to shoot a rhino and then, with a royal priest in attendance, climb into the disembowelled carcase laid on its back, so that the monarch, dressed all in white, could offer its blood to his father.

In our less gory operation, speed was of the essence, for there was a danger that if our victim lay too long in any one position, his sheer weight would crush internal organs. The specialists therefore went quickly to work. As the rangers fitted a new radio on a thick strap around his neck, another man poured water over him to stop him over-heating, and Eric Dinastiner, a biologist from the Smithsonian Institution in Washington, measured his incisors. His head was tilted to one side, and when I asked the American if he would like me to roll it over, so that he could tackle the teeth on the lower side, he said, 'You can try, but I don't think you will.' Sure enough, it took three of us to turn the head and neck, which alone weighed several hundred pounds.

After twenty minutes Hemanta cried, 'Time's up!', and everyone remounted their elephants while he administered an antidote with an outsize hypodermic syringe. We watched from on high as the hulk stirred and struggled to his feet, before moving off, unsteadily at first, then at a normal pace. Hemanta announced that henceforth he would be known as Radio Duff: and even if the monotonous, two-tone call given out by his collar was not very entertaining, it would at least enable researchers to build up an accurate picture of his movements and his territory.

Next day, with no word from the royal camp, Hemanta proposed a similar operation with a tigress. Like the rhino, she had shed a radio collar, and he wanted to replace it. Early in the morning one of the rangers had seen her go into a block of tall grass, and as it seemed likely that she would lie up there for the day, the chances of catching her were good. The block was triangular, covering several hundred acres, with a clear track running down each side of it to the apex, which was formed by a stand of big trees with open ground beneath them. Along the tracks rangers set out white tapes, the idea being that the tigress, when driven by a line of beaters, would be funnelled by the unfamiliar decoration as she moved forward, until she passed under the trees, in which a dart-gunner would be perched.

After a heavy session on Gurkha rum the night before, Hemanta and I were both feeling a little fragile when, at mid-morning, we were decanted from elephant-back into one of the trees. 'Here you are,' he said, attempting to hand me the dart-gun. 'You shoot the bloody tiger.' 'No, thanks,' I replied – and I precluded further argument by scrambling higher into the branches, mindful of the fact that tigers can, if pressed, climb pretty well.

From aloft there was a good view straight down onto the bare floor of the clearing; but the grass, ten or twelve feet high, blocked our outlook to the front. If the tigress came forward as we hoped, we would not see her till the last minute.

We waited, in silence except for the harsh calls of hornbills. Sunlight filtered down through the leaves, and the temperature was comfortable. Then, in the distance to our front, an amazing cacophony broke out: shouts, whoops, yells, drum-beats and above all the sharp rattle of stones shaken in tin cans. Although we could not see them, we knew that ten elephants had started advancing towards us in line-abreast, and that each carried three or four noise-generating humans.

As the wall of sound edged closer, tension mounted. Directly below me in the tree Hemanta sat motionless in a fork, holding the dart-gun at the ready. After a few minutes, between the shouts, we could hear the *swash* as each elephant swept thick, dry stalks of grass down with its trunk, clearing itself a path.

Swash, crash went the elephants as they plodded on. *Swash, crash.* Still we could not see them, but soon, judging by the noise, they were no more than a hundred yards off. I had been hoping that the tigress – if she was there – would come forward steadily and give the chance of a shot; but now, I realised, she must be under intense pressure, and if she bolted, would come like a rocket.

Excitement built steadily. I found I was breathing fast. This, I thought, is exactly like a Victorian or Edwardian tiger shoot, except that we're trying to knock the quarry out rather than kill it. On came the elephants. Suddenly, from our left, one of them let fly a tearing scream. Moments later another trumpet-call erupted straight in front of us, then one to our right. The tigress was there, moving along the line, trying to break back.

The human beaters stepped up their racket. More elephants trumpeted. Their screams showed she was moving back to the left – and then suddenly at last out she came at full stretch, hurtling across our glade in a couple of bounds – a beautiful streak the colour of apricot jam. She was gone in a flash – far too quickly for Hemanta to aim or fire. A watcher outside the apex of the block behind us saw her sail over the white tapes to freedom. So the elaborate manoeuvre ended in anti-climax; but by heck, it had been thrilling.

A message from the King's ADC said we should move up to the royal camp, and after a drive of a couple of hours, we arrived there in the evening, Someone had warned Hemanta that the facilities would be fairly primitive – for instance, that it was the custom for the staff to dig communal drop-pit latrines, and that in the morning one might find oneself perched beside the Prime Minister or some other high Government official. We were therefore agreeably surprised to find that we had been allocated our own tent, with a private lavatory close-by. Our beds, we had to admit, were rather basic – each being a six-foot sheet of plywood resting on trestles.

We were given a fine welcome by a Gurkha colonel; but as we chatted, I noticed that he was looking me up and down with an air of anxiety (at

6′ 2″ I was about a foot taller than him). After a few minutes he said, 'I'm anxious about your bed. It's going to be too short for you.'

'Please don't worry,' I protested. 'I'm sure it will be fine. We've got sleeping bags – everything,'

'No, no,' he said. 'We must get it seen to.'

With that we went off to supper in the mess tent; and when we returned an hour later, we found that carpenters had been in action. My bed now consisted of two sheets of plywood carefully joined together, with an overall length of eight feet.

In the morning reveille was sounded at 7 am by a blast of music from Radio Nepal, roared out over the camp loud-speakers. Breakfast was *al fresco,* in a compound surrounded by canvas walls, where two cooks were labouring over a wood-fired clay stove. The Prime Minister was indeed present – a diminutive figure wearing a tweed jacket over his high-necked shirt and tight trousers, eating an omelette off a tin plate, at the walk.

The first event of the day was the opening of a new wire factory down in the Terai. As the royal party arrived in a Super-Puma helicopter – white, with two red bands along each side – the assembled throng rose to its feet, and the King appeared wearing a beautifully-cut jacket of cinnamon silk over his Nepalese shirt and trousers. He and Queen Aishwarya, in a pale mauve sari, advanced along a red carpet to a dais brilliant with crimson, yellow and bright blue. Ropes of marigolds snaked up and down its pillars. Garlands and gifts were presented, but the King and Queen merely touched them in token reception before they were whisked away by uniformed ADCs, and the monarch moved on to unveil a plaque.

The day's main target was the town of Birganj, close to the border with India. There, after a review of irrigation projects, the royal party proceeded to the sports stadium, which was a fantastic sight, packed with people inside and besieged by a multitude without. Altogether the crowd was estimated at 200,000, among whom I was the only *angres* (white man). From the royal box, high in the stands, the king gave a short address, which was greeted with polite applause; but then, with the start of a vast procession, real fervour burst out.

Anti-clockwise round the running track came a surging tide of humanity, with hands and banners waving. Some groups were from factories and agricultural enterprises, but most represented the manifold ethnic types that inhabit the central region of Nepal. There were aboriginal Tharus with crimson head-bands from the jungles of the Terai. There were Sikhs in orange turbans, and whirling dervishes from the hills. There were *jhankris,* or witch doctors, with shaking head-dresses of peacock plumes, gyrating wildly to the thud of their flat leather drums.

As each contingent came in line with the royal box, its members slowed down, as if to prolong their contact with majesty, heaping up garlands, dancing, playing instruments, above all shouting *'Jaya! Jaya! Jaya!'* - 'Live! Live! Live!' The roars rolled up in mighty waves. Raucous horn blasts and the rattle of primitive percussion seared through the general uproar. In that cauldron of national fervour the display went far beyond mere loyalty: it was adulation, worship.

That evening came the final celebration of the winter camp: Mess Night. The tents had been lit up like Blackpool, with festoons of coloured bulbs, oil lamps twinkling along the paths, and a huge log fire blazing before the royal pavilion. Bugle-calls sounded the arrival of Land-Rovers, and the royal party walked in along a red carpet, preceded by two bagpipers in full tartan regalia, squalling out a slow march. After a film show, the entertainment progressed to home-made cabaret, with members of the Government doing turns. Waiters plied the guests with whisky, rum, beer and chunks of a much-prized delicacy, wild boar.

Next came the dancers – exotic, barefoot creatures in long, sheath-like dresses of hot orange and gold. They looked like lissom girls, but someone whispered to me that half of them were men. Was that a joke? The undulating figures looked wildly exotic, with their high cheek-bones and boldly-painted eyes flashing in the firelight.

A call went out for all ranks to join the dance. Maybe it was the rum, or the wild boar, or the high, white moon overhead – whatever the cause, I suddenly found myself on the floor. Close contact proved that some at least of the dancers *were* men: their hands were rough, their bodies hard. Equally, some of them were girls, and excellent instructors.

The party really took off. The floor was packed. I found myself hand in hand with the little Prime Minister, spinning in some sort of Nepalese eightsome reel. A scuffle broke out. Royal ADCs burst in among us, carving out a circle. Into the space came the King and Queen, and as they danced everyone else smacked out the rhythm with their hands. Then another figure entered the ring: Crown Prince Dipendra, a lithe and skittish fourteen-year old, going like a dervish with the most sinuous of the dancing girls.

Next morning I was at last summoned to my audience. I hastily tried to make myself presentable by donning a blazer, rather crumpled after its sojourn in the jungle, and walked along duckboards into the royal enclosure. The first person I saw was the Queen, standing in the garden. Immediately there came into my head the scene at the annual dinner of the Nettlebed cricket club, when in our cups we performed a ribald version of the nursery rhyme 'Sing a song of sixpence', which ended up with most of the company silently miming the verses. I *knew* that the lines really went:

The Queen was in the parlour, eating bread and honey,
The maid was in the garden, hanging out the clothes ...

but I heard them as 'The *Queen* was in the garden ...' In my confusion I attempted a bow in her direction, fell off the duckboards and tottered into the King's office tent.

He received me with the utmost friendliness and civility. Wearing an open-necked shirt, with two orange ball-points stuck in the breast pocket, and speaking perfect English with no trace of an accent, he was far more lively and amusing than his unbending public posture would give anyone to expect. He sent greetings to friends in England, and emphasised how much he was looking forward to the imminent visit of Queen Elizabeth and the Duke of Edinburgh, who were due to call in on their way to New Zealand in the New Year.

When I asked how he looked back on his time at Eton, he replied that he wouldn't have missed it for anything, because it had given him an understanding of British values. He talked freely of Nepal's problems –

the poverty of the hill villages, the lack of communications and medical facilities, and – most serious of all – the deforestation of the hillsides, which meant that every monsoon washed millions of tons of irreplaceable topsoil down into the rivers and rendered further cultivation impossible on the denuded slopes.

I asked if he thought that, at some time in the future, roads would be built to every village, and he said, 'No – it can't be done. The terrain is just too difficult.' I mentioned the tremendous enthusiasm manifest at the Birganj rally. 'That feeling exists throughout Nepal,' he replied. 'It's just there. I don't have to go to a big rally to find it. I can walk into a village house, and it's there. But this in itself creates a great responsibility. Between the people and myself there is an inner understanding – a trust – and I have to do what I can to live up to it. To them I represent Vishnu, the Preserver – and that's how I see myself, as the preserver of our country.'

When I asked why a monarch as modern as he should perpetuate the ancient, initiation ritual of entering the rib-cage of a dead rhino, he replied with engaging simplicity: 'It's something that every king has to do once in his life-time, and I just felt I ought to do it. No matter how aloof you may pretend to be, you're part of nature, and this was a way for me to make close contact with the natural world.'

For a final question, I asked why it was that such a deep friendship existed between his kingdom and Britain. 'Through the Gurkha connection, obviously,' he replied. 'Our people have been fighting for you for 150 years. But I think it's also because we were never colonised, and don't have any chip on our shoulder.'

Back in England, I wrote an enthusiastic article, which was prominently displayed in the *Sunday Telegraph* on 16 February 1987. I was delighted to hear that when the Queen and Prince Philip came down the steps of their aircraft at Kathmandu next morning, she was carrying a copy of the paper, and that she greeted King Birendra with news of a marvellous article about him and Nepal which had just appeared in England. Little can either sovereign have suspected that the author had set up the project partly in order to secure an exotic winter holiday.

I never saw Hemanta again, for he went off to live in America, where he worked for leading conservation bodies, including the Smithsonian Institution and the World Wildlife Fund. In 2008 he published *The Soul of the Rhino,* an admirably thorough study of the animal to which he had devoted much of his career.

King Birendra was less fortunate. In June 2001, at a party in one of the Kathmandu palaces, his son Crown Prince Dipendra, crazed by drugs and alcohol, ran amok and shot nine members of the royal family, including the King and his wife. Having caught a glimpse of the immense popularity which Birendra had enjoyed, I sensed that the massacre would be the beginning of the end for the royal family – and so it proved. His brother Gyanendra succeeded as King, but he was widely detested, and in 2006 he was forced to abdicate. Nepal became a federal republic, riven by competing political parties.

CHAPTER TWENTY

War Stories
1991-2005

Ghosting strikes me as a slightly degenerate activity, less admirable than original writing. Telling someone else's story is less demanding than telling one's own. On the other hand, it requires a certain amount of skill and a good deal of tact, and it puts one in close contact with interesting people. Also, it can be financially rewarding: if publishers come begging help get a story into print, brandishing large cheques, it is difficult to refuse their overtures. The disadvantage is that, if you keep your name off a ghosted book, as I always have, you disappear from public view for the duration and appear to be producing nothing.

At the end of October 1991 I got a call from General Sir Peter de la Billière, asking if I would drive over to discuss a book on which he was working. I was immediately intrigued because, although I did not know him well, having met him only a few times, I had read and heard accounts of his legendary exploits as a leader of the SAS; and now he had crowned his military career with his successful command of British forces in the first Gulf War. If that was the subject of his book, it surely was a first-class project, and I jumped at it. He lived only an hour away, so I said, 'Certainly I can come over. When are you thinking of?'

'Tomorrow afternoon?'

'No problem.'

'There's just one thing. I'm afraid I haven't read any of your books. Could you bring a couple with you?'

'Of course.'

I don't think anyone meeting Peter for the first time could guess that he was the most highly-decorated officer in the British Army, with a DSO, two MCs and a cluster of other medals. At 57 he was slender, wiry, quick-moving and self-deprecating, with a schoolboyish sense of humour – epitomised by his habit, while at Harrow, of tossing a handful of live .22 bullets into the fire in a friend's study and then departing just before they started to explode, showering the room with red-hot coals

Together with his wife, Bridget, he welcomed me to their handsome, Georgian farm house in Herefordshire. I knew nothing about Bridget, except that she too came from a family with military background; but after introductions, I handed her the two books which I had brought – one of them my biography of Peter Fleming – and she settled her own Peter and me with cups of tea in arm chairs in front of the fire at one end of the long drawing-room.

Our conversation went easily. Peter explained that he wanted to produce a personal account of the Gulf war, but that as he himself 'had never been very good at joined-up writing', he had engaged the services of a colonel versed in Army public relations. The arrangement had not worked: the colonel could not hit the tone Peter wanted, and he was now looking for someone else to take the job over. There were, he emphasised, certain difficulties, not least the fact that some of his material was classified: he was anxious not to contravene the Official Secrets Act, and any typescript would have to be submitted to both the Ministry of Defence and the SAS for clearance. I said I did not think that should produce any serious problem.

He talked until dusk, letting fall many riveting details about the war, during which he had worked alongside the American Commander-in-Chief of the Allied forces, the 6'3", 17-stone General Norman Schwarzkopf, known to the American contingent as 'the CinC' (*Sink)* – Commander in Chief – but to others as 'Stormin' Norman.' Peter gave no hint that he himself had ever done anything out of the ordinary, in this latest war or earlier; on the contrary, he assigned credit for any success to colleagues with whom he had served. His narrative did, however, reveal what an enormously challenging task his Gulf command had been.

By glancing to my right I could see that Bridget, sitting at the other end of the room, was concentrating intently on one of my books, and I kept thinking that, apart from the fact that I had written a good deal, my only qualification for acting as ghost to a general would be that I had gained some slight military experience from two years of National Service. Then, as Peter began to wind down and say, 'Well – many thanks for coming over. We'll have to let you know ...' I looked right again and saw that Bridget was making vigorous, thumbs-up gestures.

Picking up her message, Peter instantly changed his tune. 'Cancel that,' he said, with a disarming grin. 'I think you'd better do it.'

So began a winter of intensive work. After a second, longer session I sketched an outline of the book, and – partly because of the author's reputation, partly because there was intense public interest in the war – we secured a substantial contract from the leading international publishers Harper Collins. With typical generosity Peter insisted that I should get forty per cent of whatever the project earned.

The war had been started by Saddam Hussein, dictator-president of Iraq, who, at the beginning of August 1990 had sent 100,000 troops to invade his southern neighbour Kuwait. In response to this unprovoked aggression, America, Britain, France, Saudi Arabia and Qatar formed a Coalition to evict the invaders. From the start this was a tri-service operation, with air forces, ground troops and warships all contributing. Among Peter's qualifications for the job of British commander-in-chief was the fact that, as Military Commissioner in the Falkland Islands during the 1980s, he had held a previous tri-service command. Furthermore, he also served and fought in several Middle Eastern countries, knew Arabs, and spoke colloquial Arabic. For him, as he said later, the war was 'another Arabian adventure.'

Again and again I drove into Herefordshire for marathon recording sessions, bringing with me drafts of what I had written since my last visit. Peter proved a lucid and accurate raconteur, and all I had to do was to smooth out his narrative into a readable text. Our only slight disagreement came at the beginning. My instinct was to kick the book off with some action-packed incident in the desert, and then revert to the circumstances of Peter's appointment to command the British forces; but Bridget insisted that we should start at the start – the point at which she and Peter heard on the car radio that Saddam Hussein's forces had invaded Kuwait. Looking back, I think she was right. In any case, Peter agreed, and we went from there.

For day after day we sat at a table in the window of the dining room, with icy draughts from the 18th-century casement whistling about our knees. In recounting his war he had one priceless private source of information: the brief letters he had written to Bridget during the campaign. Forbidden, like all servicemen, to keep a diary, he had managed to scribble a few lines in a blue air letter almost every day, never giving away anything of importance, but recording enough of his movements to provide invaluable *aides memoires* after the war, and these kept his narrative on track.

His war headquarters were on the first floor of a modern office block in the Saudi capital, Riyadh, which frequently came under attack from Saddam Hussein's Scud missiles, and for the first few weeks he had to live in the five-star Sheraton Hotel, in the city centre, which he much disliked. Then he settled into a villa normally reserved for employees of a bank: the house was in a compound, and with it, to his delight, came a swimming pool, in which he tried to put in twenty or thirty lengths first thing every morning.

His aim was to visit as many of his soldiers, airmen and sailors as possible, and he kept constantly on the move, dropping in on ships, airfields and army units in the desert. He was greatly helped by the loan of an HS125 seven-seat executive jet, which enabled him to cover immense distances with minimal fatigue, and he dealt with an amazing variety of people, from the rulers of the Gulf States to the humblest squaddie in a slit trench. Several times he took his sleeping bag with him and spent the night on the sand in the desert – which he described as 'a welcome reversion to an earlier way of life.'

Most of the information for the book came directly from him, but he also arranged for me to meet some of his outstanding commanders, among them Brigadier Patrick Cordingley (Commander, 7th Armoured Brigade), Commodore Christopher Craig, (Senior Naval Officer Middle East) and Lieutenant Colonel Arthur Denaro, Commanding Officer of the Queen's Royal Irish Hussars (and another SAS stalwart) – all highly impressive men.

As Peter put it, the Coalition's initial task was 'to create out of thin air an immense, multi-national force with which to repel a criminal lunatic whose vast army was dug in along the frontier [between Iraq and Kuwait] barely 200 miles to the north.' Much of his narrative described the gradual build-up and training during the autumn and winter of 1990. Then, after months of preparation, the air war kicked off in the early hours of 17 January 1991, as allied aircraft and Cruise missiles launched all-out attacks on Saddam's communications facilities, air bases and Scud launch sites. By breakfast time that morning 352 sorties had been flown, and only one aircraft lost.

For five weeks the air war continued relentlessly, with low-level attacks by the Coalition fighter bombers reinforced by high-level, attritional bombing by giant B-52s. After this prolonged softening-up, the ground war at last began on Sunday, 24 February, when, at 0400, Arthur Denaro, a keen hunting man, set his tanks in motion across the Iraqi frontier with the order 'Move now!' and a yell of 'Tally Ho!' as an old dog fox jumped up ahead of the leading Challenger.

The conflict that followed proved surprisingly short. After only five days of what Saddam had promised what would be 'the mother of battles', his army was routed and destroyed. Later, much controversy raged over the Coalition's decision not to press further into Iraq and take Baghdad; but Peter agreed with Schwarzkopf's decision to stop short, pointing out that, among other things, Saddam would have evaded capture by fleeing to some safe haven.

All this he described without inhibition; but when he began to talk specifically about Special Forces – of which he had been Director from 1978 to 1982 – I sensed that we were on more difficult ground. In the middle of January, against the inclination of Stormin' Norman, he had become determined to insert SAS patrols deep into the Western Desert of Iraq, the principal aim being to prevent Saddam deploying mobile launchers to fire more Scud missiles into Israel. Then, and later, Peter was convinced that one or two more Scuds landing in Tel Aviv or Haifa might have provoked Israel into full-scale retaliation against Iraq, and that any major intervention by Israeli forces would fatally damage the Coalition.

In a separate operation, a patrol by the Special Boat Service succeeded in blowing up a stretch of the main Iraqi communications network and carrying off a section of cable – a success which delighted Schwarzkopf and vindicated Peter's use of special forces. Then in the Western Desert the vehicle-mounted patrols which he sent in achieved such a success in hunting and destroying mobile Scud launchers that after 26 January no further missiles were fired at Israel. But two eight-man patrols fared less well. One, flown deep into enemy territory by Chinook helicopter, was aborted immediately when the commander opted to return to base, having seen the extremely dangerous nature of the landscape, which was lethally open and quite without cover.

The second patrol, designated Bravo Two Zero, was also flown in at night, and went to ground in a dry wadi, where the eight men lay up for most of the next day; but then, in the afternoon, a goat-herd stumbled on their position, and they were forced to make a run for it, leaving behind their food, water and almost all their kit in their heavily-loaded bergens.

Having put in a feint to the south – back towards the Kuwait border – they turned north and marched all-out, but in the dark the patrol split. After numerous evasive measures, two men died of hypothermia, one was shot and four were captured, leaving a single man, a Geordie corporal called Chris Ryan, on his own. Heading north, he aimed to reach the Euphrates, and then to follow the river north-west until he reached the border of Syria, where he hoped he would be safe.

Afterwards, his escape was reckoned one of the most heroic that any SAS man had ever made. For seven nights he walked in freezing temperatures, and for seven days he lay up in the hostile desert, without food or water, hunted by hundreds of Iraqi troops. By the end he was *in extremis,* nearly dead from hunger and thirst, plagued by hallucinations, his feet pulped – but sheer guts, and the arduous training he had done before the campaign, carried him through to freedom.

Knowing of his epic feat, Peter was keen to include some account of it his book – especially as it redounded to the credit of the SAS. I expected that the Regiment, with its habitual avoidance of publicity, would turn down our request for an interview – but in fact it was quickly granted, and I met Ryan at SAS headquarters in Hereford.

Anticipating some degree of supervision or censorship, I was agreeably surprised when his commanding officer ushered us into the spacious, semi-circular auditorium of the lecture theatre and left us alone. We sat side by side in the centre of the front row. After minimal introductions I switched on a tape-recorder and invited Chris to talk. He proved an admirable raconteur, and he told his story so well that I hardly ever needed to ask a question. When I came to write his words down, the narrative flowed, and although a good many expletives had to be deleted, it made an excellent, self-contained chapter.

The whole text of the book amounted to 140,000 words – enough for a substantial tome – and Collins at once began to prepare it for publication. Meanwhile we submitted it for clearance to both the SAS and the Ministry of Defence. The Regiment came back promptly with some reasonable requests for excisions – which we made – but the MoD prevaricated endlessly. Word came out that someone in the building had run-off ninety copies of the typescript, and any number of bureaucrats, having scrutinised every syllable, made demands for fiddling changes that seemed designed only to enhance the roles that functionaries in the Ministry had played during the conflict. We agreed to change or omit anything that might conceivably be damaging, but refused to meet the more meretricious requests.

In advance of publication we sold serial rights to the *Sunday Telegraph,* and it was no surprise that the newspaper chose as one of its extracts the story of Chris Ryan's escape. But as Collins's deadline drew near, the MoD still declined to give clearance for the book as a whole. Stalling to the last, they never did give the go-ahead. Collins published without it, under the title *Storm Command,* and no official recrimination followed.

The result was highly gratifying: interest in the Gulf War, and in Peter's role in it, was so strong that the book went straight to the head of the *Sunday Times* best-seller list and stayed there for weeks, selling 80,000 hardback copies. Flushed with this success, Collins commissioned Peter to write his autobiography – and so we once again got down to work.

The material for the second book was no less rich than for the first, and the title I conceived for it – *Looking for Trouble* – accurately described its author's main preoccupation in life. From the moment when three boys were killed in a fire at his prep school, his life had been full of incident and danger.

In 1953, by falsifying his age – by pretending he was nineteen when still only eighteen – he had managed to take part in the Korean War as a platoon commander in the Durham Light Infantry, and it was in the desperate night-fighting with the Chinese that he learnt to control his fear. After service in Egypt he transferred into the SAS, and sought out danger wherever he could find it – fighting terrorists in the Malayan jungle, then rebels on the heights of the Jebel Akhdar in Oman, where, as a 24-year-old troop commander, he won his first MC.

In the secret Dhofar campaign of the early 1970s he played a prominent role in the SAS's successful struggle to turn back the tide of Communism from Southern Arabia, and was awarded a DSO. After commanding 22 SAS, in 1978 he rose to be Director of the SAS Group, and in that role he commanded the highly-charged siege of the Iranian Embassy in Kensington in May 1980, as well as, in 1982, the deployment of SAS patrols in the Falkland Islands six weeks before the main landings. There followed a – for him – relatively quiet assignment as Military Commissioner and Commander of British Forces in the Falklands, which were still settling down after the war. As his tour there was coming to an end in the autumn of 1990, he was beginning to make plans for retirement, when suddenly Saddam Hussein's forces invaded Kuwait, and presented him with what he called the biggest challenge of his life.

He had any number of hair-raising escapades to recount, none more gripping than the SAS's assaults against rebels established on Jebel Akhdar, the Green Mountain, in Oman. During that campaign, conducted in pulverising heat, the British became immensely fit, going up and down the great mountain, in the memorable phrase of Peter's comrade-in-arms Tanky Smith, 'quick as a whore's drawers'.

In the first night attack, having led his troop up precipitous slopes, Peter reached his objective just before dawn and deployed his men among rocks within range of the rebels' headquarter cave. As the light came up, he waited till several *adoo* (enemy) had emerged, then gave the order to fire. The SAS opened up with rifles and Bren guns, augmented by heavier fire from a rocket launcher and a Browning .30 machine gun which Tanky had managed to borrow. After a lively battle the raiders withdrew without serious casualties, leaving some twenty enemy dead. A month later, another desperately strenuous nocturnal raid – which even Peter described as 'a supreme physical effort' – finally flushed the rebels from the plateau on top of the mountain, and put an end to the crisis threatening Oman.

Soon after *Storm Command* came out, Peter and Bridget gave a dinner party to which they invited the survivors of Bravo Two Zero, the patrol which had been broken up – together with their wives and girlfriends. Generous and well-meant as it was, the occasion was not altogether a success. Peter himself carved a magnificent leg of pork, bred on his farm, and there was a certain amount of superficially cheerful banter; but there was also an undercurrent of tension, for the guests were not used to dining in the home of a senior officer, and memories of their mates who had been lost were still raw. As the survivors left, one of them, a sergeant, muttered to me, 'Well – the general's written a book. *I'm* going to write a fucking book, as well.' 'Good on yer,' I replied. 'Go for it.'

So he did. Andy McNab's *Bravo Two Zero,* his account of the patrol, came out in 1993, and became an enormous best seller – as did Chris Ryan's story of his escape, *The One that Got Away,* published in 1995.

Other books about SAS operations soon followed – and undoubtedly it was the appearance of *Storm Command* which set this train in motion and touched off a highly disagreeable reaction.

From members of the SAS, present and past, Peter came under fire for having broken the tradition whereby its members never wrote about the Regiment. He defended himself vigorously by pointing out (a) that the SAS had helped him with research, not least by allowing me to interview Chris Ryan; (b) that his text had been submitted to, and cleared by, both the SAS and the MoD; (c) that he had excised any passage that was considered a threat to security, and (d) that he had given £10,000 of his royalties to the SAS Association. This silenced some critics, but others remained implacably hostile, maintaining that *any* public description of special forces' methods was unacceptable, as it gave away potentially damaging information about methods and tactics from which intelligent enemies might gain some advantage.

The result was that the Regiment turned its back on its most celebrated hero, and banned Peter from its headquarters in Hereford. This, for him, was a bitter blow – and one which caused him lasting hurt. The ugliest manifestation of hostility occurred in August 2003 when he went to the funeral of Tanky Smith, his old troop corporal and close friend, with whom he had fought so memorably in Malaya, on the Jebel Akhdar and elsewhere. He and Bridget were allowed to attend the service in church, which was outside the barracks, but when they went on to the wake, in SAS headquarters, a senior officer came up to Peter and told him he was not welcome there. Arthur Denaro, who was standing nearby and overheard the conversation, was so shocked that he walked out with the de la Billières, taking his wife Maggie with them. Other contemporaries were no less deeply disgusted, and deplored such insensitive behaviour; but for the time being the Regiment could not find the magnanimity to relent. Besides, a new edict barred all members from ever writing about their experiences.

I myself got a taste of the prevailing bitterness when least expecting it. At one of the cricket matches staged by J. Paul Getty II on his lovely ground at Wormsley, in the Chilterns, guests had lunch, as usual, in a marquee poised on the raised lawn above the boundary. As we stood up from our round tables at the end of the meal, I found myself back-to-back with Viscount Slim, son of the celebrated second world war commander Field Marshal Slim, and at that date second-in-command of the SAS. When we both turned round and someone said, 'Oh – do you know Duff Hart-Davis?', Slim replied loudly, 'HOW VERY NICE TO MEET YOU. GOODBYE' – with which he spun round on his heel and walked off.

Naturally I was dismayed to have played a part in damaging an unique reputation. But whenever someone told me that I should not have helped Peter write his books, I replied that he was determined to go ahead with them, and that if I had not lent a hand, he would have found somebody else to dot his i s and cross his t s.

I am glad to say that we have remained good friends. In 2005 we collaborated on another book, *Supreme Courage,* his study of the Victoria Cross and its winners, published to mark the 150th anniversary of the medal. This never achieved the roaring success of his two best-sellers, partly because the subject was a difficult one to encompass, and partly because so many other authors had been mining the same seam. Yet it did enable Peter to examine a subject that had long fascinated him – the nature of courage – and to remind readers, with characteristic understatement, that courage is a quality which he himself has always possessed in exceptional abundance.

It is good to be able to record that in October 2017 the Regiment at last agreed to lift the ban which had blighted Peter's retirement, and re-admitted him to its ranks.

CHAPTER TWENTY-ONE

A Few Shots
1990s

I was born with a strong hunting gene, and an urge to spend as much time as possible out of doors. Where this came from, it is hard to say, for my father had no wish to shoot any bird or animal, and took as little exercise as possible. If ever a book-worm existed, it was he. My mother was intensely practical, but she too neither shot nor fished. Luckily I inherited some of her energy, and spent as much time as possible playing cricket and football, or, when at home, pursuing game.

In this I was strongly encouraged by Peter Fleming, on whose estate we lived in the Chilterns. When I was twelve, he began taking me with him on two-man shooting forays, and we devoted countless autumn and winter afternoons to what he called 'death marches', patrolling outlying stretches of his 2,000 acres in search of partridges, pheasants, pigeons and rabbits. I also spent much of my school holidays with Harry Brown, the gamekeeper, going round his vermin traps, ferreting rabbits and lying in wait for crows – and from these activities I derived a lifelong fascination with birds, animals and nature in general.

Now that ninety per cent of British people live in cities or towns, it is not surprising that a high proportion of them disapprove of field sports, for they retain no trace of the instinct which upon which our distant ancestors depended for survival. On the other hand, those who do still have the hunting gene find it hard to explain to urban types why they enjoy killing birds and animals.

With the notable exception of grouse-shooting, which actively promotes the conservation of heather moorland, bird shooting –

especially the massacre of reared pheasants or partridges – is hard to justify. One can argue that well-run lowland shooting estates enhance the landscape, because hedges and woods are planted and maintained to encourage game, and that by suppressing predators such as foxes, rats, crows and magpies gamekeepers promote the welfare of many desirable bird species. Such benefits, however, carry little weight against accusations of excess.

Hunting people justify their activity by saying that it keeps the fox population down. This is true up to a point. But what they should admit is that being carried across country faster than one would wish, with the chance of getting seriously injured or even killed at any moment, is extremely exciting. This is the real point of hunting: the thrill and the danger. The exercise is a ludicrously expensive form of predator reduction, and even though hunts do help keep down fox numbers, especially in hill country like Wales, control by snaring and night-shooting is far more cost-efficient.

Deer control, in contrast, needs no defence, for in Britain it is an ever-more-essential activity. The number of deer is constantly increasing, and the animals, graceful though they are, inflict severe damage on crops and trees. For more than half a century I have actively pursued fallow, roe and muntjac in the wooded hills of Oxfordshire and the Cotswolds, and red stags on autumn migrations to many a Highland forest. I do not regret having spent thousands of hours walking, creeping, crawling, sitting in wait, on the ground or in high seats, on culling operations in lowland woods and on Scottish mountains. On how many hundred winter dawns have I eagerly watched deer come over the skyline on their way back to the wood, black silhouettes outlined against a glowing red sky? How many times have I been drawn by the magical sound of a fallow buck calling in the rut, or a red stag roaring across the glen?

As I have already written about stalking in my book *Among the Deer,* here I will just record three bird-shooting expeditions sharpened by the fact that they took place in countries that were Communist, or had recently been so.

Siberia

Partridges in Siberia? It sounded improbable, but worth a punt – and so it was that in August 1990 I found myself on board a flight to Moscow, in the company of Ian Haddon, from Somerset, Chairman of the National Woodcock Club, and Peter Bromley, the well-known BBC racing correspondent. We were guests of Roxtons, the agency which arranges game-shooting, and was then hoping to establish operations in Russia, where President Gorbachev's *perestroika,* or restructuring of the political system, was well under way. Our destination was Charysh, a small town on a river of the same name in the southern Altai Mountains, some 1,500 miles east of the Soviet capital, where, it was said, we could shoot unlimited numbers of partridges, blackcock and quail.

I knew neither of my companions, but before we left England I rang up my wife's cousin John Oaksey, the celebrated amateur jockey and racing commentator, to ask what sort of a fellow Peter Bromley was. 'Oh,' said John, 'he's quite OK, but watch him, as he's sometimes likely to throw a wobbly.'

On the British Airways plane Peter showed no sign of nerves; nor did Ian. Both were friendly, and we had a convivial flight. In Moscow, however, we hit trouble, for Roxtons had mentioned that the area for which we were heading held Maral – very large red deer – besides game birds, and Ian had brought along a handsome new .308 match rifle, besides a shotgun. This was too much for the Customs official, who said, 'One weapon only', and after a brisk argument Ian was obliged to leave the rifle behind.

Our onward flight to Barnaul was anything but convivial. We left Moscow in the middle of the night, with our biological clocks already three hours adrift, and droned on eastwards for three-and-a-half more hours. The Aeroflot jet was noisy and cramped, but easily its worst feature was that one or more of the lavatories, at the back, had got blocked, with the result that a devastating stink crept inexorably forward through the cabin. Luckily our seats were in the front row, as far as possible from the source of the smell, but even so the atmosphere became highly unpleasant.

Only the miniatures of whisky and ginger ale which we had brought along enabled us to survive in a relatively cheerful state.

It was a huge relief when the sky began to lighten and the plane started its descent. I was much stirred by glimpses of the mighty River Ob, winding northwards through gigantic bends and ox-bows on its 2,000-mile course to the Arctic Ocean. In the dawn there was something epic and doom-laden about the size of it, the seventh longest river on earth.

Staggering out into fresh air at Barnaul, we were surprised to see a Lufthansa cargo plane sitting on the tarmac – a reminder that there was a large German colony in the town, and that their supplies were regularly flown in. We were met by the young and friendly Yevgeny, speaking excellent English, who announced himself as our guide for the whole trip, got us some coffee and rolls for breakfast (by then it was 7 am) and bundled us into a modern 4 x 4 vehicle.

Four hours later, and 150 miles to the south-east, we were decanted at our hunting camp – a scatter of wooden huts in a grassy meadow. Stunned though we were by the journey, we were no less stunned by the landscape: a river running swiftly beside our camp field, and grey-green mountains on every side: immense open spaces, with not a house in sight. No wonder some Swiss said that the Altai mountains were like the Alps before tourists discovered them.

The huts were so new that the untreated wood was still beautifully pale: our living quarters, which had four bedrooms, a central room, a bathroom and a separate lavatory, smelt deliciously of fresh pine. Across the grass was another large hut containing a dining-room, and a kitchen occupied by two splendid girls, who seemed to spend most of their time paralysed by fits of laughter. This was quite understandable, for we were the first Westerners that they, or any of the men, had ever seen.

The environment was on a grand scale. Our camp in the valley was about 2,000 feet above sea level, but all round it the mountains went up to 6,000 feet or more, making me think of the Brecon Beacons writ large. When asked about the size of the area over which we had permission to shoot – How many hundred hectares? How many thousand? – our hosts could give no answer: there were no limits, and we could go wherever we liked.

There were no farm animals, and no fences; some areas in the hollows of the hills had grown corn and been harvested, but most of the land was untouched, covered with coarse, knee-high grass, among which grew a great variety of herbs – oregano, licorice, bergenia, Jacob's ladder and the aphrodisiac golden root, which our companions cheerfully described as 'good for making babies.' We occasionally saw people out picking the herbs, no doubt for medicinal and general culinary purposes, but often just for *Altaiski chai* - Altai tea.

A pattern was quickly formed. After breakfast we would set out in military-type, cross-country vehicles and drive to some vantage point. Each of us was assigned a beater-cum- picker-up (probably armed), and we would walk in line-abreast, with a couple more beaters spread between us, several of them with dogs, all out of control. In truth, there was very little to shoot: we did see one good covey of partridges, and quite a few blackcock and quail, and one morning Peter shot what he claimed was a partridge, but turned out to be a corncrake. Most of the birds were put up out of shot by the ill-disciplined dogs ranging far ahead. If we returned to base exhausted with a bag of half a dozen, we felt we were doing well. The strange fact was that game-birds seemed to be out-numbered by raptors – goshawks, sparrowhawks, kestrels – which we saw every day. One day, in the far distance, we spotted three very large red deer – almost certainly Maral – which made Ian mourn the confiscation of his rifle.

We had expected Siberia to be cold, but in fact the weather was fine and hot – 25 C or more during the day – so that in the evening a visit to the ramshackle hut which housed a sauna, and to the totally *al fresco* shower close by it, was very inviting. The girls proved excellent cooks, and I still have delicious memories of their blackcock casserole. We were amused to find that they both slept jammed up against each other like sardines in a tiny cubicle – little more than a horizontal slot in the kitchen wall. With no shortage of vodka and wine, we had rollicking evenings in the big dining room; as we were the first non-Communists with whom the local hunters had made contact, they were eager to find out how shooting was conducted in England, and Yevgeny was constantly called-upon to translate technical terms. They were also very curious about the person they called 'your first lady' – not the Queen, but Margaret Thatcher.

We were equally curious about life in Siberia, and asked, particularly, what things were like in winter. The answer was that once the snow had come in November, it stayed right through until the spring, lying maybe a metre deep, and the surface of the river froze so hard that lorries could drive over it. In that case, what happened to all the birds? Did partridges migrate? It seemed unlikely, and yet some survived.

By the third day we were getting a little tired of walking hard with scant result; but we had noticed that a high, vertical face in a hill beyond the river was alive with rock pigeons; and when Ian asked if we could tackle them, the answer was 'Of course'. So across the river we went, on board a lorry which forded the stream without difficulty, and proceeded to have a tremendous shoot. The birds were flitting about the rock face, in and out of caves, and offered challenging targets. My clearest memory is of scrambling up on to a ledge; as I was about to peer over the side, a shot went off below, immediately followed by a sharp hiss as pellets zipped up vertically past my nose. We went back to camp with a bag of thirty birds, some of which we ate, but most of which we distributed among our retainers, to their surprise and delight.

Next day Ian expressed a wish to shoot capercaillie. 'No problem,' said Yevgeny. 'We will go to a special forest. There you will shoot capercaillie and hazel grouse.' We set off at mid-day, expecting to drive for half an hour, but in fact the journey lasted nearly two hours – and after sixty miles, we were still within our authorised beat. The forest looked endless and enticing: stretching away into the distance along a steep hillside, it consisted mainly of dark pines and spruce with wonderfully slender, pointed tops – shaped that way by nature so that they would shed snow – and birch with bark so smooth and white that I longed to write on it with black ink and an italic nib. Our guide warned us that numerous bears lived in the forest; but he assured us that they were not dangerous, as they would move off when they heard us coming.

We started with a kind of beat – three of us in line, and our guide on the right. Almost at once I had a stroke of luck. I was in a relatively open patch when a large bird flapped out of a tree ahead of me. Firing instinctively, more or less from the hip, I brought down a hen capercaillie. Whether or not it was in season, we were by no means sure, but it was too late to worry – and on we went. The trees and undergrowth were so dense that we soon became separated from each other and fought our individual ways through the thickets. Every now and then I came on a clearing, and there in the open spaces were growing the most luscious red currants I had ever seen. The size of grapes, they hung in magnificent clusters, ripe and sweet beyond one's dreams, and incredibly refreshing when eaten by the handful.

Quickly it became clear that we were not the only creatures enjoying the fruit. The grass in the glades was carpeted with droppings, which could charitably be described as 'loose', and were scarcely less red than the currants. Obviously the bears were also gorging. Now and then I heard heavy disturbances ahead of me, but never anything close. By far the loudest noises were the double shots that kept going off lower down the mountain. I supposed that my companions were finding a good many birds to shoot at – whereas I got only three hazel grouse. Not until we all emerged into the open did I discover that Peter, fancying himself menaced by bears, had shot nothing at all, but had been loosing off both barrels repeatedly to keep his supposed pursuers at bay.

After struggling through undergrowth for several hours, we were glad to sit down on the ground for a picnic tea, toasting sandwiches and sizzling slices of Polish Spam over a small wood fire. Then, back at camp, we had the problem of where to put the capercaillie. Ian was keen to take it to England and have it mounted, but the weather was so hot that we feared it would not last out the two remaining days of our stay: all we could do was lay it on the floorboards in the coolest room – the small lavatory cubicle – and there it stayed, instantly known as the caper in the crapper.

On our last morning we went into town for a tour of the museum, which contained an extraordinary assortment of local treasures, from geological and archaeological specimens to Cossacks' costumes, badly-stuffed animals and sundry artefacts. Then came a ceremonial lunch at the home of one of our shooting hosts. I think we were all slightly embarrassed to be entertained by a family whose means were modest, to say the least; their house was walled with upright wooden boards, and the roof was of corrugated iron. But the warmth of their greeting was such that inhibitions soon melted, and they gave us a sumptuous meal of *pelmeni* – little dumplings stuffed with meat – and salads of many vegetables chopped together, which we ate watched at point-blank range by two fair-haired boys of about seven and nine and a girl of five. At the end of seven energetic days, it was the friendliest possible send-off.

After the clear air and exhilarating space of the mountains, it was a shock to land back in Moscow at midnight, with the temperature about 35 C – and maybe it was the heat that caused Peter to throw his one real wobbly of the trip. As we changed planes, through the window of the arrival hall we could see our luggage coming in on a trailer. But then, a few minutes later, we spotted our guns being wheeled away on a hand-trolley. Instantly deciding that they were being stolen, Peter gave a shout and dashed out of the building.

The next thing we saw, he was walking vaguely about the apron, weaving his way between passenger jets which were manoeuvring to park or take off. Ian and I thought he was about to be killed, or at least severely injured by blast from the engines – but then, miraculously, a few minutes later he reappeared none the worse, loudly claiming that the weapons had been appropriated by the KGB, the airport staff or common criminals. Of course, nothing of the sort had happened: the guns had been put in a secure room, and presently they were returned to us to check in for London, along with Ian's confiscated rifle, which he had feared he would never see again.

Throughout the homeward journey – four hours by road to Barnaul, two hours in the airport there, three hours in the air to Moscow, two hours there, and over three hours to London – the capercaillie had been crammed into Ian's suitcase. At Heathrow it passed undetected through the green channel, and eventual exposure to the air in Somerset revealed that it had somehow survived the journey in miraculously good condition. Ian then had it mounted by a taxidermist, and today, thirty-odd years later, it still graces his sitting room, an elegant memento of our sojourn in Siberia.

Hungary

As Communism crumbled and the Berlin Wall was breached in November 1989, field sports organisations in Eastern Europe became eager to attract shooting parties from the West; and so it was that in January 1990 I joined a group of six others on an experimental trip to eastern Hungary. We went under the auspices of Hungarian Sporting Developments, a British company which had secured the shooting rights on a large area, and we were led by Peter Merrikin, a farmer from Bedfordshire, who was keen to set up some sort of agricultural enterprise in former Communist territory.

Having flown to Budapest, we were driven 200 miles eastwards through a snow-laden landscape to a State farm almost on the Russian border. The temperature was -10 C, the country depressingly featureless. None of us knew what to expect, but we had all read of the great bags of partridges which used to be made in the 1930s on the Hortobagy plain, and we were encouraged by the knowledge that the Hungarians were doing their best to restore game shooting to something like its former level.

Our base was a converted villa on the edge of a town called Mátészalka, heated to an insufferable temperature but otherwise comfortable; and the best surprise in it was Gyorgyi Makadi, our dazzlingly attractive interpreter. Not only did she speak first-class English: she also had a perfect grip of sporting terms: over-and-under, picker-up, runner, flush – she was at ease with them all. As we found at supper, the food in the villa was rich and abundant – and so was the Bull's Blood (otherwise Egri Bikavér) with which we washed it down.

To brief us, in came the Head Keeper, Istavan Papp – rather pale, serious and in his late thirties, with a neat red beard. He explained that the State farm extended to 30,000 acres, of which 40 percent was hardwood forest, mostly acacia. He had twelve keepers working under him, and parties of guns, provided they booked far enough in advance, might shoot 1,000 pheasants or duck in a day. His ground also held gold-medal roebuck, wild boar, a few red deer and a herd of 200 fallow, which had been imported a year earlier.

Under the Communist regime most of the shooting had been reserved for high-ranking party functionaries and their guests; but in recent seasons teams of Germans and Italians had been coming to shoot pheasants. No doubt because walked-up birds are less challenging, they had opted for them, rather than driven – and our hosts seemed rather surprised that Peter had asked for drives.

In the morning, after a gargantuan breakfast, which included hotly-spiced sausages and black bread, we were away by 8 am in a little convoy of jeeps. The air was bitterly cold, the sky overcast, the trees rimed with frost. The terrain, was disappointing, being almost entirely flat, but we were delighted by the rocketing flight of any pheasant that got up, and by the faintly outlandish manner in which proceedings were conducted.

As one of the guns remarked, it was not quite the same as a day in the Home Counties. For one thing, most of the beaters were very small, dark Magyar gyspies, not much more than five feet tall. They had no sticks with which to rattle tree-trunks and bushes, and, being new to the game, had little idea of keeping in line, but rushed hither and thither letting off fiendish yells. Drives began and ended with melodious horn-calls, blown by Tibor, a dashing young man with a down-swept moustache.

Each gun was allotted a loader. Mine, Ernesto, was a likeable young fellow, but clumsy at handling cartridges – and his faltering efficiency was constantly undermined by his dog, a young Viszla called Ali, who felt it necessary to retrieve every bird in sight, no matter how many times it had been retrieved already. The result was that whenever I fired a shot, broke the gun and looked round for another cartridge, I usually found that Ernesto had run off in pursuit of his hound. A further disadvantage was that, every time I killed a bird, he shouted 'BRAVO!' and gave me a tremendous clout between the shoulder-blades, which threw me off balance for another shot. In spite of these problems, we got on splendidly, helped by the fact that he spoke a little German, so that minimal communication was possible.

The morning was repeatedly enlivened by the appearance of wild boar, which kept us on our toes by erupting from cover at high speed and hurtling between us as we stood in line. There were plenty of birds, and marksmanship was decent – which was just as well, for we felt rather as if we were on show, representing Great Britain, and our hosts were watching closely to see how we would perform.

At about mid-day snow began to fall, and when we heard that lunch was to be *al fresco,* spirits faltered – but only for a few minutes. In an attractive little dell dominated by an ancient willow, a long wooden table had been elaborately laid. Two roaring bonfires blazed. Goulash steamed in our plates, Bulls' Blood flowed and snowflakes hissed as they perished in the leaping flames. To ward off the vapours, we dosed ourselves liberally with peach brandy.

It may have been this fiery *digestif* that led to a memorable incident in the afternoon. During one drive, across an open stretch of ground, I spotted a single cock pheasant heading straight for me, high and fast. More by luck than by good judgment, I killed it well out in front – and instantly saw that its descent was going to bring it down right onto me. In those few seconds rugger memories suddenly kicked in. Having survived a clout in the back and a cry of 'Bravo!', I handed Ernesto my gun, saying '*Halten sie das!*' and braced myself for the arrival of the dead bird. Down it came, smack into my arms and solar plexus, and at the impact I shouted 'MARK!'

In retrospect, I realised what a foolish thing it was to have done. The pheasant weighed probably three kilos; alive, it had been travelling at 30 mph, and falling from a height, it had a lot of kinetic energy. It also had a very sharp beak. Had I misjudged the catch, I could have been quite badly injured. As it was, my jacket was covered with blood and feathers, and I had to try to explain to my loader (in German) the rudiments of this crazy English variant of football – in which you may only pass backwards, but if you bring off a catch like I had, and simultaneously ram your heel into the ground, you get a free kick. From then on he kept eyeing me closely, as if for further signs of possibly dangerous eccentricity.

With the winter evening already closing in, the shoot ended at 3.30 pm. Our bag of 170 pheasants was laid out, cocks and hens separately, within a rectangle of pine branches. Everyone lined up – guns to one side, keepers and loaders opposite, beaters to our left – and hats came off as Tibor sounded three echoing calls on his horn.

Three more days followed much the same pattern – although one was punctuated by a startling incident. As we were walking along a single-track railway line, a train came hurtling towards us. The party hastily scattered, right and left, and the driver, far from slowing down, gave a few merry toots with his whistle – to which Tibor blew a quick riposte. Health and safety? Unheard of then.

On the last morning, as we were driving to a new beat, a feature in the landscape struck me as oddly familiar. Out to our right, fields rose gently towards woods on a distant hill. Closer to us, a few specimen trees – the remains of an avenue – led in line up the slope to a small plateau, on which nothing was growing. Suddenly I found myself thinking of *Macbeth,* and King Duncan's observation when he comes to Dunsinane: 'This castle hath a pleasant seat.' Here in the east of Hungary I was looking at a pleasant seat, and I sensed that a grand country house had stood there.

'Istavan,' I said, pointing up the hill. 'Was there a house there once?'

The keeper stared at me as if I was somehow psychic and had sensed some invisible remnant of the past.

'Yes,' he replied uncomfortably, 'it was a castle. That was the home of Count X, a Jewish man. He went to America when things started looking bad in Germany, before the war.'

'And what happened to the building?'

'Local people destroyed it. They took away the stones for their own homes.'

Too late, I remembered that the Nazis had made Mátészalka one of the most notorious ghettos in Hungary, and that thousands of people had died there. Evidently the count had left just in time. Later we passed several similar relics – ruined castles, or patches of cleared ground.

We also saw what damage the Communist regime had done to the environment, by ripping out hedges and creating fields of 200 acres or more – a foretaste of what was now happening in East Anglia.

Our expedition was reckoned a success: we established that game shooting on a generous scale was entirely feasible for foreign visitors, and relations with our hosts were as friendly as anyone could wish; but to have been pampered in a country ground-down by Communism for nearly half a century gave me a curious feeling. It was if our party were members of the old aristocracy who had miraculously returned to their former haunts, and found many of their old retainers still happy to do them service.

Poland

It might have been the set for a wildly extravagant production of *Il Trovatore.* Frost-bound snow glittered under foot, and on a ridge high above my left shoulder the walls and towers of a ruined medieval castle loomed black against the sky. All around, the hardwood forest lay silent, as if in expectation of some tremendous opening chord. Then, in a gap between the battlements, a lone figure appeared, and a horn-call came echoing down through the bare branches..

This was January 1991. Together with three Americans, two Swiss and two Germans, I had come to south-west Poland at the invitation of an eccentric, engaging entrepreneur from Co. Wicklow, Robert Clotworthy. A big, tall, tousle-headed fellow in his forties, with a true Irish gift of the gab, he had been drawn to the area by reports of exceptional big-game shooting: bison, elk, red deer, wild boar and wolf were all available. But when he saw the country –steep hills clad in oak, larch and pine – he realised that the area would be ideal for showing the high, driven pheasants which international musketeers pay thousands to shoot. Research on the ground showed that the cost of producing birds would be less than half that in Ireland or England; so he persuaded the American agency, Dunn's, to set up a joint venture company in Warsaw.

I think he underestimated the difficulties involved. Not only did the

Poles have no experience of the kind of shoots he was planning; worse, the country was struggling to free itself from the stupefaction imposed by forty-five years of Communist rule. Prices were certainly low, but so were standards of transport, accommodation and service, and a crippling general lethargy prevailed.

In spite of it, Robert had already achieved a good deal. He had leased the bird-shooting rights in a block of State-owned woodland, brought over an English gamekeeper, built release pens and bought poults from the nearest State farm, which had been exporting birds to France. He had also galvanised the managers of the Hotel Sudety– a dreary, 1960s concrete box in the town of Walbrzych – forcing them to redecorate the foyer and some of the rooms, and to issue the girls on the reception desk with new blouses.

In all this he was greatly helped by Maria Skierniewska, a small, lively woman in her forties, who had spent two years in England. She had also worked with the State travel agency Orbis, on the hunting side, so that she had numerous contacts in the Polish countryside.

In the woods, hazards abounded. One was the extraordinary number of goshawks, which greatly appreciated the sudden appearance of gormless young pheasants, and, being a protected species, could not be combated. Another, even more damaging element was the influx of amateur poachers – townspeople who poured out into the forest when they heard that an unprecedented supply of easily-caught dinners had mysteriously become available.

Nevertheless, the first shoot, held the previous November, had been an encouraging success. In four days a team of Americans had shot nearly 800 pheasants and declared the quality of the birds 'amazing'. But in the background there had been trouble. The gamekeeper, proving inadequate, had been sent home. In his place Robert had appointed two local lads, one a tailor, the other a boy just out of school. Both were enthusiastic about their new role, but so inexperienced that he had been obliged to spend countless hours instructing them on the ground. By the end of the year he had made fourteen trips to Poland.

Thus it was with high expectations, but also some apprehension, that he welcomed his second team of guns at the beginning of January. Two Swiss and three Germans turned out in normal European hunting gear, of green or grey Loden, but the three Americans wore beautifully-tailored tweed knickerbocker suits, and a few minutes' conversation established that they were immensely experienced shooting men who spent fortunes on their sport. Robert Mann, President of his own financial company, had flown from Texas with his old hunting pal Dr Robert Maurer, a radiologist from San Antonio. In the past six winters these two had made seventeen separate trips to shoot pheasants in England, Scotland and Wales. From Ann Arbor, Michigan, came Richard Barch, President of an investment bank, who had first gone hunting in Africa more than thirty years earlier, 'when the British still ran Kenya'.

All three had beautiful weapons: Bob Mann a pair of custom-built 20-bores, Bob Maurer his favourite matched pair of Francotti 12-bores, custom made in Belgium, Dick Barch a custom-built Perazzi MX-8 12-bore with gold-plated ducks on the sides of the action and a portrait of his favourite Labrador engraved on the bottom. This, he confided, was one of between eighty and 100 sporting weapons which he kept at home in an armoured room under the stairs. I could not help noticing that Bob Mann's watch was a gold Rolex, also custom made, with a walnut face, the hours picked out in diamonds, and a complete ring of diamonds round the perimeter.

I scored a point or two by talking up my own gun – a side-by-side 12-bore sidelock made by the well-known firm Henry Atkin in 1906. The antiquity of the weapon impressed the Germans, but greater distinction derived from the fact that it had been ordered as No. 2 of a pair by H.H.Asquith, when he was Chancellor of the Exchequer, and shortly before he became Prime Minister. The fact that for some unknown reason he never took up the order detracted slightly from the story, but all the same my fellow guests handled the weapon with reverence.

Beside the sartorial paragons from the United States, the beaters looked a ragged lot, in jeans and old anoraks. Most of them were lads from the State farm, earning £75 a month and accustomed to start work at 6 am. By the time we arrived in the forest at 8.30, they were clustered round a blazing bonfire, and with that as a cheerful background Robert Clotworthy read the riot act. With Maria interpreting, phrase by phrase, he spelled out what he wanted.

'We have a common object, and that is to drive very high sporting birds over the guns ... Each drive starts and ends with a horn call ... The important thing is for you to stay in line with each other ... Keep looking at your neighbours to left and right ... This is a bit of an experiment, so things may easily go wrong ... I get very excited, and I blow up at least twice a day, so if I start to roar at you, don't worry.'

With that, we moved off for the first drive, and I took up station on the left of the line, beneath the gaunt ruin. Then the horn sounded, and soon pheasants began to come over. Very high they were, too – some twisting through the trees, but many above them, all exciting targets. For me, no small part of the enjoyment lay in the fact that the lie of the land was entirely novel, the texture and feel of the woods somehow different from those in England. The highlight of my day was the first drive in the afternoon, at which I found I was in the hot spot and fired eighty cartridges in less than twenty minutes at some of the highest birds I had ever engaged.

All three days of our shoot went pretty well, although the number of birds tailed off, and in all we shot 460, instead of the 600 advertised. The shortfall was partly due to the fact that another German gun, who joined for the second and third days, could hit practically nothing. He had shot deer and boar innumerable, but, as he cheerfully admitted, these rocketing pheasants were beyond him. Needless to say, he kept drawing prime position in the line. The Swiss-German contingent were so impressed by the proceedings that they immediately booked to come again.

Lunch each day was *al fresco* – wonderfully thick soup, bread, tea and vodka, brought out to the fire – and in the evenings we dined lavishly in the panelled banqueting room of the hotel, where (we were told by George, the head waiter) leading Polish Communists had entertained foreign notables who came to hunt. It was strange to reflect that the capacious oak chairs had been occupied by the behinds of (among others)

Marshal Tito of Yugoslavia and Eric Honecker of East Germany. Tito, George confided, was a real gentleman, Honecker anything but.

Talk turned repeatedly to the abundance of big game in Eastern Europe, and to the way Communist apparatchiks had kept the best of it for themselves. The most luxurious shooting lodge that any of our hosts had ever seen was in the 27,000 hectare reserve called Awamov, on the Russian border, where members of the Politburo disported themselves in marble halls.

One evening we visited the magnificent castle of Ksiaz – an eighteenth-century, baroque pile now dismally decrepit, poised above plunging ravines. Once the home of the Princes of Pless, it had been chosen as a bolt-hole for Hitler during the Second World War, and slave labourers from a nearby concentration camp had hacked a tunnel and lift-shaft out of living rock so that the Führer would be able to come and go undetected.

It was hard to tell what the Poles made of Robert's strange, multi-national invasion. We managed to exchange plenty of jokes with the locals, and when the beaters saw that the guns could bring down the highest birds, they saluted their good marksmanship. At the same time they made it clear that they did not regard the massacre of driven pheasants as very sporting. They described it as *strelanie,* or sport-shooting, as opposed to *polowane,* or hunting – the more energetic and traditional pursuit of game by one or two men with a dog. Nevertheless, they welcomed the innovation – not least because the beaters were each paid £4 a day, and got a bottle of vodka at the end.

One certain fact is that they loved Robert Clotworthy. No matter that in moments of stress he might yell *'Hollera!' (Rubbish!)* or even *'Kurva'* – a term better not translated here. So easy was his manner, so winning his way with people, that by the end of the shoot he had become a father figure to his young team.

As I headed for home, at the security check in the airport a dreadful-looking woman, with hair dyed bright orange, who would instantly have found a role in a James Bond film, was exchanging insults with a colleague. So preoccupied was she with her feud that she continued cursing for several minutes before she snatched my precious gun and threw it down the steel chute with a crash. Luckily it was in a padded sleeve, and survived undamaged; but I didn't know this until I recovered it in London, and so had an uneasy homeward flight.

CHAPTER TWENTY-TWO

Dealing with the Palace
1984-1996

When Sir Alan Lascelles (always known as 'Tommy') died in 1981, at the age of 94, many authors and editors were keenly aware that he had left diaries of the highest historical and social interest. As Private Secretary to Edward Prince of Wales from 1920 to 1929, to King George VI from 1942-1952, and briefly to Queen Elizabeth II from 1952-53, he had twenty years' intimate experience of the Royal family, and outsiders were eager to discover what he had written about them. He himself had always maintained absolute discretion, knowing that his duty was to keep silent about royal affairs, and accepting that his journals could not be published during his lifetime. Nevertheless, as a writer *manqué,* he very much hoped that they might at some time in the future see the light of day.

It was my great good fortune that in the 1970s I got to know him during the last years of his life. I met him through my father – who had long been a friend – and as we got on well, he sometimes invited me to lunch at his grace-and-favour flat in Kensington Palace. By then he had ceased to shave, and had grown a big, bushy beard, which gave him the look of an Old Testament prophet. As I soon found, his memory was astonishing, and wholly unimpaired by age. All his life he had read voraciously: he knew most Shakespeare plays by heart, loved quoting passages of Homer in ancient Greek, and had read the novels of Anthony Trollope so often that he had compiled a *Who's Who* of the author's characters.

I never asked him about his diaries, for although I knew they existed,

I did not, at that stage, imagine there was any chance of their being published. Nor did I question him about his career in royal service, for I feared that to do so would seem inquisitive, if not impertinent. Sometimes he did tell anecdotes about his travels with the King, but usually we talked about congenial subjects such as the Lit Soc (the Literary Society) – a dining club of which he had long been a member, and I the Secretary. Other regular topics were shooting and deer-stalking, at which he had excelled in his youth. A favourite story was of my godfather Duff Cooper shooting at Belvoir and missing almost everything, until at last out of the covert came a pure white albino pheasant, which he managed to hit. So excited was he that he shouted out, 'By God, I've shot the Holy Ghost!'

When I sent Tommy a draft of my book *Monarchs of the Glen* – a history of the Highland deer forests – he replied with a letter which included useful suggestions and a vivid account of how he had shot his own first stag. A further bond was his admiration of my other godfather, Peter Fleming; in 1972 he helped me while I was doing research for my biography, and then, when the book was published, congratulated me on hitting the right note. A photograph of Peter – the one on the jacket of the book – stood on the mantelpiece in his sitting-room to the end of his life.

Imagine my excitement when, in 1983, Tommy's daughters, Caroline Erskine and Lavinia Hankinson, suggested that I should edit his papers for possible publication. We knew there would be opposition from the librarians and private secretaries who kept guard over all documents involving royalty, so we proceeded with patience, planning to start by bringing out a volume of Tommy's early letters and diaries, from boyhood to his marriage in 1920, which we hoped would soften-up future resistance from Buckingham Palace, should we seek to publish the much more important journals covering his years of royal service.

As we expected, the attitude of the Queen's librarians and private secretaries was defensive and slightly hostile. One of their most effective weapons was delay: when I wrote to Sir Robin Mackworth-Young, the royal librarian, with some early request, he took ten months to send a negative reply.

Tommy's papers were then housed in a locked black box in the royal archive at Windsor, and when Caroline wrote to Sir Robin in January 1984, saying that she and Lavinia had given me permission to look at them, she received a typically cautious reply. There were two particular envelopes, Nos. 12 and 26 (Sir Robin wrote) which he would rather I did not see. Would Caroline and Mrs Jenkinson [*sic*] agree that he should remove them from the box before my first visit? He also reminded Caroline of her father's recorded wish that no public use should be made of his diaries without the approval of the Sovereign.

Early in March Caroline went to Buckingham Palace to see Sir Philip Moore, the Queen's Private Secretary. 'He said he would prefer to talk to me on my own,' she warned me in a letter ... We must get him to read drafts. I will be in touch after seeing him, if I don't get sent to the Tower!'

Her report of the interview was discouraging: Moore told her that *nothing* should be published, now or in the foreseeable future. No word, he said, must appear in print that revealed the nature of the relationship between the Sovereign and the Private Secretary. 'Obviously, by invoking that argument, he can kill everything,' I wrote to my father. 'I fear he has poisoned the water pretty thoroughly.' Nevertheless, Caroline and I decided to press ahead and see if we could fashion a volume out of the early, non-contentious journals.

I am not sure what shifted the block. But I soon received permission to see the black box's contents (though not those of the two hot envelopes). So it was that I gained access to the Royal Library in Windsor Castle, and there I spent many days, working in the circular reading room at the top of the Round Tower, lulled by the faint chatter rising like smoke from hordes of Japanese tourists as they shuffled over the cobbles far below. Sir Robin would occasionally come past my table, a dry, ascetic figure, not actively hostile, but radiating disapproval of our project.

By ranging back and forth through the letters and journals, I got to know the outline of Tommy's life. His background was aristocratic, to say the least. His father, the Hon. Frederick Lascelles, was the younger brother of the fifth Earl of Harewood, whose son Harry Lascelles (Tommy's contemporary) married Princess Mary, only daughter of King

George V. Tommy always rejected accusations of snobbishness, but he did not mind admitting that he valued good breeding as much in humans as in horses. Sent to Marlborough, where he had won a scholarship, he hated the school for its philistine attitude, and lamented the fact that he had not gone to Eton. When he went up to Trinity College, Oxford to read Greats (Classics), almost all his friends were old Etonians, and he called Oxford 'the beloved city.'

I much enjoyed the physical feel of his early diaries – small, solid volumes bound with black leather and fitted with silver locks. Several of them opened with an incantation designed to scare off snoopers:

There are 29 distinct damnations
– one sure if another fails –
awaiting anyone who reads this
book unbidden.

Whether or not this echo of ancient Egyptian tombs had had any effect, the author clearly did not want contemporaries to read what he was saying about them. He began the first volume when he went up to Oxford in the autumn of 1905, and cheerfully recorded the disgraceful behaviour in which he and his friends indulged: releasing a young pig into Balliol, stringing chamber pots overhead across the Trinity Quad.

By then he was 6′1″ tall and unusually slim, weighing no more than ten stone. With his regular features, and dark hair parted in the centre, straight over the top of his head, he cut a commanding figure, later emphasised by the dark suits he habitually wore when he went into royal service.

I soon found that my greatest difficulty was going to be to select from the mass of material available, for Tommy's social life, both at university and in the vacations, had been astonishingly full: 'Lady Dartmouth's ball ... the Duchess of Leeds's ball ... Henley regatta ... Zoo party ... danced at old Lady Bute's ... lunch with the Bigges in St James's Palace ... To Lady Bath's ball – amusing enough ... Dined at Lady Sheffield's ... Dined 10 Downing Street ...' In the country he stayed at one great house after another.

There was nothing in the early diaries to alarm the Palace. In spite of his formidable intellect, Tommy's early career was riddled with disappointments. Hoping for a First in Greats, he came down from Oxford with a Second. He sat and failed the Foreign Office exam. He tried for a job in journalism, but could not land one. Becoming a stockbroker, he much disliked life in the City.

Nor was there anything contentious in his reminiscences of the First World War, in which he joined the Bedfordshire Yeomanry as a cavalry officer and was posted to France. There, too, he was frustrated, for the regiment spent much of the war in reserve, and he could only watch in distress as, one after another, his closest friends – Raymond Asquith, Hugo and Ivo Charteris, Billy and Julian Grenfell, Edward Horner, Charles Lister, John Manners, Patrick Shaw-Stewart, Mark Tennant – were killed in action or died of wounds. All the same, he did fight, was wounded and won a Military Cross.

After the war his luck changed, when his brother-in-law Sir George Lloyd (married to his sister Blanche) was posted as Governor of Bombay, and took Tommy with him as one of his A.D.C.s. During a keddah, or catch-up of wild elephants in Mysore, he fell in love with Joan Thesiger, daughter of the Viceroy, Lord Chelmsford, and married her at a grand wedding in Delhi in March 1920. To his astonishment his cousin, Harry, Viscount Lascelles, gave him an endowment of £30,000 (in today's values about £1.4 million), remarking that 'it ought to provide biscuits and margarine, if not bread and butter.'

When the couple returned to England in July, Tommy again scratched around for a job, until to his rescue came a friend, Letty Elcho, bringing 'an unofficial offer from the Prince of Wales that I become his assistant secretary at £600 per annum.' This seemed an immense stroke of good fortune, for Tommy had 'a very deep admiration for the Prince,' and was convinced that 'the future of England is as much in his hands as those of any individual.' So, on 29 November 1920 he went to St. James's Palace and made his bow to H.R.H. 'He won me completely,' he wrote. 'He is the most attractive man I've ever met.'

This seemed a good point at which to conclude our first volume, which was published in 1986. *End of an Era* received enthusiastic reviews, but caused no controversy. For our second volume, we planned that the centre-piece should be the section covering the Prince's official tours of America, Canada, and East Africa, between 1924 and 1928. Although once again styled 'Letters and Journals of Sir Alan Lascelles', the collection consisted entirely of letters – to Joan, to other members of the family, and to various colleagues – for he had ceased to keep a diary during those years.

My task now became more difficult, for after a honeymoon period during which Tommy continued to admire the Prince, his opinion had gone sharply downhill. In 1928, during the official tour of East Africa, his disillusionment became complete: he now saw his royal employer as an irresponsible playboy and womaniser, with little or no sense of duty, and thought him utterly unfit to become king. His despair reached a climax one night in Tanganyika when a telegram from Stanley Baldwin, the Prime Minister, caught up with the royal train, begging the Prince to come home at once, as in England his father King George V was lying dangerously ill. Passing the message off as 'some election dodge of old Baldwin,' the Prince ignored it and spent the night 'in the successful seduction of a Mrs Barnes, wife of the local commissioner.' He himself told Tommy so next morning.

That was too much for his Private Secretary. In January 1929, back in England, Tommy resigned from Edward's service and gave him an hour's severe dressing-down, telling him that if he did not mend his ways, he would lose the throne of England – a warning to which the Prince responded by presenting him with a new car.

Next, in a cooling-off period, Tommy lived for two years at the family home in Dorset, and then, from 1931 to 1935, became secretary to the Governor-General of Canada, Lord Bessborough.

In Ottawa he was delighted to discover that the natives were still stirringly loyal to the King of England, fired by what he called 'astonishing patriotism' – which meant that a large part of his job was to promote the ideal of monarchy to a receptive audience. He got on well enough with Bessborough, and when Joan brought out their two girls and son John, the family settled comfortably into Rideau Cottage, a timber-clad building with a verandah that looked out over a lake in the grounds of Government House. For Tommy, the peaks of his time in Canada were his summer expeditions to the gin-clear Bonaventure river in the Gaspé peninsula, where he enjoyed the best salmon fishing he had ever known: during one four-week visit he caught a hundred fish weighing 1,405 lbs.

The excellence of his work in Government House drew extravagant praise from the next Governor-General, the novelist John Buchan, who told him in a letter: 'You have left a mighty reputation here, and you are quoted as Roman lawyers quoted Justinian. I need not tell you how grateful I shall be if you can ever find time to send me a line.'

In England again, Tommy was quickly approached with the offer of a job as Assistant Private Secretary to George V. At first he refused, fearing that if the ailing King soon died (which seemed likely), he would find himself once again working for the man whom he had come to despise; but when other members of the staff assured him that the old monarch had several good years to run, he changed his mind and rejoined the royal household – only for his worst apprehension to be fulfilled, when George V died six weeks later.

This meant that Tommy witnessed, from close quarters, the protracted Abdication crisis of 1936, which he described as 'a real tragedy' in his own life. It is posterity's loss that he kept no journal during what he called 'those nightmare years'. He did, however, record that Edward called him 'an evil snake' and regarded him as one of his worst enemies at Court – a ridiculous distortion of the truth.

When I submitted the text of our second volume to the Palace for clearance, I was expecting a sharp blow-back, for the book included a forthright account of Tommy's experiences with the Prince of Wales in Africa. I was therefore agreeably surprised when it passed the royal censors with only a few requests for minor cuts. *In Royal Service* was published in 1989, to be greeted by a volley of sensational newspaper headlines: 'Portrait of the Duke as Womaniser', 'No Trust in this

Prince,' 'A Prince Not so Charming', 'Mrs Simpson did us all a favour,' and so on.

Not until the beginning of June 1942 did Tommy resume his earlier habit of making daily entries in a journal. But, once started, he continued for the next four years, always writing in ink, with extraordinary fluency and precision, never changing a word or crossing one out. The result was an unique record of the Second World War observed from the cockpits of Buckingham Palace, Westminster and Windsor – for by then he had become Private Secretary to the King. He saw the monarch almost every day, greeted every important person who came for an audience, and had frequent dealings with the Prime Minister, Winston Churchill.

The war journals contained any amount of riveting material; but there was one explosive passage which made everything else look humdrum. On the evening of 3 March 1943 – when Tommy was living in Buckingham Palace – the Editor of *The Times* sent across a proof of the paper's standing obituary of the Duke of Windsor, formerly Edward VIII. The aim was to solicit Tommy's view of the article; this it achieved, but his reaction went far beyond mere comments, and took the form of a thunderous broadside, 4,000 words long, denouncing the man who, he wrote, 'had wasted the best years of my life' in trying to make him fit to be king.

Those twelve pages amounted to a devastating indictment of the Prince's character – his childishness, his selfishness, his lack of any sense of duty, his reckless pursuit of women, his enslavement to Wallis Simpson. Among other shocking stories, Tommy related how the King (as he then briefly was) had gone to inspect the glass-houses in the kitchen garden at Windsor and ordered the old Scottish gardener to cut all the peach blossom – thus destroying the year's crop, to the gardener's despair – and send it to Mrs Simpson and friends for the embellishment of their drawing-rooms in London. At another point Tommy described how, in a secret meeting with Baldwin, he said he sometimes hoped that, for the good of himself and the country, the Prince would break his neck hunting or riding in a point-to-point – to which the Prime Minister replied, 'God forgive me. I have often thought the same.'

On my first-run through the archive I had at once seen that this outburst would make a stunning serial extract in one of the national newspapers. I had therefore tried, by stealth, to attach the passage to the end of our Volume Two, on the grounds that although it had been written in 1943, it described the author's involvement with Edward in the 1920s and his behaviour during the Abdication crisis. I was disappointed, but not surprised, when the Palace detected my ruse and forbade publication until some later date, if ever.

In spite of this prohibition, we decided to press ahead with work on Volume Three. By 1990, at Caroline's request, Tommy's papers had been transferred from Windsor to the Archive Centre at Churchill College, Cambridge, where they would be more easily available to researchers. This made things awkward for me, in that every visit meant two 150-mile cross-country journeys; but compensation came in the fact that the atmosphere in the reading room was congenial, and that the Director of the Centre, Allen Packwood, far from obstructing our enterprise, was thoroughly helpful from the start.

In a series of all-day sessions, sometimes staying overnight in one of the college rooms, I transcribed selections from the three wartime diaries and put together a text of some 200,000 words, besides creating hundreds of footnotes, to explain the identities and roles of all the people mentioned in the text. Once the family had cleared the draft, I submitted it to the Palace with a covering letter and settled down to wait.

After seven months had passed without an answer, I wrote again to the Private Secretary, asking if anything could be done to expedite matters. The response was a suggestion that Caroline and I should come to Buckingham Palace to discuss some difficult points. Thus one afternoon we presented ourselves at the Palace side-gate. Arriving on a bicycle, I asked the duty policeman if I might chain my steed to the railings. 'No, Sir,' he replied. 'But you can take it through. We'll look after it for you.' So, having wheeled it across the forecourt, I propped it against the Palace, unsecured, and in we went.

The meeting took place in the Chinese Dining Room – which blazes with startlingly garish oriental reds and yellows – and proved a fiasco. The Private Secretary who had been dealing with the matter was unfortunately not available, having gone away for the day, and his place was taken by a deputy who had not been properly briefed and kept sifting helplessly through a pile of papers. After some futile discussion we departed, my only consolation being that my bike had spent an hour leaning on the north wall of the Palace – a contact which I felt gave the machine some distinction.

In due course, after more exchanges, we agreed to make some minor cuts. The text, including the nuclear passage, was at last cleared for publication, and in 2006 the book came out with the title *King's Counsellor*. As I expected, it created a huge clamour in the national newspapers. *The Times* ran serial extracts; reviews were long and enthusiastic; nobody was sent to the Tower, so much had official attitudes softened. Twenty-three years after its inception, our project reached a satisfactory conclusion, and Tommy's secret ambition – to become a published author – was at last fulfilled.

CHAPTER TWENTY-THREE

Hess or not Hess?
1978-2017

One day in the summer of 1978, as we sat finishing lunch at Rathenny, our rented house in Co. Tipperary, the post van drew up outside. 'You'll have a glass,' I said, handing a beaker of cold Chardonnay out through the dining-room window. 'God, I will,' replied Charlie gratefully, passing in a package and a couple of letters. ''Tis fierce hot weather, is it not?' As usual, he was in no hurry: the sun streamed in through the high, Georgian casements, and a few minutes' agreeable chat ensued before he went on his way.

No sooner had his van disappeared down the avenue than I found he had delivered a bit of a bombshell. In the package was a tired-looking typescript and a letter from my literary agent, Richard Simon, in London. His note explained that an Army Consultant Surgeon called Hugh Thomas was aiming to write a book about Rudolf Hess, Hitler's deputy before and during the Second World War. The would-be author had not managed to make the text saleable, but he had an astonishing theory – that the man who flew to Scotland on 10 May 1941, claiming to be Hess and trying to make peace with England, was not the Deputy Führer at all, but a double. 'Either the author's a fantasist,' Richard wrote, 'or else there's a tremendous story here.'

I read the typescript that afternoon, with rapidly-increasing excitement. Thomas claimed not only that the lone aviator was an impostor, but that the British knew it; further, that they kept him in confinement until the war had ended, sent him for trial at Nuremberg in 1946, and acquiesced in his confinement at Spandau, in Berlin, until his death in August 1987 at the age of ninety-three – all in the knowledge that he was the wrong man.

At several points I found it hard to believe what I was reading. Had the author not made half this up, and stretched or manufactured evidence to suit his case? There was only one way to find out – and that was to meet him.

Down he came from the north of Ireland, where he was working, to stay for a couple of nights – a small, voluble man in his forties, with a strong Welsh accent and a penetrating tenor voice. I soon saw that he was no fantasist, but rather a human terrier with his teeth clamped on a mystery of the utmost fascination.

When I asked what it was that had set him off on his quest, he said, 'Scars – or the lack of them.' Looking straight at me, he went on, 'I see you've had a tumour removed from your cheek, and you split your left eyebrow when you were a boy.' Clearly, he could read old scars as easily as most people read newspaper headlines.

He explained that, as a British Army surgeon working in Belfast, he had operated on numerous victims of sectarian violence after they had been shot. From this experience he knew exactly what damage a rifle or pistol bullet can cause, and what scars a wound will leave. The real Rudolph Hess had been shot through the left lung, fore to aft, by a rifle bullet during the First World War, but the man in Spandau, whom Thomas had examined, had no bullet-wound scars on his chest or back. It was this startling fact that had led him to pursue research into Hess's life – and the further he went, the more anomalies he found, the more convinced he became that he had hit on a gigantic deception.

Gripped, yet fairly sceptical, I listened as he outlined his story. Several times he brought out something so startling that I interrupted and said, 'Are you sure you're not exaggerating?' To which he replied, 'Look, I'm a surgeon. In my work I have to be absolutely precise. I can't fudge anything. If I did, I might kill the patient. It's the same when I'm doing research for the book.'

After several long sessions of talk, I agreed to help knock his draft into shape, and to join in further research. So began my involvement with a story which has run, on and off, for forty years, and has not yet reached its end. Spandau's Prisoner No.7 is long dead, but the mystery of who he was remains very much alive.

My first task was to prepare a coherent outline, together with an opening chapter. Hugh, throughout his draft, had referred to the central character as 'Hess'. But, as I pointed out, his claim was that the man in captivity was *not* Hess. We were dealing with two different people: the real Rudolf Hess, last seen in 1941, and from then on, his double. Therefore we must refer to the man who reached Scotland as 'the prisoner', 'the double', or, as he became known in Spandau, as 'Prisoner No. 7'.

On the strength of my two introductory pieces we obtained a contract from the London publishers Hodder & Stoughton. I then began straightening out Hugh's prose, much of which was unnecesarilyfacetious. For instance, with the appearance of Hermann Goering in the story, he had written: 'It is now time for the fat man to make his entrance. Welcome, Mr G.' Why, with so serious a subject, had he made these silly interjections? Hugh replied that he found the act of writing tedious, and resorted to humour to cheer himself up. In spite of that, we got on well from the start, and never had a serious argument.

Soon I became familiar with the bones of his story, which had begun in 1972, when Hugh was posted to the British Military Hospital in Berlin as Consultant in General Surgery. Spandau Prison was a short distance from the hospital; Prisoner No. 7 – last of the Nazi leaders who in 1946 had been given life sentences at the Nuremberg trials – was then 75, and Hugh knew that if the old man fell ill, he would have to treat him. As a precaution he read two biographies of Rudolf Hess to pick up background information, as he would of any patient of whom he was about to take charge.

Both books confirmed that Hess had been shot through the left lung by a rifle bullet while serving as a young rifleman on the Rumanian front in 1917. The wound was serious: the patient needed blood transfusions, and spent four months in hospital; he was lucky to survive, for a bullet is liable to draw dirt and fragments of cloth into a wound, and in those days, without antibiotics, he might easily have succumbed to a lethal infection. Although he recovered, he was never again fit enough to rejoin the army, but trained as a pilot.

Armed with this information, Hugh became eager to examine the last inmate of Spandau, to determine the sites of the entry and exit wounds, and the track of the bullet through the lung. His chance came when Prisoner No. 7 was admitted to the British Military Hospital for a barium meal, to check intestinal problems – and Hugh was astonished to find no trace of any bullet wound. The discovery precipitated him into further research, and – to cut short a long story – every new facet of the case that he turned up lent weight to his argument.

There was no doubt that Hess had taken off from Augsburg, near Munich, on the evening of 10 May 1941 in a Messerschmitt Bf 110 – a twin-engined, three-seater heavy fighter; known as a *Zerstörer,* or destroyer; but where he went, or what happened to him, was far from clear.

One of the first British reactions that aroused our suspicion came from Winston Churchill. On 11 May 1941 the news that a lone aviator had reached Scotland was urgently rushed south, but the Prime Minister at first showed very little interest, preferring to watch a Marx Brothers film before discussing the matter. On 13 May, however, he urgently telegraphed the consultant physician in Glasgow who had temporary charge of the prisoner, asking him to confirm that 'no injury exists new or old to the chest'. Next day the doctor replied: 'No lesion new or old.'

Everything suggests that Churchill had been expecting a strange arrival, and that he had secret information about the airman's identity. What else would have led him to ask about the man's scars? Duff Cooper, then Minister of Information (and my godfather), strongly suggested that professional photographs should be obtained of the aviator, so that if the worst occurred and he escaped, the British would at least have proof that they had captured him. Churchill vetoed the project, and moreover ordered that no photograph was to be taken of the man while he was in England.

A show was made of verifying the German's identity, but – with one exception – men who had known Hess before the war were not allowed to see him. The only one who *had* known him well was Richard Arnold

Baker, born a German aristocrat, Werner Richard von Blumenthal, but since 1938 Anglicised and serving as an officer in MI6. Posing as 'Captain Barnes', he visited the prisoner within days of his arrival and came away declaring that the man was not Hess at all, but a 'pathetically poor double.'

With publication drawing closer, we decided to try for an interview with Ilse Hess, to see if we could glean any more details of her husband's life and behaviour. To our surprise she agreed to see us at her home in Bavaria. We therefore flew to Munich, hired a car and drove out to the village of Hindelang in the foothills of the Alps. We were both fairly nervous, not knowing how she would react to questioning, but the tension was let down when suddenly, as we drew near our target, we passed through a small town and spotted a board standing on a bank at a jaunty angle, adorned in huge letters with the single word WANK! It was the exclamation mark that set us off. '*What?*' we said. '*Here? Now?*' (Alas, it was just the name of the place.)

Frau Hess was anything but welcoming. Then in her late 70s, grey-haired, short and stocky, she exuded hostility. She was astonished by Hugh's assertion that the man in Spandau was not her husband, and poured scorn on his questions about Hess's war wound, his dietary habits, his physical well-being, his mental state. Hugh had decided in advance not to reveal his key evidence – the absence of wound scars – in case Frau Hess leaked it to one of the German news magazines, and spoilt the impact of our book before it came out. Even so, the truth several times came very close to the surface.

'Why do you keep going on about his health?' she demanded. 'Of course he could climb hills. His wound made him short of breath for the first few hundred metres of an ascent, but after that he was fine.' Then she added: 'Another thing you might like to know: his handwriting has never changed. He writes now just as he always did. I have dozens of his old letters in the loft.'

'That's fascinating,' Hugh replied. 'Could we see some of them?'

'Not now. I can't get them down immediately. But if you give me your address, I'll send you one or two.' When I asked if her husband had been in good health before he left, she again became indignant. 'Of course he was well,' she said. 'He was in very good spirits – and he was so ebullient that on the day before he left he vaulted over that chair you're sitting in.' Of course I did not say that her account made Hess sound nothing like the neurotic, physically decrepit man who landed in Scotland, and was described by a British doctor as 'gaunt, hollow-cheeked, pale and lined.'

Fortunately her son Wolf-Rüdiger Hess – then 40 – was present at our interview. Large, solid, reasonable, he spoke good English and lowered the temperature by showing strong interest in our questions. When I asked what he remembered about his father, he replied, 'I'm afraid I'm not a very good witness, because I was only three when he disappeared.' But several times, when he began to volunteer something, his mother shut him up.

Our interview, though far from conclusive, gave us several good new points. Yet I still had dreadful doubts about the validity of Hugh's claim: could it really be that a deception of this magnitude had lasted unexposed for nearly half a century? Then, about two weeks later, came a thunderbolt – a letter from Frau Hess, which said that she was sorry, but in the event she could not find any of her husband's pre-war correspondence. She then returned to the subject of the wound. She confirmed that it was a *Lungendurchschuss,* or shot through the lung, and that it had ended Hess's career in the infantry; but she also wrote, 'In normal life the only things that reminded him of the wound were the scars which he bore on his body, front and back.'

There it was – a sudden, unsolicited vindication of Hugh's claim. Further confirmation came from medical records found in Munich, which showed that the wound had been caused by a bullet entering Hess's chest just below the left shoulder and exiting high in his back near the spine. My doubts dissolved, and we went all-out to complete our text. Many other points lent weight to our argument:

- Hess had been mainly a vegetarian, but the prisoner ate all kinds of meat with relish.
- The prisoner refused to play tennis, saying he did not know the rules – whereas Hess had been a keen player.
- The prisoner refused to see any member of the Hess family until 1969 – twenty-eight years after Rudolf had flown out of Germany.
- When Ilse did see Prisoner No. 7, she remarked that his voice was much deeper than she remembered – whereas an old man's voice almost invariably goes up rather than down.

The book came out in the autumn of 1979 under the title *The Murder of Rudolf Hess,* with a judicious foreword by the veteran author Rebecca West, who, after expressing some scepticism, agreed that the story was extremely odd, and concluded that 'In this book Hugh Thomas has begun the unravelling of the greatest mystery of the Second World War.' We offered serial rights to the *Observer,* whose editors spent nearly six weeks trying to pick holes in the story, before deciding that they didn't believe it. We then switched our attack to the *Sunday Telegraph,* which aroused widespread interest by printing three major extracts. These led to a question in the House of Commons; but the Government made no move towards setting up an inquiry, still less towards releasing the last, lonely inmate of Spandau, who was already eighty-five and very frail. Ilse Hess rejected Hugh's account with scorn and declared him crazy. '*Dieser Kerl hat nicht alle Tassen im Schrank,*' she said to one newspaper journalist. 'This fellow hasn't got all his cups in the cupboard.'

I, by then, had been diverted on to other projects; but Hugh, pressing ahead relentlessly with more research, kept unearthing new details which strengthened his theory – for instance that on the night 10 May 1941 two Czech pilots, flying with the RAF from Aldergrove, had closed on a Messerschmitt Bf 110 over the West Coast of Scotland and were about to shoot it down, when, to their chagrin, they were called off by their controller. Again, two independent sleuths confirmed Hugh's belief that if the plane which crashed in Scotland had indeed taken off from Augsburg, it could not have completed the flight without refuelling.

Normally a second crewman, in the rear seat of a Messerschmitt Bf 110, pumped oil into the engines from a reserve tank – but in this case there *was* no second crewman – and in any case the oil reserve pipe was sealed with a wired-up brass cap.

By the time the aged prisoner eventually expired in Spandau, on 17 August 1987, Hugh's contacts and knowledge were such that he was able reconstruct the circumstances in detail. The official version was that Prisoner No 7 hanged himself in a hut in the prison garden by attaching the flex of a reading lamp to the window catch. Hugh quickly despatched this claim by pointing out (a) that the old man was far too bent and frail to have hung himself; (b) that the catch was too low – only 4′ 7″ from the ground – for *anyone* to have hung himself from it; and that (c) that marks on the dead man's neck showed clearly that he had been strangled, not hung. Further, an enormous bruise on the back of his head could not possibly have been caused by hanging.

Further suspicion derived from the fact that two unidentified strangers, in unmarked uniforms, had been seen hanging about the garden, and then that Lt. Col. A.H. Le Tissier, the British Military Governor, had ordered the hut burnt that same night, thus eliminating the scene of death before any coroner could examine it. When Wolf-Rüdiger Hess asked what had happened to a length of yellow flex found in the hut, Le Tissier told him , 'I threw it on the fire,' thus destroying what had probably been the murder weapon. It also became clear that the British had been anticipating the prisoner's death, for, under the top-secret Operation Royston, a Hercules transport aircraft and crew had been on standby at RAF Lyneham, ready to take off at short notice and evacuate the body swiftly to England. In the event, the aircraft did fly to Berlin, but returned to base when the French rendered removal of the corpse impossible by blocking the rear entrance of the British Military Hospital with a collection of vehicles.

Two separate post-mortem examinations were carried out by highly-qualified specialists, one British, one German. The first confirmed beyond doubt that the prisoner had never been shot through the lung. The second showed that he had been throttled, rather than hung, and that one of his injuries was a severe contusion on the back of the head, which could not have been caused by hanging. Hugh's conclusion was that the man had been murdered by the two strangers seen in the garden. Who had commissioned them? It was impossible to say.

In the past, whenever somebody suggested that the ancient prisoner should be released, it had been assumed that it was the Russians who vetoed the proposal. But more recently researchers had begun to believe that it was the British who were exercising the veto. When President Gorbachev suggested it was time to show clemency, the British, it seemed, feared that if the old man came out of gaol he might at last tell the truth.

For seven months the body was kept in the mortuary at Wunsiedel, the Hess family's home town in Bavaria, the official reason for the delay being to prevent the interment becoming a focus of Nazi fervour. Finally it was buried – but not all the evidence went with it, for frozen blocks of tissue from the body had been retained. When Hugh asked that a comparison should be made between the DNA of the prisoner and that of the Hess family, his request was refused, by both the family and the Foreign Office – a final denial, and a final endorsement of his belief.

All this new material was incorporated into a second edition of our book, now entitled *Hess: a Tale of Two Murders,* which came out in the spring of 1988. Again, a parliamentary question was framed, this time by Dale Campbell-Savours, the Labour Member for Workington. But this time the question was never asked; rather, it was suppressed, on the grounds that it was inadmissible, because of the sensitive nature of the subject. When Campbell-Savours wrote to the Foreign Secretary, Sir Geoffey Howe, seeking an answer, he received a letter from Mrs Lynda Chalker, Minister of State at the Foreign and Commonwealth Office. Asked to confirm that one of the post mortem reports indicated 'no bullet scars on the left part of the torso of the prisoner,' she replied:

> No. Both the interim report and the full report drawn up by the pathologist indicated scarring on the left part of the torso consistent with bullet wounds.

Doubtless this was the information she had been given, but in fact it was an outright lie. The prisoner had no scars 'consistent with bullet wounds' on his chest. There had been no scars of any kind until, on 4 February 1945, he pulled a pinch of skin away from his ribs, twisted it upright, and pushed the blade of a kitchen knife through it, pretending he had tried to stab himself in the heart – and perhaps deliberately creating scars which he hoped to pass off as the result of a war wound. The self-inflicted injury left two parallel, horizontal scars, barely an inch long, and quarter of an inch apart. These, and stitching marks, were recorded by an American military doctor at Nuremberg in 1945, by Hugh in Spandau in 1973, and again by a British specialist at the second autopsy in 1987. The prisoner had claimed that these tiny scars were the result of a bullet wound – but their shape made that impossible, and in any case, a bullet passing through his chest at that point would have killed him immediately. When Hugh gave an illustrated talk to the Royal College of Surgeons in Manchester, the audience – all experts – agreed by 76 votes to nil that the prisoner could not have been Hess.

I found, and find, it disturbing that a Minister can lie so blatantly in the face of so much evidence. The key question is: Why does the Government persist in ignoring the medical facts? Is it still trying to keep some dreadful secret buried? Other researchers, following up Hugh's lead, suggest that in 1941 Churchill and MI6 contrived a monstrous plot, designed to accelerate the launch of Operation Barbarossa, the invasion of Russia which Hitler was already planning. This began on 22 June and ultimately proved fatal to Germany, and to millions of combatants and citizens on either side.

For decades historians both amateur and professional eagerly awaited the release of files on Hess held in the Public Record Office and closed in 1947 for seventy years. But when some were opened in 2017, they contained no revelations of any significance. Many documents had been so heavily redacted, with pages and whole sequences removed, that they gave nothing away. One file at least remained closed until 2032 – and when that eventually opens, the odds are that it will divulge nothing, so that the great mystery will gradually fade into oblivion.

ENVOI

Looking back, I seem to have been extraordinarily fortunate. I have never suffered a serious injury or illness, never had a bad car-crash, never broken any large bone. I regret that I have spent so much time on country matters, and I am all too well aware that I have always lacked the grand ambition of Tennyson's Ulysses:

To sail beyond the sunset, and the baths
Of all the western stars, until I die.

Nevertheless, I still look forward to tackling new projects, from whatever source they may derive, and I am encouraged by the fact that now and then an idea for a story has come to me ready-made. I was once (for instance) working on a book designed to accompany a television documentary about the training of fast-jet pilots. Flying in Hawk jet trainers had been sensational, but the project was labouring to a rather dull conclusion, and I was longing to finish it. Then, in the middle of the night, I woke up abruptly with the plot of a thriller ready-made in my head. I had not been looking for a new subject; nor had I been thinking about Scotland – but suddenly, here was a whole story, ready to be written.

An ex-special forces man is on the run in the Western Highlands. An explosion during his military service has left him slightly unbalanced, and now he is driven by a grudge against the Forestry Commission, which he blames for blanketing the mountains with serried ranks of conifers. He seeks to work off his anger by setting fire to plantations – and a nation-wide man-hunt ensues.

The book almost wrote itself – not least because I knew and loved the background in which I set it – and when it came out to good reviews under the title *Fire Falcon,* it attracted the attention of a film producer, Chris Chrisafis. Fired by enthusiasm, he hired a helicopter to reconnoitre locations, and we had some thrilling flights. On our way north we found Robin Fleming, proprietor of the great deer forest Black Mount, stranded for lack of transport at Glasgow airport; so we magnanimously gave him a lift home. When we landed close to the lodge, the pilot offered three of the estate staff a brief joy-ride; and as Hamish the Head Stalker cautiously eased his magnificent backside down between the arms of the little seats in the back, one of his colleagues made the immortal remark, 'I'm thinking if Hamish rises, the helicopter will rise with him.' Alas, the film was never made, but the story, materialising from nowhere, put fire into our lives, not least when our pilot took us wheeling like an eagle off the towering cliff-faces beyond the head of Loch Nevis.

Who knows where such ideas come from? Who knows what others may arrive out of the blue? As it is, I have one published novel ready-made for a Russian billionaire film-promoter with a passion for horse-racing. *Horses of War* embroiders the true story of how in 1919 an English jockey, Joseph Clements, walked two former winners of the Epsom Derby, Minoru and Aboyeur, through the Ukraine in the middle of the Russian civil war and got them evacuated on a ship sailing for Constantinople. Glamorous horses, bitter fighting, the noise and colour of the crowds at Epsom, winter on the Steppes, Cossacks desperately riding their horses out to sea ... what more could a film producer want?

For good or bad, I have written or edited more than fifty books, thirty my own, twenty ghosted. Add to them well over a thousand newspaper articles, and it will be clear that I have been lucky enough to have had a marvellously diverse career. I may not have earned millions, but I have certainly enjoyed myself, and I hope I have given some fun and enlightenment to others.

INDEX